C0-AWU-494

SOCIAL-COGNITIVE DEVELOPMENT IN CONTEXT

SOCIAL-COGNITIVE DEVELOPMENT IN CONTEXT

Edited by
Felicisima C. Serafica
The Ohio State University

DISCARD

BF
723
.S6
S64
1982

The Guilford Press
New York
London

INDIANA
UNIVERSITY LIBRARY

JUL 2 1984

NORTHWEST

© 1982 The Guilford Press
A Division of Guilford Publications, Inc.
200 Park Avenue South, New York, N.Y. 10003

All rights reserved

No part of this book may be reproduced, stored in a retrieval system, or transmitted, in any form or by any means, electronic, mechanical, photocopying, microfilming, recording, or otherwise, without written permission from the Publisher

Printed in the United States of America

Library of Congress Cataloging in Publication Data
Main entry under title:
Social-cognitive development in context.
    Includes bibliographical references and index.
    1. Social perception in children.   2. Cognition in
children.   3. Social interaction in children.   4. Emotions
in children.   I. Serafica, Felicisima C.
BF723.S6S64   1982   155.4′18   82-2913
ISBN 0-89862-623-4

Contributors

DAVID J. BEARISON, PhD, Doctoral Programs in Educational and Developmental Psychology, The Graduate Center of the City University of New York, New York, New York, and Department of Psychiatry, Harvard Medical School and The Children's Hospital Medical Center, Boston, Massachusetts

DALE A. BLYTH, PhD, Department of Psychology, The Ohio State University, Columbus, Ohio

STEVEN BRION-MEISELS, EdD, Laboratory of Human Development, Harvard University, Cambridge, Massachusetts, and Judge Baker Guidance Center, Boston, Massachusetts

MICHAEL J. CHANDLER, PhD, Department of Psychology, University of British Columbia, Vancouver, British Columbia, Canada

SUSAN HARTER, PhD, Department of Psychology, University of Denver, Denver, Colorado

DEBRA REDMAN LAVIN, EdD, Laboratory of Human Development, Harvard University, Cambridge, Massachusetts, and Judge Baker Guidance Center, Boston, Massachusetts. Present address: Cornell University Medical Center, Valhalla, New York

ROBERT L. SELMAN, PhD, Laboratory of Human Development, Harvard University, Cambridge, Massachusetts, and Judge Baker Guidance Center, Boston, Massachusetts

FELICISIMA C. SERAFICA, PhD, Department of Psychology, The Ohio State University, Columbus, Ohio

CAROLYN UHLINGER SHANTZ, PhD, Department of Psychology, Wayne State University, Detroit, Michigan

MYRNA BETH SHURE, PhD, Department of Mental Health Sciences, Hahnemann Medical College and Hospital, Philadelphia, Pennyslvania

Acknowledgments

The publication of this book was made possible by the assistance of several organizations and individuals.

Above all, thanks are due to the Foundation for Child Development for its financial support, through the Society for Research in Child Development, of the SRCD Study Group on Social Cognition. This support is another manifestation of the Foundation's commitment to research as an essential base for improving the status of children and their families. We are also very grateful to the SRCD Executive Officer, Dr. Dorothy Eichorn, and her staff. The Study Group on Social Cognition was able to meet because the SRCD Committee on Summer Institutes and Study Groups recognized the value of such a conference. We are deeply indebted to the Committee, particularly to Drs. Frank B. Murray and Ross D. Parke.

The use of The Ohio State University facilities is warmly appreciated. To Karen Kreutzfeld goes a special note of thanks for her able handling of the many details involved in organizing the Study Group meetings. Jane Chapman and Viki Thompson also deserve our thanks for their efficient typing and careful attention to detail.

Finally, to the editors of The Guilford Press goes a sincere expression of deep appreciation and gratitude for their commitment and contributions to the production of this book.

Contents

SOCIAL-COGNITIVE DEVELOPMENT IN CONTEXT

Introduction

FELICISIMA C. SERAFICA

The relationship between the cognitive and social spheres of human functioning and their context has long been regarded by social and behavioral scientists as a central theoretical issue. Baldwin (1906) asserted that the dialectic of personal growth is manifest in social interaction, particularly in the give-and-take that characterizes the infant–caregiver transactions. According to Mead (1934), both mind and self evolve in a social context. In his view, the transformation of the biological organism into a reflective individual with a strong sense of selfhood occurs through the medium of language; in turn, language presupposes the existence of a certain kind of society. It has been contended, too, by Marx (1953) that man's consciousness is determined by his social being. For Marx, human thought is founded in human activity and in the social relations brought about by this activity.

The critical role that social interaction plays in the development of higher mental functions was also emphasized by Vygotsky (1978). He proposed that all higher functions originate from actual relations between human individuals, with interpersonal transactions becoming transformed into intrapersonal mental processes. Every function appears first at the social or interpsychological plane and only later emerges at the individual or intrapsychological plane. Social relations, particularly peer relations, have been implicated in cognitive development, too, by Piaget (1932/1965). He suggested that peer interaction exposes children to viewpoints different from their own or those of their parents, thereby generating cognitive conflict which, in turn, precipitates cognitive restructuring and progression to higher and more mature levels of thought.

The foregoing theoretical propositions have inspired a number of empirical studies which, directly or indirectly, elucidate further the meaning of this important relationship. The chapters that comprise this volume represent some contemporary attempts to advance our scientific understanding of the interface between cognitive and social

FELICISIMA C. SERAFICA. Department of Psychology, The Ohio State University, Columbus, Ohio.

1

functioning. This introduction is intended to provide a background for them by presenting the major theoretical concerns and a brief history of research in this area.

Before proceeding further, a word must be said about the use of the term "social relations" in this book. In the developmental literature, the referent of the term "social relations" seems to vary with the issue under consideration. When invoked in discussions of the relationship between cognitive and social development, it is often used specifically to mean interpersonal relationships, either dyadic relations such as attachment or friendship, or group relations. When used in regard to the relationship between cognition and social behavior, it is often treated as a synonym for social interaction. In this case, the way people interact with one another is referred to as social relations. Last, the term "social relations" has been used to denote a particular social structure that serves as the context of both behavior and development. As used in the various chapters that make up this book, the term "social relations" assumes any of these three different meanings, reflecting the diversity of opinion among contemporary investigators.

Major Theoretical Concerns

The central hypothesis regarding a significant relationship between cognitive and social functioning and their context can be differentiated further into three specific issues: (1) the relationship between structural levels of cognitive and social development, (2) the relationship between cognition and social behavior per se (as distinguished from a particular social-developmental level), and (3) the role of contextual factors in ontogenesis.

Cognitive and Social Development

The relationship between cognitive and social development has sometimes been characterized as one of reciprocal interaction; certain developments in cognition are viewed as necessary though not sufficient conditions for specific achievements in the social sphere, and vice versa. This viewpoint guided early attempts to establish the relationship between development of the object concept and development of the infant–mother relationship (Bell, 1970; Decarie, 1965).

Alternatively, Piaget (1981) conceptualized the relationship between cognitive and social development as an instance of formal parallelism. He maintained that cognitive and affective or social development are inseparable and that parallels may be found, stage by stage, between cognitive structures and levels of affective or social development. Both behaviors related to objects and behaviors related to people have structural aspects. For example, just as the cognitive schemata that are initially centered upon the child's own actions become the means whereby he/she constructs an objective and decentered universe, similarly, and simultaneously, the initial lack of differentiation between self and others is replaced by the construction of a group of exchanges of emotional investments that link the differentiated self to other persons (Piaget & Inhelder, 1969). From this perspective, the research strategy for investigating the relationship between cognitive and social development involves looking for correspondences between levels of the two processes.

It should be noted though that while Piaget in his later writings stressed the existence of a functional parallelism between evolutions in the intellectual and affective or social domains, he also acknowledged an interaction between logical and social development, particularly in his early work (Piaget, 1932/1965, 1928/1966). Thus, these two positions on the relationship between structures in cognitive and social development are not antithetical to one another. Within such frameworks, the important research aims are to determine which lines of social development are most likely to parallel cognitive-developmental trends, and to ascertain whether cognitive and social development intersect at specific points.

Cognition and Social Behavior

The relationship between cognition and social behavior per se has often been construed in unidirectional causal terms. Along this line, some investigators have advanced what Cairns (1979) calls the "cognitive primacy hypothesis." For example, Kohlberg (1969) has suggested that the child's cognitions of him/herself and others are the primary determinants of his/her behavior. Similarly, Schaffer (1971) has asserted that the nature of the cognitive structure at a particular age sets limits on the kinds of social behavior that one can expect at a given stage of development. Cairns (1979) has stated that there is now ample justification for rejecting the cognitive primacy hypothesis in its simple form, that is, that behavior is merely a reflection of cognition.

On the other hand, it has also been proposed that social behavior, the child's own and that of significant others with whom he/she interacts, determines cognitive growth. An extreme version of this "behavior primacy hypothesis," to paraphrase Cairns, is held by advocates of reinforcement theory (e.g., Lovitt, 1975). Within a Piagetian framework, social interaction is also viewed as a facilitating condition for transitions in cognitive development (Botvin & Murray, 1975). However, this position differs from the behavior primacy hypothesis in that it considers the developmental level represented by a particular social act as the critical variable. Hence, the important issue for cognitive-developmental theorists is still the relationship between structural levels of cognitive and social development.

Social Context and Ontogenesis

The role of contextual factors in development has been stressed by scientists representing different disciplines and diverse theoretical persuasions (Berger & Luckman, 1966; Bronfenbrenner, 1977; Gewirtz, 1971; Piaget, 1970). From a life-span perspective, context has been defined in temporal, social, and historical terms (Elder & Rockwell, 1979). In a more molecular fashion, situational variables and specific external stimuli, including individual characteristics and behaviors as well as environmental contingencies, have been identified as the relevant contextual variables by those who subscribe to a mechanistic world view (Reese & Overton, 1970). Cognitive-developmental theory, too, emphasizes that development is the outcome of organism–environment interaction. However, for the most part, its proponents have confined definitions of context to general statements about social interaction and subject–object relations. In fact, according to Kuhn (1978), cognitive-developmental theory can rightly be accused of conceptualizing the environment as passive, in much the same way that mechanistic theories have been accused of considering the organism as passive; the environment has been treated in cognitive-developmental research as a neutral context within which ontogenesis takes place.

In spite of the avowed theoretical importance of the hypothesized relationship between cognitive and social functioning and context, there have been relatively few studies on this topic. This lacuna in our scientific knowledge has been attributed by Kuhn (1978) to the propensity of investigators who hold different world views (Reese & Overton, 1970) to narrowly apply their respective paradigms to the particular phenomena they handle best—the development of social behavior in the case of the mechanistic paradigm and cognitive development in the case of the organismic paradigm. Kuhn suggests that differences in

theoretical orientation may have kept investigators of social development from communicating with researchers interested in cognitive
development, thereby limiting progress in studying the relationship
between these two separate yet interrelated processes. To this I would
add that Piaget's preoccupation with the acquisition of knowledge
about the physical rather than the social world also precluded more
rapid advances in our attempts to understand what Piaget himself has
called the functional unity between the cognitive and social domains
(Piaget & Inhelder, 1969). Thus, the important task of conceptualizing
environment and empirically verifying its role in development still confronts proponents of cognitive-developmental theory. For instance, we
know relatively little about how cognitive and social functioning differ
as a function of context. Nor do we know precisely what constitutes environment in a particular organism–environment transaction. We also
do not know much about the "cognitive maps" that children form
about their social world. If cognitive-developmental theory is to provide a more complete description and explanation for development, it
must address these and other issues.

Developments in the Study of Social Cognition

Within cognitive-developmental theory, relatively little attention was
initially directed toward specification of hierarchically ordered levels of
social functioning that might be systematically linked to levels of
cognitive development. According to Flavell (1977a), some early attempts (e.g., Cook, 1972) to demonstrate the cognitive–social linkage
failed precisely because there was a lack of specificity about the
"degrees" or developmental levels of the social phenomenon under
investigation. However, when other investigators (Feffer & Gourevitch,
1960; Flavell, 1968) began to extend Piaget's cognitive-developmental
theory to cognition of the self and the social world, they opened a new
avenue to the study of the interface between cognitive and social
functioning. It seemed highly conceivable that the cognitive abilities
employed in making inferences about the self and other human beings
might be organized in the same manner as the cognitive structures
constructed from the organism's interactions with the physical world.
If this were the case, then parallels and/or interactions between cognitive and social development might be more easily identified and the
impact of contextual factors on cognitive and social phenomena might
be more readily observed.

Social Cognition as Social Inference

Starting in the mid-1960s and continuing into the next decade, there occurred one of those ground swellings in science which culminate in the definition of a new field of study; several separate lines of research converged to form the domain that is now popularly known as social cognition. One of these research trends was the study of person perception, or the ability to represent others; the rest dealt with the development of social inference, that is, the ability to infer the thoughts, emotions, intentions, and viewpoints of others. Hence, when it first attained visibility within the scientific community, the study of social cognition was defined as the study of the child's intuitive or logical representation of others, particularly his/her abilities to characterize others and to make inferences about their covert inner psychological experiences (Shantz, 1975).

The social-inferential abilities that have received the lion's share of researchers' attention are the abilities to represent other people (person perception) and to infer their thoughts (cognitive or social perspective taking, also referred to as role taking), visual perceptions (also known as perceptual or spatial perspective taking), feelings (empathy or affective perspective taking), and motives or intentions (intentionality). In the following paragraphs, early research on the development of social cognition is selectively discussed. The intent here is not to present a comprehensive review of the available theoretical and empirical literature but rather to provide a historical background focusing on the critical "turning points" in the field which led to the different lines of research endeavor presented in this book that, it is hoped, bring us closer to a better understanding of the relationship between social cognition, social relations, and context. For a more thorough coverage of research on social cognition and a more elaborate discussion of conceptual and methodological issues, the interested reader is referred to reviews by Shantz (1975, in press), Chandler (1977, 1982), Flavell (1977b), and Hoffman (1977), and to books edited by Keasey (1977a), Damon (1978), Glick and Clarke-Stewart (1978), and Flavell and Ross (1981).

Not surprisingly, early research on social-inferential abilities was directed toward identifying developmental trends. These early studies were undertaken to obtain empirically based descriptions of age-related changes in children's abilities to represent people or to infer their visual perceptions, thoughts, feelings, intentions, and motives. For each of the social-inferential abilities mentioned above, developmental sequences have been identified (e.g., Barenboim, 1977, 1981; Borke, 1971, 1973; Cox, 1978; Erwin & Kuhn, 1979; Feshbach & Roe, 1968; Flavell, 1968; Flavell, Everett, Croft, & Flavell, 1981; Hebble, 1971; Hughes, Tingle, & Sawin, 1981; Keasey, 1977b; King, 1971; Mossler, Marvin, & Greenberg, 1976; Peevers & Secord, 1973; Selman, 1971; Selman & Byrne, 1974; Strayer, 1980; Urberg & Docherty, 1976; Whiteman, 1967; Wood, 1978). This phase of research on social cognition has not occurred without controversy. Much of the debate centers around the age of onset for some inferential abilities, such as empathy or affective perspective taking (Borke, 1971, 1973; Chandler & Greenspan, 1972) and intention (Karniol, 1978; Keasey, 1977b), but there has also been some disagreement about the generality of social-inferential abilities (Kurdek & Rodgon, 1975; Rubin, 1973). Upon closer scrutiny, these inconsistencies among findings regarding age of onset have been found to be related to definitional and measurement issues (Brandt, 1978; Chandler & Greenspan, 1972; Hudson, 1978; Kurdek & Rodgon, 1975; Liben, 1978; Rubin, 1978; Shaklee, 1976). Quite often, apparent contradictions between results of different studies could be reconciled if conceptual and methodological differences were taken into account.

Of particular interest here are the results concerning the relationships between social inference and logical operations, structural levels of social development, social behavior, and contextual factors. Several studies have found positive relationships between various social-inferential abilities and logical operations (Feffer & Gourevitch, 1960; Keating & Clark, 1980; Rubin, Attewell, Tierney, & Tumolo, 1973; Turnure, 1975). The magnitude of this relationship varies from study to study, but the accumulative effect of the data from these studies is to empirically support the notion of a link between social inference and logical thinking. Furthermore, although a relationship does exist between the two domains, social-inferential abilities correlate more highly with one another than they do with logical relations (Hollos, 1975; Hollos & Cowan, 1973), suggesting that these two domains are distinguishable from one another while remaining related.

There is less solid empirical justification, however, for the hypothesized parallelism between structural levels of social inference and social-behavioral systems such as attachment and altruism. Identifying the nature and occurrence of the parallels between these two lines of development has proven to be a difficult enterprise, handicapped by both conceptual and methodological problems. To begin with, we lack precise definitions of social-interaction patterns that represent different structural-developmental levels of social-behavioral systems. Furthermore, adequate measures of these different levels of social-interaction patterns have yet to be constructed. Moreover, even if one could adequately identify and measure different levels or stages of social-interaction patterns, there remains the problem of determining exactly when and how the ontogenetic parallels are manifested.

To those interested in the link between cognitive and social functioning, research into the relationships between social-inferential abilities and social behavior initially seemed to offer a bright promise. The results have not quite lived up to expectations, however. Although there are consistent findings showing a positive relationship between perspective taking and communication effectiveness (Glucksberg, Krause, & Higgins, 1975; Greenspan, Barenboim, & Chandler, 1976; Piche, Michlin, Rubin, & Johnson, 1975), conflicting results have emerged from studies of the relationship between perspective taking and popularity. Investigations of this hypothesized relationship have yielded either no support (Finley, French & Cowan, 1973), partial confirmation (Rothenberg, 1970; Rubin, 1973), or inconsistent findings (Gottman, Gonso, & Rasmussen, 1975; Rubin, 1972). These findings are not really surprising, since research has shown that peer acceptance is influenced by many factors, including names (McDavid & Harari, 1966), body build (Staffieri, 1967), facial attractiveness (Dion, 1973; Dion & Berscheid, 1974; Langlois & Downs, 1979), and rate of maturation (Ames, 1956; Jones, 1957). However, when popularity is assessed through direct observation (e.g., Deutsch, 1974), it is found to be positively related to social inference, significantly so. Similarly, other studies that used behavioral measures (e.g., communication behavior, cooperation) to represent social behavior have yielded evidence for the hypothesized relationship. Thus, how one conceptualizes and measures social behavior appears to be a critical issue.

One attempt at a reformulation of the nature of the relationship was advanced by Deutsch (1974). She suggested that in development there may be a curvilinear relationship between communication as an index of perspective taking and a sociometric measure of popularity because there is no difference between perceived and actual popularity for kindergarten and second graders, whereas there is a difference between the two measures for fourth and sixth graders. She found that among preschoolers, communicative egocentrism was related significantly to an observational measure of peer popularity, even when IQ was partialed out, but not to a sociometric measure of popularity. Certainly, the findings regarding a positive relationship between social-cognitive measures and social-behavioral assessments in young children have been more consistent. Rubin and Maioni (1975) found that empathic role taking and spatial egocentrism were significantly related to popularity, and spatial egocentrism was related to dramatic play as well among preschoolers. Also for this age group, Jennings (1975) found that summary scores on tests of social knowledge (Wechsler Preschool and Primary Scale of Intelligence comprehension score, role taking, empathy, sex-role knowledge, and moral judgment) were related significantly to peer popularity and to several qualitative aspects of social behavior, such as the ability to function as a peer leader, forcefulness in pursuing goals, being self-starting and self-propelled, and the ability to get along with others. Another relevant finding was that, regardless of the amount of time spent in social interaction, children who were more effective in these interactions were also more likely to be advanced in social knowledge. Last, a study by Levine and Hoffman (1975) showed a significant relationship between empathy and cooperation in 4-year-olds. Among older age groups, however, the scientific evidence accumulated thus far provides merely weak support for the hypothesized interaction between social inference and social behavior.

Another attempt at a reconceptualization was made by Barrett and Yarrow (1977), who suggested that the effect of social-inferential abilities on social behavior is mediated by other variables, for example, assertiveness. The role of mediating variables therefore needs further exploration. The conflicting findings regarding the status of social-inferential level as a necessary though not sufficient condition for social functioning may be due in part to our lack of conceptual clarity as to exactly which levels or stages of social-inferential development logically constitute the cognitive underpinnings for particular kinds of social behavior or new attainments in the social domain. One possibility is that social-inferential abilities such as perspective taking underlie the way children organize their ideas about social relations such as attachment or friendship. Piaget (1981) has said that there is a structure to social knowledge which comes from taking consciousness of social relations and organizing them. These organized patterns of thinking about social phenomena, in turn, influence the conduct of social relations and, reciprocally, are influenced by such social experiences. Furthermore, if there are indeed parallels between structural levels of cognitive and social development, perhaps they are more likely to be found between particular cognitive structures and specific levels of social-concept development.

It must also be noted that although it is generally assumed that the relationship between social inference and social behavior is a reciprocal one, the focus of research to date has been the assessment of the impact on a particular level or mode of social interaction of the developmental status of a given cognitive ability or its absence thereof.

Assuming that we can specify the social-inferential abilities that might be implicated in certain kinds of social behavior, we must still be cautious about positing a one-to-one correspondence between social-inferential level and level of social behavior. Research on moral behavior (Biasi, 1980) suggests that there are other factors besides cognitive level that determine behavior in specific situations. Situational determinants also seem to play an important role, yet not enough attention has been paid to this variable in social-cognitive research.

Research to date on the role of contextual factors in the development of social inference has been based on the premise that variations in the quality and/or organization of social environments lead to differences in the level of individual competence. Furthermore, it has been assumed that language mediates this impact of the way social relations, dyadic or group, are organized. Within this framework, for example, differences in linguistic environments associated with maternal communication styles (Bearison & Cassel, 1975) or amount of social interaction, particularly of a verbal nature (Hollos, 1975; Hollos & Cowan, 1973), are viewed as important influences on development of social inference.

Bearison and Cassel (1975) hypothesized that when interpersonal relations are based primarily upon individuating psychological properties (i.e., are person-oriented), the ability to coordinate listener–speaker perspectives is apt to develop more than when interpersonal relations are based primarily upon the socially ascribed status or position of the members (i.e., are position-oriented). In turn, the ability to coordinate perspective contributes to effective communication. Support for this hypothesis was obtained from a study that showed that on each of five measures (game information, inadequate referents, number of words, verbal description, and verbal–gestural reference) assessing the form and context of messages to sighted and blindfolded listeners, 6-year-old children from person-oriented families showed greater evidence of accommodating their communication to the listener's perspective than did same-age peers from position-oriented families.

The role of social setting (and, by implication, of amount of verbal and social interaction) in the development of logical operations and perspective taking was studied by Hollos and Cowan (1973) in 7-, 8-, and 9-year-old children from three different Norwegian communities: town, village, and dispersed farm community. Factor analysis yielded two main factors—a logical-operations factor involving all classification and conservation tests and a role-taking factor involving all multiple perspective-taking and communication tests. Age effects were prominent in logical operations while setting effects predominated in role taking. Farm children, the most socially isolated, received relatively low scores on role-taking tasks, but performed as well as or better than village and town children on logical operations. A replication of this study in Hungary yielded similar results (Hollos, 1975). The authors interpreted this finding as disconfirming Bruner's (Bruner, Olver, & Greenfield, 1966) hypothesis that language stimulation and schooling are the major determinants for the development of logical operations. Instead, they suggest a threshold hypothesis; that is, some minimal level of experience in verbal–social interaction appears to be sufficient for the development of logical operations and perspective taking, and the threshold for the latter may be higher than for the former.

The studies cited above have dealt with the effect of the child's sociolinguistic environment on social cognitive development, an important topic certainly, but we also need to know more about how contextual factors affect the relationship between social cognitive level and social behavior. In this regard, one problem is to identify different structural levels of the social environment. Another is to specify precisely the mechanisms whereby experiences in social interchanges and in social systems give rise to organized forms of social knowledge, create expectations about social behavior and affect actual behavior in specific situations.

Social Cognition as Social Knowledge

Coincidentally, at about the time that research data challenging the prevailing conceptualization of the relationship between perspective taking and social behavior emerged, the study of social cognition was also moving into a different phase from its initial emphasis on development of social inference to a new focus on the development of social knowledge or organized forms of thought about social phenomena. At about the mid-1970s, people began to raise the question, What is social about social cognition? Doubts were expressed about investigating social cognition as if it were limited to the application of cognitive abilities to people (e.g., Chandler, 1977). For instance, Selman (1976) argued that the nature of social cognition involves an understanding of relations within persons (i.e., relations between feelings, thoughts, actions) and between persons. A coherent approach to the development of social cognition must include a thoroughgoing examination of the structural shifts in the organization of social concepts, as well as in the ability to coordinate perspectives. In general, it was thought that there are ways in which interpersonal strategies, behaviors, and social interactions of a nonverbal as well as verbal nature are logically structured and developmentally ordered. If social behavior can be characterized developmentally, then its relationship to social reasoning might be investigated more successfully.

This new approach to the study of social cognition received its impetus from theory and research on the development of the understanding of concepts about social convention (Turiel, 1975), the self and self–other relations (Selman, 1976), and authority (Damon, 1977). Turiel (1975) proposed a theoretical distinction between social convention and morality. He also hypothesized that ideas about social-conventional concepts undergo the following developmental progression: (1) convention as descriptive of social uniformity (6 to 7 years); (2) negation of convention as descriptive of social uniformity (8 to 9 years); (3) convention as affirmation of rule system; early concrete conception of social system (10 to 11 years); (4) negation of convention as part of rule system (12 to 13 years); (5) convention as mediated by social system (14 to 16 years); (6) negation of convention as societal standards (17 to 18 years); and convention as coordination of social interactions (18 to 25 years). Empirical support for this hypothesized progression has been found (Turiel, 1978).

Along a similar vein, Damon (1977) suggested that the development of the child's concept of authority might be understood best through an examination of age-related changes in the child's thinking about two crucial issues: legitimacy and rationale for obedience. Both are relevant to the child's concept of authority because, according to Damon, the kinds of social power traits that a child believes to be legitimate are aligned with his/her rationale for obedience. He described a hierarchically ordered sequence consisting of three major levels, each one subdivided further into two. This sequence begins with the notion that authority is legitimized by attributes that link the authority with the self, either through affectional bonds or identification, and that obedience ensues from a primitive association between the authority's commands and the self's desires. The sequence culminates at a level where authority is legitimized by the possession of attributes that enable a person to command in one specific situation, though not necessarily in others, and obedience is viewed as a situation-specific cooperative effort. Damon (1977) reported evidence from both cross-sectional and longitudinal studies indicative of a strong association between age and authority reasoning level.

The work of Selman and his collaborators (Selman, 1976; Selman & Jaquette, 1977; Selman, Jaquette, & Lavin, 1977) seemed particularly germane to the issue of the relationship between cognitive and social functioning. From a structural-developmental framework, he had undertaken a broad investigation of developing conceptions of persons, dyadic relations, group relations, and parent–child relations. For each of these content areas or domains of knowledge, he proposed a developmental sequence consisting of five hierarchically ordered stages. For example, the concept of peer group was conceptualized as evolving in the following progression. At Stage 0, the peer group is viewed as a series of physical connections or linked activities that hold the group together. In the next period, Stage 1, the peer group is characterized as a series of unilateral relations. At Stage 2, the child begins to think of the peer group as comprised of bilateral partnerships. However, at this stage, the child is still unable to view the group as something more than the sum of dyadic relations which comprise it. By Stage 3, the idea of the peer group as a community has been abstracted from the specific relations between its members, but it remains essentially a homogeneous community. It is not until Stage 4 that the peer group comes to be viewed as a pluralistic organization in which individual differences are recognized and integrated in the pursuit of common goals. Preliminary findings from this comprehensive research project showed empirical support for the hypothesized sequences. More importantly for our own specific concern with the relationship between cognitive and social functioning and how it is affected by context, Selman (1976) also reported some encouraging results about relations between social perspective taking and ontogenetic changes in each domain, between interpersonal concepts and logicophysical reasoning, and between interpersonal reasoning and the ability to relate to others (through a comparison of normal children with children who are experiencing problems in interpersonal relations).

The work of these three investigators showed that the cognitive aspects of relationships with other people could be studied by examining developmental changes in the maturing child's ideas about social relations and their regulation. These demonstrations of structural changes in forms of social knowledge suggested an alternative approach toward determining the relationship between cognitive and social development. Perhaps, through this paradigm, one might be more likely to observe the parallels between cognitive and social development and the points at which they interface, if any. Conceivably, too, it might facilitate the discovery of how conceptual level of development interacts with context to produce a particular level of social behavior. The role of context cannot be ignored because the individual's acquisition of social knowledge and his/her social behavior does not take place in a vacuum. The social interactions out of which social knowledge is constructed occur within a social milieu that also has its own intrinsic organization. From an interactional perspective, it is equally important to identify contextual factors, categorize them, and understand how they influence cognitive and social development, A viable approach to these tasks is greatly needed.

The SRCD Study Group on Social Cognition

From June 18 through July 1, 1978, a Study Group on Social Cognition funded by the Foundation for Child Development through the Society for Research in Child Development (SRCD) met at The Ohio State University to discuss these new trends in research on social cognition and the problem of studying context. Its aims were (1) to review current theoretical and empirical knowledge of selected social-cognitive topics; (2) to specify, whenever possible, the sequence of normal development in these areas; (3) to discuss shared conceptual and methodological problems, and how these might be resolved; (4) to define heuristic approaches to the study of contextual factors and their role in development; (5) to identify new directions for research; and (6) to explore ways in which different lines of research might be integrated so as to facilitate theory building about the development of social cognition and social relations in context.

The composition of the SRCD Study Group was planned so as to bring together researchers working in different yet related lines of investigation that have important implications for a contextually based understanding of the relationship between cognitive and social functioning. Although their specific research interests differ, all of these investigators subscribe, in varying degrees, to an organismic world view. Therefore, they are committed to an interactional perspective on development. Also, they tend to conceptualize development as a hierarchically ordered sequence of structural transformations resulting from organism–environment interactions. This shared metatheoretical orientation facilitated communication while the diversity of research interests and disciplines (psychology and sociology) ensured a rich exchange of different, even contradictory, ideas. That most of the participants also happened to be developmental psychologists with clinical interests enhanced the coherence of the dialogue. This clinical–developmental perspective adds a dimension of social relevance to their conceptualization of developmental issues and the research methods they employ.

The chapters that comprise this book were first presented at the Study Group meetings. The specific topics were chosen because they represented either different domains of social knowledge or innovative ways of describing the social environment and examining its role in ontogenesis.

The development of a child's self-knowledge is represented by Harter's chapter on children's understanding of affect and trait labels and by Selman, Lavin, and Brion-Meisels's chapter on troubled children's use of self-reflection. Another commonality between these two lines of research is their roots in clinical practice. Both of these chapters illustrate how clinical observations can give rise to exciting research ideas and how knowledge gained through research can illuminate clinical practice.

It is generally acknowledged that cognition and affect are equally important, yet there has been relatively little research on children's emotional development and on the link between affect and cognition, particularly from a cognitive-developmental perspective. Within this framework, the study of affect would entail an examination of the structural aspects of feelings (Piaget, 1981). This is precisely the task that Harter has undertaken—a developmental analysis of children's comprehension and construction of the emotional concepts that define the affective sphere of their lives. Her pioneering work differs from previous studies in this area because instead of assessing children's ability to infer emotion, she has chosen to study the development of children's understanding of emotions and the manner in which conventional emotional labels are applied to the self and others (in this case, parents). Of particular interest to Harter are the development of children's understanding that two emotions can co-occur and the dimensions underlying such understanding. This interest grew out of her clinical observation that young children have difficulty in expressing simultaneously what seem to be contradictory or conflicting feelings.

The approach employed in studying children's understanding of emotions is extended to the study of their use of trait labels. Again, a specific focus of the study is the co-occurrence of different polar attributes such as smart and dumb, and the developmental changes in the manner whereby these trait labels are applied to the self. Additionally, the relationship between children's use of trait labels and the development of self-concept is discussed. Relevant to the development of self–other relations, Harter presents some interesting data on age-related changes in children's reasoning about the source or cause of a particular parental emotion. These specific results bear on the important theoretical issue of the relationship of content domain to the developing cognitive structure; they suggest that the child's interpretation of the causes of parental emotion is a function of the emotion in question. Like Selman, Harter is concerned with the child's construction of a theory of self, but she approaches the problem through the child's perception over time of both stability and change in those characteristics that define his/her own theory of self.

According to Mead (1934), the distinguishing trait of selfhood resides in the capacity of the thinking organism to be the object of his/her own reflective action. The chapter by Selman, Lavin, and Brion-Meisels deals precisely with this important human capacity for self-reflection. First, they present the developmental sequence in the capacity for self-awareness, based on normative research that employed hypothetical social dilemmas and clinical-interview procedures to elicit children's and adolescents' verbalized conceptions (concept-in-theory) about how human beings reflect on their inner experiences. They then proceed to examine in greater detail the themes and aspects of self-awareness that emerge at one stage (Stage 2), as an introduction to a demonstration of how this particular form of understanding can be expressed in the spontaneous self-reflective verbalizations (concepts-in-use) under naturalistic conditions of group discussion. They conclude with a discussion of the implications of research on reflective understanding for the study of practical understanding in troubled children. Thus, like Harter, Selman and his associates emphasize the need for normative data as a backdrop against which individual differences can be assessed. Additionally, they address the important issue of variations in levels of social-cognitive functioning in different contexts.

Just as the child constructs a theory of self so does he/she formulate conceptions about relations with others. Knowing about self–other relations encompasses several domains or content areas. Perhaps the earliest acquisitions involve the ordering of relations between the self and the primary caretaker. However, that responsiveness to peers is manifest even in the first year of life suggests that early on, children begin to deal as well with peer relations in general and, some years later, with the particular form of dyadic relations known as friendship. The development of children's conceptions of friendship and friendship interaction patterns is the topic of Serafica's chapter.

In this chapter, contemporary research on conceptions of friendship and friendship interaction are reviewed selectively in order to delineate conceptual and methodological issues, identify possible links between these two lines of research, and suggest new directions for future investigations. The issue of whether there are systematic, hierarchically ordered transformations in children's ideas about friendship is discussed from two different yet related viewpoints—structure-oriented and content-oriented approaches—as is the critical question regarding what organizing principles underlie the observed developmental trends; structure-oriented approaches posit that development of perspective taking, particularly the ability to coordinate perspectives, is the organizing principle, whereas for those who employ a content-oriented approach, it is the child's increasing capacity for abstraction. Last, the issue of individual variations in children's conceptions of friendship is discussed in relation to sex, peer status, and clinical classification.

In probing the nature of the relationship between thought and action within the domain of friendship, Serafica takes three approaches. First, she looks for consistency in level of social reasoning across situations. Second, she searches for correspondence between level of concept development and behavioral interaction between friends. Third, she examines the influence of interactions with friends on concept development and vice versa. These explorations lead to the conclusion that there is a hiatus between the study of friendship concept development and the study of friendship interaction patterns. The conceptual and methodological problems associated with this gap are discussed and directions for future research are proposed.

The theoretical issue regarding the relationship between social-cognitive abilities and social behavior is given a fresh new look by Shure in her chapter on interpersonal problem solving, or what she calls children's thinking skills—that is, the ability to think through and solve typical everyday interpersonal problems. She describes several interpersonal cognitive problem-solving (ICPS) skills. Drawing from studies of young children, she presents evidence relevant to three important issues: (1) individual differences in ICPS skills, (2) the relationship between ICPS skills and social behavior, and (3) the function of ICPS skills as mediators of social adjustment and interpersonal competence. Additionally, she deals with the critical problem of the generalizability of process training to behavior in natural, real-world settings. If ICPS skills are critical for social relations and psychological adjustment, then how they develop and what factors influence their development are questions which require serious consideration. Using data from her own research, done in collaboration with George Spivack, and from the work of other investigators, Shure describes developmental trends in specific interpersonal problem-solving skills and in the overall process of coping with social dilemmas. The issue of what factors affect ontogenesis is addressed in three different ways: (1) through an examination of the relationship between a mother's ICPS skills and those of her child, (2) through an investigation of the facilitative effects of training, targeted directly at the child's ICPS skills or indirectly through mothers and teachers, and (3) through a review of studies that have assessed the relationship between social-inferential abilities and ICPS skills. Other issues considered are the relative merits of quantitative versus qualitative methods of measuring social-thinking skills and the significance for social adjustment of process (or form) of problem-solving thinking as compared to content (or substance).

The development of the child's knowledge about the world beyond the boundaries of the self is the topic of the chapter by Shantz. In addition to constructing a theory of self and self–other relations, the child also acquires an understanding of social rules and their functions. The construction of social reality involves, among other matters, identification of domains that are rule-governed and a comprehension of the origins, generality, and changeability of rules, and of the consequences of particular rule violations. In her chapter, Shantz examines first- and second-grade children's reasoning about social rules. She presents an empirically based description of this particular age group's (1) ability to distinguish between conventions and moral principles, (2) types of reasoning, and (3) variations in reasoning as a function of the type of violation and age. The results of her study are relevant to the broader issues of whether children's ability to distinguish between conventions and moral principles is an age-related phenomenon and, if so, when in ontogenesis the majority of children make such a distinction. One intriguing finding gives rise to the interesting question of whether the various patterns manifested in this narrow age span represent developmental differences or individual differences in social reasoning.

The interactional perspective is reflected by Shantz's assertion that the construction of social reality is a bidirectional process involving the social environment as well as the child. Relative to this, she discusses the possible relations between social-rule understanding and the social context within which the child operates. Noting that very little attention has been paid by theorists or researchers to the manner in which social organization is manifested to the child, she proposes that the "perturbation" in the social system enhances the salience of rules for the child. Drawing from the findings of recent studies, she discusses some factors that draw the child's attention, facilitate discrimination of rules, and give meaning to the rule. The chapter ends with a presentation of several alternative approaches to the study of the relationship between social-cognitive development and context.

In his chapter on social interaction and cognitive growth, Bearison contends that early conceptions of social cognition as referring to a particular class (i.e., social) of knowledge have promoted dubious distinctions between physical and social knowledge, created theoretical confusion regarding the social origins of all knowledge, and resulted in empirical problems, including a misleading approach to the study of the relationship between social knowledge and social behavior. He proposes instead a more expanded view of social cognition that recognizes social interaction as a cognitive process that develops in tandem with the cognitive-structural status of the individual.

Bearison's thesis is that cognitive development cannot be adequately explained solely in terms of children's solitary reflections on hypothetical problems since knowledge is not constructed independently of the social contexts in which it is shared, validated, and used to mediate social discourse. Moreover, he adds, instead of merely assuming that the cause of mental development is the cognitive conflict generated by children's exposure to viewpoints different from theirs, investigators must establish the presumption of cognitive conflict in the course of social interaction and problem solving. In keeping with his position, Bearison suggests that a method involving systematic observations of how children socially interact while attempting to solve cognitive problems might reveal more about the process of cognitive change than the verbal outcomes of children's solitary reflections. More specifically, such a method would permit the identification of the particular aspects of social interaction that reflect levels of cognitive conflicts co-occurring within the individual and within the interaction, as well as the ensuing intra- and interindividual coordinations directed toward resolving such conflicts at different levels of cognitive organization.

A study based on the foregoing assumptions is presented to illustrate the usefulness of the paradigm shift being advocated. On the basis of its findings, several interesting directions for future research on the reciprocal relationship between cognitive–organismic and social–contextual structures and its effects on cognitive development, are discussed.

The scarcity of heuristic models for describing the organization of the social environment in developmentally meaningful ways has long been a major obstacle to the proper study of organism–environment interaction. Both Chandler and Blyth address this important issue, but do so from different orientations. Chandler approaches it from the viewpoint of structural-developmental theory while Blyth contributes a sociological perspective.

Chandler's chapter on social cognition and social structure begins with a critique of what he calls a "one-sided constructivism" that pays lip service to the importance of both organism and environment in development and behavior yet in practice treats all constructions of reality as if they were solely the products of the human mind, reflecting nothing of the stimulus world. Because, he says, it is a subject-centered psychology where organization, when observed, is assumed to be imposed by persons rather than inherent in the objects or tasks with which they interact, it has excluded from systematic study the organized character of targeted objects of knowledge.

Other writers (Kuhn, 1978) have made similar criticisms. What is unique about Chandler's analysis of this problem is his assertion that this restriction of scientific investigation to the subject pole of organism–environment interactions was made possible in part by the nature of impersonal cognition. Moreover, he suggests that the inherently recursive character of social cognition offers a means of redressing this lack of balance in the study of organism–environment interactions.

The theme of the chapter by Chandler is that the outcome of children's transactions with different facets of their social environment are best understood as resulting from an interaction between their current level of cognitive organization and independent but comparable social structures. Within the interpersonal domain, the intended objects of knowledge (who happen to be subjects in their own right) also possess an inherent structure of their own, quite apart from the structure possessed by the cognizer. Thus, both subjects and objects can be characterized as varying along a common dimension of increasing organization or complexity. The study of social cognition therefore permits, as well as requires, a dual and equal focusing of research attention on the structural features of both subject and object. Some recent studies, undertaken from this proposed binocular perspective, are described to illustrate the feasibility and usefulness of this approach.

Blyth, too, is concerned with characterizing the structural organization of the social environment. His sociological approach to this problem entails an examination of the organization of children's social relations. He presents a review and critique of some techniques currently employed in studying a person's social world: classical sociometric techniques, social-network techniques, and techniques involving the identification of an individual's significant others. Concisely, he discusses each technique, how it is distinct from others, and some particular problems associated with it.

The central focus of the chapter, however, is a proposed conceptual framework for viewing a child's social relations in a manner which can be related to the structural features of his/her environment and the development of cognitive abilities used to interpret that environment. Its basic assumption is that a child's social relationships have differential meaning and salience over the course of ontogenesis that are reflected in the way social networks are formed at different developmental periods. Attention is focused on four major questions that arise in regard to mapping children's interpersonal relationships: What is the social world one is attempting to define? How does one define a social relationship? Who acts as the definer? How does one summarize or describe the individual's social map? Having established the background, Blyth then describes three basic social-mapping techniques: relationship, structural, and combined. The discussion is organized along methods for eliciting significant others and the kinds of information to be gathered for each of these important others. Within this context, he reports illustrative data from programmatic research on the social world of adolescents designed to depict a meaningful portrayal of adolescents' important social relationships and adequately characterize them.

Social-mapping techniques, Blyth suggests, allow the investigator to describe the social world of different sets of people in different contexts and to explore whether or not social worlds change as a function of the individual's development and/or the changing environment in which people find themselves. Social maps, therefore, can serve as independent, as well as dependent, variables. Their use, however, must be guided by careful consideration of three potential problems, discussed in the last section of the chapter: (1) the effects of different levels of cognitive development on the resultant social maps, (2) whether it is possible to talk about important people globally rather than talk about importance in specific areas, and (3) the stability of an individual's social world.

Together, the topics covered in this book present a coherent picture of the development of aspects of the self and self–other relations, and how these two lines of development interact within a given context. The development of a child's understanding of him/herself is represented by Selman *et al.*'s chapter on self-awareness and by Harter's presentation of children's understanding of emotions. Progress in understanding self–other relations is portrayed by Serafica's discussion of friendship and by Shure's work on interpersonal problem solving. The child's differentiation of the broader social world is depicted by Shantz's research on social rules, roles, and relations. All of the foregoing deal only with development of social cognition. The relationship between cognition and social behavior is delineated by Bearison. Finally, the contextual factors that influence this interaction are discussed by Chandler and by Blyth. The metaphor of a camera lens might be used to describe the relationship between the different chapters. All contributions attempt to portray the child's developing awareness of the self in relation to the social world but the camera lenses vary. Some researchers use a zoom lens, focusing intensively on one aspect of the self such as the emotions; other investigators use a lens with a wider angle and are thus able to capture dyadic interactions. Blyth, the lone sociologist in the group, uses the lens with the widest angle and captures the broader social network. Each view contributes to an integrated portrayal of the child as a developing social being within a social world.

REFERENCES

Ames, R. A. *A longitudinal study of social participation.* Unpublished doctoral dissertation, University of California, 1956.
Baldwin, J. M. *Social and ethical interpretations in mental development.* New York: Macmillan, 1906.
Barenboim, C. Developmental changes in the interpersonal cognitive system from middle childhood to adolescence. *Child Development,* 1977, *48,* 1467–1474.
Barenboim, C. The development of person perception in childhood and adolescence: From behavioral comparisons to psychological constructs to psychological comparisons. *Child Development,* 1981, *52,* 129–144.
Barrett, D., & Yarrow, M. R. Pro-social behavior, social inferential ability, and assertiveness in children. *Child Development,* 1977, *48,* 475–481.
Bearison, D., & Cassel, T. Cognitive decentration and social codes: Communicative effectiveness and the coordination of perspectives in young children. *Developmental Psychology,* 1975, *11,* 29–36.
Bell, S. M. The development of the concept of object as related to infant–mother attachment. *Child Development,* 1970, *41,* 291–313.
Berger, P. L., & Luckman, T. *The social construction of reality.* New York: Doubleday, 1966.

Biasi, A. Bridging moral cognition and moral action: A critical review of the literature. *Psychological Bulletin*, 1980, *88*, 1–46.

Borke, H. Interpersonal perception of young children: Egocentrism or empathy? *Developmental Psychology*, 1971, *5*, 263–269.

Borke, H. The development of empathy in Chinese and American children between three and six years of age: A cross-culture study. *Developmental Psychology*, 1973, *9*, 102–108.

Botvin, G. J., & Murray, F. B. The efficacy of peer modeling and social conflict in the acquisition of conservation. *Child Development*, 1975, *46*, 796–799.

Brandt, M. M. Relations between cognitive role-taking performance and age, task presentation, and response requirements. *Developmental Psychology*, 1978, *14*, 206–213.

Bronfenbrenner, U. Toward an experimental ecology of human development. *American Psychologist*, 1977, *32*, 513–531.

Bruner, J. S., Olver, R., & Greenfield, M. *Studies in cognitive growth.* New York: Wiley, 1966.

Cairns, R. B. *Social development: The origins and plasticity of interchanges.* San Francisco, Freeman, 1979.

Chandler, M. J. Social cognition: A selective review of current research. In W. F. Overton & J. M. Gallagher (Eds.), *Knowledge and development* (Vol. 1: *Advances in theory and research*). New York: Plenum, 1977.

Chandler, M. J. Social-cognitive development. In B. Wolman (Ed.), *Handbook of developmental psychology.* New York: Prentice-Hall, 1982.

Chandler, M. J., & Greenspan, S. Ersatz egocentrism: A reply to H. Borke. *Developmental Psychology*, 1972, 7, 104–106.

Cook, N. L. *Attachment and object permanence in infancy: A short-term longitudinal study.* Unpublished doctoral dissertation, University of Minnesota, 1972.

Cox, M. V. Order of the acquisition of perspective-taking skills. *Developmental Psychology*, 1978, *14*(4), 421–426.

Damon, W. *The social world of the child.* San Francisco: Jossey-Bass, 1977.

Damon, W. (Ed.). *Social cognition.* San Francisco: Jossey-Bass, 1978.

Decarie, T. G. *Intelligence and affectivity in early childhood.* New York: International Universities Press, Inc., 1965.

Deutsch, F. Observational and sociometric measures of peer popularity and their relationship to egocentric communication in female preschoolers. *Developmental Psychology*, 1974, *10*, 745–747.

Dion, K. K. Young children's stereotyping of facial attractiveness. *Developmental Psychology*, 1973, *9*, 183–189.

Dion, K. K., & Berscheid, E. Physical attractiveness and peer perception among children. *Sociometry*, 1974, *37*, 1–12.

Elder, G. H., & Rockwell, R. C. The life-course and human development: An ecological perspective. *International Journal of Behavioral Development*, 1979, *2*, 1–22.

Erwin, J., & Kuhn, D. Development of children's understanding of the multiple determination underlying human behavior. *Developmental Psychology*, 1979, *15*, 352–353.

Feffer, M., & Gourevitch, V. Cognitive aspects of role taking in children. *Journal of Personality*, 1960, *28*, 383–396.

Feshbach, N. D., & Roe, K. Empathy in six- and seven-year olds. *Child Development*, 1968, *39*, 133–146.

Finley, G. E., French, D., & Cowan, P. *Egocentrism and popularity.* Paper presented at the 14th Inter-American Congress of Psychology, Sao Paulo, 1973.

Flavell, J. H. *The development of role-taking and communication skills in children.* New York: Wiley, 1968.

Flavell, J. H. *Cognitive development*. Englewood Cliffs, N.J.: Prentice-Hall, 1977.(a)

Flavell, J.H. The development of knowledge about visual perception. In C. B. Keasey (Ed.), *Nebraska symposium on motivation 1977* (Vol. 25). Lincoln: University of Nebraska Press, 1977.(b)

Flavell, J. H., Everett, B. A., Croft, K., & Flavell, E. R. Young children's knowledge about visual perception: Further evidence for the level-1 level-2 distinction. *Developmental Psychology*, 1981, *17*, 99–103.

Flavell, J. H., & Ross, L. (Eds.). *Social and cognitive development*. New York: Cambridge University Press, 1981.

Gewirtz, J. L. Mechanisms of social learning: Some roles of stimulation and behavior in early human development. In D. A. Goslin (Ed.), *Handbook of socialization theory and research*. Chicago: Rand McNally, 1971.

Glick, J., & Clarke-Stewart, K. A. (Eds.). *The development of social understanding*. New York: Gardner Press, 1978.

Glucksberg, S., Krause, R. M., & Higgins, T. The development of communication skills in children. In F. Horowitz (Ed.), *Review of child development research* (Vol. 4). Chicago: University of Chicago Press, 1975.

Gottman, J., Gonso, J., & Rasmussen, B. Social interaction, social competence, and friendship in children. *Child Development*, 1975, *46*, 709–719.

Greenspan, S., Barenboim, C., & Chandler, M. J. Empathy and pseudo-empathy: The affective judgments of first- and third-graders. *Journal of Genetic Psychology*, 1976, *129*, 77–80.

Hebble, P. W. The development of elementary school children's judgment of intent. *Child Development*, 1971, *42*, 1203–1215.

Hoffman, M. L. Personality and social development. *Annual Review of Psychology*, 1977, *28*, 295–321.

Hollos, M. Logical operations and role-taking abilities in two cultures: Norway and Hungary. *Child Development*, 1975, *46*, 638–649.

Hollos, M., & Cowan, P. Social isolation and cognitive development. Logical operations and role-taking abilities in three Norwegian social settings. *Child Development*, 1973, *44*, 630–641.

Hudson, L. M. On the coherence of role-taking abilities: An alternative to correlational analysis. *Child Development*, 1978, *49*, 223–227.

Hughes, R., Jr., Tingle, B. A., & Sawin, D. B. Development of empathic understanding in children. *Child Development*, 1981, *52*, 122–128.

Jennings, K. D. People versus object orientation, social behavior, and intellectual abilities in preschool children. *Developmental Psychology*, 1975, *11*, 511–519.

Jones, M. C. The later careers of boys who were early or late maturing. *Child Development*, 1957, *28*, 113–128.

Karniol, R. Children's use of intention cues in evaluating behavior. *Psychological Bulletin*, 1978, *85*, 76–85.

Keasey, C. B. (Ed.). *Nebraska symposium on motivation 1977* (Vol. 25). Lincoln: University of Nebraska Press, 1977.(a)

Keasey, C. B. Children's developing awareness and usage of intentionality and motives. In C. B. Keasey (Ed.), *Nebraska symposium on motivation 1977* (Vol. 25). Lincoln: University of Nebraska Press, 1977.(b)

Keating, D. P., & Clark, L. V. Development of physical and social reasoning in adolescence. *Developmental Psychology*, 1980, *16*, 23–30.

King, M. The development of some intention concepts in young children. *Child Development*, 1971, *42*, 1145–1152.

Kohlberg, L. Stage and sequence: The cognitive-developmental approach to socialization. In D. A. Goslin (Ed.), *Handbook of socialization theory and research*. Chicago: Rand McNally, 1969.

Kuhn, D. Mechanisms of cognitive and social development: One psychology or two? *Human Development*, 1978, *21*, 92–118.

Kurdek, L. A., & Rodgon, M. M. Perceptual, cognitive, and affective perspective taking in kindergarten through sixth-grade children. *Developmental Psychology*, 1975, *11*, 643–650.

Langlois, J. H., & Downs, C. A. Peer relations as a function of physical attractiveness: The eye of the beholder or behavior reality? *Child Development*, 1979, *50*, 409–418.

Levine, L. E., & Hoffman, M. L. Empathy and cooperation in 4-year-olds. *Developmental Psychology*, 1975, *11*, 533–534.

Liben, L. S. Perspective-taking skills in young children: Seeing the world through rose-colored glasses. *Developmental Psychology*, 1978, *14*, 87–92.

Lovitt, T. Applied behavior analysis and learning difficulties: Part I. *Journal of Learning Disabilities*, 1975, *8*, 432–443.

Marx, K. *Die fruhschriften*. Stuttgart: Kroner, 1953.

McDavid, J. W., & Harari, H. Stereotyping of names and popularity in grade school children. *Child Development*, 1966, *37*, 453–459.

Mead, G. H. *Mind, self and society*. Chicago: University of Chicago Press, 1934.

Mossler, D., Marvin, R. S., & Greenberg, M. T. Conceptual perspective taking in 2- to 6-year-old children. *Developmental Psychology*, 1976, *12*, 85–86.

Peevers, B. H., & Secord, P. F. Developmental changes in attribution of descriptive concepts to persons. *Journal of Personality and Social Psychology*, 1973, *27*, 120–129.

Piaget, J. *The moral judgment of the child*. London: Kegan Paul, 1965. (Originally published, 1932.)

Piaget, J. *Judgment and reasoning in the child*. Totowa, N.J.: Littlefield, 1966. (Originally published, 1928.)

Piaget, J. Piaget's theory. In P. H. Mussen (Ed.), *Carmichael's manual of child psychology* (Vol. 1). New York: Wiley, 1970.

Piaget, J. [*Intelligence and affectivity: Their relationship during child development*] (T. A. Brown & C. E. Kaegi, Eds. and trans.). Palo Alto, Calif.: Annual Reviews, 1981.

Piaget, J., & Inhelder, B. *The psychology of the child*. New York: Basic Books, 1969.

Piche, G. L., Michlin, M. L., Rubin, D. L., & Johnson, F. L. Relationships between fourth graders' performances on selected role-taking tasks and referential communication accuracy tasks. *Child Development*, 1975, *46*, 965–970.

Reese, H. W., & Overton, W. F. Methods of development and theories of development. In L. R. Goulet & P. B. Baltes (Eds.), *Life-span developmental psychology* (Vol. 1). New York: Academic Press, 1970.

Rothenberg, B. Children's social sensitivity and the relationship to interpersonal competence, intrapersonal comfort and intellectual level. *Developmental Psychology*, 1970, *2*, 335–350.

Rubin, K. H. Relationship between egocentric communication and popularity among peers. *Developmental Psychology*, 1972, *3*, 364.

Rubin, K. H. Egocentrism in childhood: A unitary construct? *Child Development*, 1973, *44*, 102–111.

Rubin, K. H. Role taking in childhood: Some methodological considerations. *Child Development*, 1978, *49*, 428–433.

Rubin, K. H., Attewell, P. W., Tierney, M. C., & Tumolo, P. Development of spatial egocentrism and conservation across the life span. *Developmental Psychology*, 1973, *9*, 432.

Rubin, K. H., & Maioni, T. L. Play preference and its relationship to egocentrism, popularity and classification skills in preschoolers. *Merrill-Palmer Quarterly*, 1975, *21*, 171–180.

Schaffer, H. R. Cognitive structure and early social behavior. In H. R. Schaffer (Ed.), *The origins of human social relations*. New York: Academic Press, 1971.

Selman, R. L. Taking another's perspective: Role-taking development in early childhood. *Child Development*, 1971, *42*, 1721–1735.

Selman, R. L. Toward a structural analysis of developing interpersonal relations concepts: Research with normal and disturbed preadolescent boys. In A. Pick (Ed.), *Minnesota symposia on child psychology* (Vol. 10). Minneapolis: University of Minnesota Press, 1976.

Selman, R. L., & Byrne, D. F. A structural–developmental analysis of levels of role-taking in middle childhood. *Child Development*, 1974, *45*, 803–806.

Selman, R. L., & Jaquette, D. Stability and oscillation in interpersonal awareness: A clinical–developmental analysis. In C. B. Keasey (Ed.), *Nebraska symposium on motivation 1977* (Vol. 25). Lincoln: University of Nebraska Press, 1977.

Selman, R. L., Jaquette, D., & Lavin, D. R. Interpersonal awareness in children: Toward an integration of developmental and clinical child psychology. *American Journal of Orthopsychiatry*, 1977, *47*, 264–267.

Shaklee, H. Development in inferences of ability and task difficulty. *Child Development*, 1976, *47*, 1051–1057.

Shantz, C. U. The development of social cognition. In E. M. Hetherington (Ed.), *Review of child development research* (Vol. 5). Chicago: University of Chicago Press, 1975.

Shantz, C. U. Social-cognition. In P. Mussen (Ed.), *Carmichael's manual of child psychology* (Vol. 3: *Cognitive development*; J. H. Flavell & E. Markman, Eds.). New York: Wiley, in press.

Staffieri, J. R. A study of social stereotype of body image in children. *Journal of Personality and Social Psychology*, 1967, *7*, 101–104.

Strayer, J. A. A naturalistic study of empathetic behaviors and their relation to affective states and perspective-taking skills in preschool children. *Child Development*, 1980, *52*, 815–822.

Turiel, E. The development of social concepts: Mores, customs and conventions. In D. J. DePalma & F. M. Foley (Eds.), *Moral development: Current theory and research*. Hillsdale, N.J.: Erlbaum, 1975.

Turiel, E. Social regulations and domains of social concepts. In W. Damon (Ed.), *Social cognition*. San Francisco: Jossey-Bass, 1978.

Turnure, C. Cognitive development and role-taking ability in boys and girls from 7 to 12. *Developmental Psychology*, 1975, *11*, 202–209.

Urberg, K. A., & Docherty, E. M. Development of role-taking skills in young children. *Developmental Psychology*, 1976, *12*, 198–203.

Vygotsky, L. S. *Mind in society: The development of the higher psychological processes* (M. Cole, V. John-Steiner, S. Scribner, & E. Souberman, Eds.). Cambridge, Mass.: Harvard University Press, 1978.

Whiteman, M. Children's conceptions of psychological causality. *Child Development*, 1967, *38*, 143–155.

Wood, M. E. Children's developing understanding of other people's motives for behavior. *Developmental Psychology*, 1978, *14*(4), 561–562.

1

A Cognitive-Developmental Approach to Children's Understanding of Affect and Trait Labels

SUSAN HARTER

Introduction

As a developmentalist, it is interesting to characterize the field of psychology in terms of its stages of scientific advancement. For many years the theoretical efforts of individuals appeared to represent exercises in *solitary play*, idiosyncratic formulations which were pursued in isolation. As we came to define ourselves as a legitimate domain of scientific inquiry, we advanced to a stage more analogous to *parallel play*. Dimly aware that other branches of the field existed, we were content to promote the growth of our own specialty, be it learning, perception, physiological cognition, affect social psychology, personality, or psychopathology. In our theoretical egocentrism we might have found ourselves occasionally talking to our colleague in the next laboratory or office, though rarely did we listen.

The 1970s seemed to represent yet another advance, to *associative conceptual play*. Theoretical battle lines were no longer so sharply drawn, nor were we quite so possessive. Rather, the tools and ideational toys, as it were, of the various neighboring subbranches took on a new appeal, and there seemed to be a desire to somehow want to play together. Nowhere has this trend been more striking than in those variegated efforts to investigate the possible links between affect and cognition.

SUSAN HARTER. Department of Psychology, University of Denver, Denver, Colorado.

Within the field of developmental psychology, the most popular attempts have involved the application of Piagetian theory to the topic of affect. In practice, these efforts typically manifest themselves in the search for those cognitive structures which are correlates or prerequisites of affect. That is, one begins with either an explicit or implicit cognitive orientation and then maps it onto the affective variables of interest. Hypotheses or predictions concerning the relationship between particular cognitive structures and affective expression are then tested within a given laboratory-experimental paradigm.

I have found my own way into this intellectual playground and share an interest in the interface between cognition and affect. However, the impetus was not a commitment to any particular hypotheticode-ductive framework. The story can best be characterized as an inductive effort which began in my clinical interactions with child clients. Only much later did the setting shift to the research laboratory. Ironically, perhaps, it began in the play-therapy room.

My orientation can best be characterized as eclectic. I shared with many schools of therapy the view that affective expression was somehow central to psychological growth. As such, play provided a natural arena for the acknowledgment, acceptance, and understanding of the nature and the implications of one's emotional life. It became increasingly apparent in my work with children that a sensitive appreciation for the child's level of cognitive development was also essential. A number of developmental questions struck me as I observed child clients who came with a variety of presenting problems. Through what type of cognitive filter does a child process information about his/her emotions? And how does one's emotional understanding change with age? What implications do possible ontogenetic shifts have for our attempts at clinical intervention?

In my own therapeutic efforts these questions were not raised in the abstract but emerged in relation to a phenomenon which began to emerge as I observed client after client. All of these young children seemed to have considerable difficulty acknowledging seemingly contradictory feelings. While one feeling might be expressed, the child could not simultaneously acknowledge its seeming opposite, in situations where one would expect both to be manifest.

A common theme among many of these children has been the smart–dumb dichotomy. For example, a bright, sensitive 7-year-old boy who had been diagnosed as dyslexic was convinced that there wasn't a smart bone in his body. He insisted that he was "all dumb." In another case, where there was a great deal of latent hostility which an

8-year-old felt toward his father, the boy insisted that he felt nothing but love and admiration for the parent. How could he possibly harbor any ill feelings toward his own father?

Another client, a bright 6-year-old boy, was referred because of a tremendous problem of acting out aggressively at both home and school, where he demonstrated extremely poor impulse control. He was convinced that he was "all bad" and that there was nothing commendable about his behavior. Another, a 7-year-old girl from an orthodox Jewish family and the third girl born to these parents, developed an extreme case of sibling rivalry when the family was finally "blessed with" a boy, the longed-for son. She could only acknowledge her extreme hate for her new brother; there was no part of her that could express any positive feelings toward him.

Elsewhere (Harter, 1977, in press-a) I have described an illustrative case in detail, the case of K. Briefly, K, who was 6 when she began therapy, was referred for school learning problems which began in kindergarten. She was an anxious child who seemed to question her competence, even though her standardized test performance was within the normal range. In short, she felt "all dumb" like the client described earlier. Factors in the home situation caused her to be particularly anxious. She had not known her natural father, and her mother remarried a man who was particularly harsh and punitive with K and her brother. Her ambivalence was marked. This became acute when the parents threatened to separate. Yet she could only acknowledge one feeling, her love for her stepfather, and she was adamant in her insistence that she felt no other emotional reaction toward him. K also had a deep fear of people leaving her, which has a basis in reality. A grandmother of whom she was very fond remarried and then moved across the country. There were other losses. A favorite uncle died, creating another emotional vacuum. In addition, there had been a constant parade of aunts temporarily moving in and out of the house because of interpersonal problems in their own lives. A common scenario was the dissolution of a relationship—they had left a husband or someone had left them. In therapy, K could only express her sadness, and much later anger, about these events; she could not acknowledge any pleasure or joy over these relationships.

Repeatedly I have seen young children adopting this kind of all-or-none conceptualization of their own affective life, accepting a very one-sided view of their feelings. They vehemently deny alternative emotions and experience great difficulty in accepting the possibility that seemingly contradictory feelings might simultaneously exist. Another related manifestation is the tendency for some young children to *vacillate* from one extreme to the other. While today they may feel "all happy," tomorrow some event may cause a dramatic shift toward the opposite pole where they can only express their strong feelings of anger. From a psychodynamic point of view it could be argued that such difficulties stem from certain environmental or familial considerations which cause these particular children to have specific adjustment problems, emotional difficulties, and conflicts in the areas cited. Given this framework, it is understandable why they should deny certain feelings and have difficulty acknowledging or expressing what appear to be contradictory emotions or polar opposites. However, it would also appear that these difficulties are a function of certain cognitive-developmental factors, namely age- or stage-specific conceptual limitations which are present in the young child. Thus, after numerous observations convinced me that the phenomenon was real, it seemed fruitful to explore what implications Piagetian theory (Flavell, 1963; Piaget, 1932) would hold for elucidating the possible cognitive underpinnings.

Implications of Cognitive-Developmental Theory

A more detailed description of the implications of Piagetian theory can be found in an earlier publication (Harter, 1977). The developmental shift in Piaget's theory that seemed particularly relevant was the transition from the stage of preoperational thought to the stage of concrete operational thought. It is this particular transition, and the gradual development and solidification of logical operations during the concrete operational period, that seems intimately related to the child's comprehension and construction of a logical system of *emotional* concepts that define the affective spheres of his/her life.

There are a number of important general hallmarks with regard to preoperational thinking which seemed relevant. Principally, the child is unable to reason logicaly or deductively. Rather, his/her judgments are dominated by his/her *perceptions* of events, objects, and experiences. A further limitation is the fact that he/she can only attend to one perceptual dimension or attribute at a time, to the exclusion of all others. Fischer (1981) provides an excellent summary of preoperational thought:

> The child does not yet have the ability to organize his thinking into coordinated systems that he can direct and control. His intelligence is

dominated by whatever thought strikes him at the moment, whatever characteristic is prominent in a situation. His thinking is egocentric because he cannot coordinate various viewpoints into a single system that takes all of them into account. . . . His thoughts run on of themselves and he flits from one idea to another, because he cannot coordinate his ideas around a single concept. . . . He cannot coordinate his knowledge of people and objects into systems that allow him to deny his immediate impressions and maintain a consistency to his interpretations. Similarly, he cannot carry out a task that requires him to coordinate his thinking unless he has the help of salient concrete clues.

What are the implications of these cognitive-developmental limitations for the child's understanding and expression of his/her emotional feelings and, in particular, the difficulty in simultaneously acknowledging seemingly contradictory emotions? An examination of the conservation task provided some initial clues. The classic water beaker experiment requires that the child make a judgment about the amount of water poured from one standard-sized glass into a second, taller but narrower glass. In his/her insistence that there is more water in the taller glass, the preoperational child's judgment is dominated by his/her perceptions of the most salient physical dimension or attribute, in this case height. Of critical importance is the fact that he/she is able to focus on only *one such dimension at a time.*

The concrete operational child, on the other hand, will assert that the amount of liquid has remained the same because, to take a typical explanation, the "new glass is taller, but it's also thinner." That is, the concrete operational child is able to simultaneously consider more than one attribute and is thus capable of understanding the reciprocal relationship between the two dimensions of height and weight.

Piaget largely restricts his theorizing to those processes that involve judgments about physical quantities and/or the mathematical sphere. He has not extended this particular type of analysis to judgments in the affective realm. However, it would seem that one can readily extrapolate certain of these principles to the child's developing system of *emotional* concepts. If the preoperational child has difficulty focusing on more than one *perceptual* dimension at a time, it may also be difficult to focus on more than one *emotional* dimension at a time Thus, when the young child is faced with judgments based on such affective opposites as smart versus dumb or good versus bad, his/her cognitive limitations make it difficult to view both as simultaneously operative. Rather, the focus is on only one of these emotional dimensions, leading to such all-or-none conclusions as "I feel like I am all dumb" or "I'm completely bad."

The general inability to coordinate various viewpoints into a single system that takes all of them into account simultaneously also suggests why the child may sometimes vacillate in his/her affective judgments. For example, the child may feel "all loving" at one moment and "all nonloving" the next. Or, yesterday's assertion which implies that "there is only one part of me, and it is happy" may then dramatically shift to the conviction that "I feel all sad" today. Just as transformations may alter prelogical children's judgments about physical quantities, it is suggested that certain transformations can also change one's judgments in the affective realm.

The examples of children's difficulty in acknowledging more than one feeling at a time were drawn from clinic cases referred for treatment. However, given the argument that stage-specific characteristics of *normal* cognitive development are in part responsible for the manner in which children conceptualize their emotions, it was essential to embark on a normative cognitive-developmental program of research.

Normative-Developmental Research

Initial Considerations

It was important at the outset to specify the domain of inquiry, since one may well question whether it is possible to phenomenologically experience two polar emotions such as love and anger at the same time. We did not address this particular question. Rather, we focused on the child's conceptualization of emotions, his/her understanding of the manner in which conventional emotional labels are applied to the self and to others. Thus, the research goal was to indicate how a cognitive-developmental approach could illuminate changes in the child's understanding of emotional concepts.

The preceding analysis focused primarily on a two-stage model, highlighting the implications of the shift from preoperation to concrete operational thought. Given the paucity of evidence relating to children's emotional understanding, however, we did not want to confine our empirical efforts to a test of the applicability of Piagetian theory. Thus, we did not predict a sequence of stages but allowed the data to dictate a sequence, if in fact it existed. To superimpose a theoretical structure upon this phenomenon seemed premature. Therefore, we began by studying the phenomenon itself, very directly, in the absence of any potential theoretical blinders.

This phenomenon was initially described in terms of the child's understanding of his/her *emotions* and the problem in acknowledging seemingly contradictory *feelings*. However, it would appear that at least two different types of personal attributions were subsumed under the general label of "emotions." While certain conflicts, such as the happy–sad dichotomy, appear to refer to actual *emotional* concepts, other dichotomies (e.g., smart–dumb) appear to reflect the domain of a child's perceptions of his/her abilities, characteristics, etc. Thus, it seemed fruitful to distinguish between the child's acknowledgment of *feelings* such as happy, sad, scared, surprised, mad, and excited; and those characteristics falling under the "self-concept" rubric—for example, smart, dumb, popular, attractive, unathletic, etc. Our research initially examined the domain of emotional or affective constructs.

Research Methodology

INTERVIEW TASK

There was some precedent in the existing literature on emotional development for the use of pictorial materials. However, the previous research did not address the question of the understanding of multiple emotions, nor was it intuitively obvious how pictorial stimuli would be selected or designed to meet this need. Thus, we decided to begin our empirical journey with an open-ended interview. In this interview, children were first asked to generate single feelings, and we then asked a series of questions about each separate emotion. A second set of questions was designed to ascertain the extent to which the child could understand how two feelings could go together. Our experience in piloting our interview is described elsewhere (Harter, in press-a). Basically we learned that we could fruitfully employ the same general interview procedure with children between the ages of 3 and 12, and could meaningfully code the data.

A child was first asked to name all of the different feelings he/she could think of, and then to give an example of a situation in which he/she would have that feeling. To date, we have focused on nine different emotions: happy, sad, mad, scared, loving, jealous, ashamed, proud, and nervous. If a child did not spontaneously mention one of these nine, we asked him/her about each feeling, and in what situations such an emotion would be experienced. These questions have provided us with information about the nature and number of single emotions which children at different developmental levels comprehend.

In the second part of our interview, we have systematically probed about the experience of two emotions, asking about what other feelings could coexist with the "basic four," happy, sad, mad, and scared. We have referred to these as the "basic four" since pilot interviews revealed that all of our subjects, including the youngest, demonstrate their verbal understanding of these feelings.

Piloting also revealed that there were two general classes of response to questions directed at how two feelings could co-occur. In some instances the emotions followed one another temporally—for example, "I was happy that I could watch television, and then mad cause I had to go to bed." Other responses expressed two emotions simultaneously— for example, "I was excited about my first airplane ride but I was also a little scared." Thus, our first interview question concerning the ex-perience of two emotions is designed to elicit a response relevant to the *temporal sequence* of each feeling. We asked our subjects: "You told me that one thing that made you happy (mad, sad, or scared) was when . . ." (and then we repeated what the child initially described as the situation making him/her happy). We then continued with "That was one feeling, but sometimes you can first have one feeling, like happy, and then you can have another feeling, a different feeling, *after* you feel happy. What feeling could you have after you feel happy?" After the child described another feeling, we asked what would make him/her feel that emotion.

In order to address the *simultaneous* expression of two emotions, we next said to the child: "O.K., now that was how you could first have one feeling and then have a different feeling after it. But sometimes you can have two different feelings at the *very same time*. Tell me how you could have another feeling at the very same time you were feeling happy?" The child's response was then followed by a question asking him/her to elaborate on the situation in which he/she would feel those two feelings.

The child was asked this same series of questions about each of the four basic emotions.

SUBJECT POPULATION

Our subjects between the ages of 3 and 13 have been drawn from predominantly middle-class and upper-middle-class families. The ma-jority of children have been individually interviewed in our laboratory facilities where their responses have been recorded on either an audio- or videotape. Over 100 subjects comprised the earlier samples on which our procedures were revised. Initial findings summarized in this chapter were based on data collected from 45 children, all of whom were given the interview previously described.

Initial Empirical Findings on the Use of Affect Labels

Range and Content of Emotions

The number of emotions generated for a given subject in our sample of 3- to 13-year-olds ranged between 3 and 18. We found that we were able to reliably code a total of 40 discrete emotions spontaneously mentioned by our entire sample. The correlation between number of emotions generated and chronological age across our sample was .38.

The youngest children, 3-year-olds, could consistently generate three emotional labels—happy, sad, and mad—and in certain cases a fourth, scared. They clearly understand all four of these feelings and can give rich and appropriate examples of events or experiences in which they have had these emotions. For the most part, our youngest subjects, in the 3- to 5-year-old range, do not have a clear understanding of ashamed, proud, nervous, or jealous. This is not to say that they have not experienced these feelings at some level. Recall that our focus is on the children's ability to conceptualize these emotions, as reflected in their capacity to verbally describe appropriate situations in which they have experienced these feelings. We return to this issue in a subsequent section.

With increasing age we find that children not only understand all of the nine target emotions we selected but demonstrate their comprehension of a wide range of additional feelings which they generate—for example, annoyed, disappointed, relieved, discouraged, anxious. These particular examples are typical of the older children in our sample, between the ages of 10 and 13. Our younger subjects typically mentioned a minimum of six feelings. Often, however, these constituted synonyms for the basic four emotions or closely related affects—for example, fine, good, great, unhappy, dizzy, hate, yukky, etc. The correlation reported for the relationship between age and number of emotions mentioned, therefore, does not reflect the increasing sophistication and differentiation of the emotional network generated by children as they become older. Thus it will become necessary, in our future data analytic efforts, to determine how to document this type of ontogenetic shift.

Co-occurrence of Two Emotions

Our initial examination of the interview data indicated that we could broadly categorize children's responses as falling into one of the following three levels:

1. Only one feeling can be experienced; two feelings cannot go together: Although the youngest children can give appropriate examples of situations in which they have felt, or might feel, single emotions, they cannot envisage any way in which two feelings could go together. This conceptual inability was manifest in a number of ways. Some children vehemently deny that one could ever have more than one feeling in the same situation—for example, "You *can't* have more than one feeling" or, for those more engrossed in the vernacular, "No way!" Other exclamations have included: "It's hard to think of this feeling and that feeling cause you only have one mind!"; "I'd be sad if my friends don't want to play with me but that's the only feeling I could have then"; and "I've never done that before, you know I've only lived six years!" Other young children gave more indirect responses such as "I don't want to think so hard" or "My brain doesn't know the answer to that one." It was clear in almost all cases that our young subjects understood the question, even if they could not produce a codable response. There were relatively few "I don't know" comments.

2. Two feelings in a temporal sequence: The first indications that a child can conceptualize two different feelings take the form of expressing them in a temporal sequence. Sample responses in this category were: "I would be sad if my friends wouldn't play with me, but then if my mommy gave me a toy I'd be happy"; "I'd feel excited about getting on the roller coaster but scared once it got going"; "I'd feel happy that the present I was getting might be something I liked and then mad if it was something I didn't like"; "I'd feel fine because my aunt and uncle were coming to my house, and later I'd feel happy because another friend came over to play with me"; and "I'd be proud 'cause I thought my report card was going to be good, but then later I'd be disappointed that it wasn't as good as I thought."

The data documented a clear developmental progression in that many of the children who could describe two feelings in sequence could not give an acceptable response to our question asking how they could have two feelings at the very *same time*. Some children simply deny this possibility—for example, "I've never had two feelings at the same time." One child exclaimed: "Another feeling with happy at the same time? That's a toughie. Well, it sure couldn't be sad or scared!" Another child came up with the general conclusion that "You just can't have opposite feelings at the same time."

3. Two feelings simultaneously: When explicitly asked to indicate how two feelings can go together at the same time, children deal with this question in a variety of ways. The following sample responses give some flavor for this diversity: "I'd feel mad 'cause my brother knocked down my blocks and sad 'cause I called my mommy and she didn't come." "I'd feel loving about going to see my grandma but grouchy about packing up to go and see her." "If I was watching a Godzilla movie I'd be scared if he attacked someone but excited to see what was going to happen." "If my friends wouldn't play with me, I'd feel sad and angry and disappointed. I'd feel sad that I couldn't play, and angry at them, and I'd also feel disappointed that I didn't try to do anything about it." "Well, if my dog was hurt I'd feel happy if her front legs were O.K., but I'd feel sad because her back legs were hurting."

Although the three levels (one feeling only, two feelings in temporal sequence, and two feelings simultaneously) provided us with the general outline of an age progression, the variations within the second and third levels gave us pause. There seemed to be qualitative differences in the manner with which different children dealt with the questions at each of these latter levels. Our next task, then, was to determine whether it was possible to categorize these different types of responses into a system which was psychologically meaningful and reliably codable, and which might reveal a more differentiated sequence with regard to emotional understanding.

Dimensions Underlying the Understanding of the Co-occurrence of Two Emotions

In keeping with the original strategy, to allow the data to dictate those categories which might define a possible sequence, we began to look further for dimensions along which we might organize children's responses. In addition to the temporal relationship between the emotions, either sequential or simultaneous, examination of the responses within each of these two broad categories suggested two additional dimensions.

Affective Valence

Children's responses varied with regard to the affective tone or the valence of the emotions described. Certain children produced two emotions which were *similar* in valence, either both *positive* (e.g., happy and excited, loving and glad) or both *negative* (e.g., sad and mad, worried and disappointed). Other responses described emotions of *different* valences; that is, one positive and one negative feeling (e.g., happy and sad, excited and scared).

This dimension seemed intriguing in light of the clinical origins of this research. Our clinic children had particular difficulty in the integration of seemingly *contradictory* feelings (e.g., happy and sad, loving and mad). The discovery of this dimension in the normative-developmental data suggested one way to operationalize the term "seemingly contradictory," namely emotions of different valence. We became interested in determining whether there might be developmental differences in the ability to generate examples of the co-occurrence of similar-valence emotion pairs in contrast to feelings reflecting different valences.

Object of the Two Emotions

In addition to temporal relationship and affective valence, a third dimension emerged from our inspection of the interview data, the object, or the target of the emotions. Certain emotion pairs were directed toward the *same* object or situation—for example, "I'd be mad because they knocked my blocks down and miserable because I'd have to build it up again." In other examples, each of the two feelings mentioned were attached to *different* events—for example, "I was frightened that my mom was going to punish me for not cleaning my room and happy 'cause I was watching TV."

The emergence of this third dimension was of interest since the examples from the child clients typically reflected their difficulty in appreciating how one can have different feelings about the same target, primarily a particular person. The client K, for instance, had difficulty realizing that she might have more than one feeling about her grandmother, toward whom she could only express feelings of sadness at the beginning of treatment. She could not consciously acknowledge the ambivalence which could be inferred from additional clinical material. Thus, we sought to examine the relevance of this third dimension to a developmental progression of emotional understanding.

Interactions among the Three Dimensions

Once having identified these three dimensions, we turned our attention to their interaction in determining children's responses. From a conceptual standpoint, we could readily map out the eight possible combinations of these three dimensions, which are given in the following list. Examination of the pool of responses revealed that these were not simply hypothetical combinations; there were clear examples of each of the eight possible ways in which these three dimensions could be combined.

Temporal relationship	Valence of the two emotions	Object of the two emotions
Sequential	Different	Different
Sequential	Different	Same
Sequential	Same	Different
Sequential	Same	Same
Simultaneous	Same	Same
Simultaneous	Same	Different
Simultaneous	Different	Different
Simultaneous	Different	Same

Sample responses for each combination are as follows:

1. *Sequential, different valence, different object*: "In the wintertime I get *sad* because I can't go swimming but then I feel *happy* because I can go ice skating."
2. *Sequential, different valence, same object*: "I was *mad* when my brother Peter got into my stuff and wrecked it—very mad—and then I was very *happy* when Peter put the stuff back to shape."
3. *Sequential, same valence, different objects*: "I'm *happy* when my cousin visits me and *excited* 'cause my aunt is going to have a baby, it's in her tummy."
4. *Sequential, same valence, same object*: "I feel *happy* when I hit a home run and then *proud* 'cause your teammates would keep on respecting you."
5. *Simultaneous, same valence, same object*: "On the roller coaster I was *scared* cause I thought I was going to fall off on the hills and turns and also *anxious* to see what it would really be like."
6. *Simultaneous, same valence, different object*: "It was raining and there was nothing to do and I was *bored* cause there was nothing to do and *mad* 'cause Mother punished me."

7. *Simultaneous, different valence, different object*: "I was *fright-ened* that my mother was gonna punish me for not cleaning my room and *happy* 'cause I was watching TV."

8. *Simultaneous, different valence, same object*: "When I went horseback riding by myself I was *glad* cause it was good to be away from my brothers and sister but I was *lonesome* all by myself cause there was no one to talk to."

Developmental Differences in the Use of Dimensions

The findings are merely summarized here. They are presented in more detail, in graphical form, in an earlier work (Harter, in press-a). Data were from 45 subjects, spanning the age range from 3 to 12.

To review our procedure: We asked each child about both the sequentiality and simultaneity of different emotions which could accompany each of the basic four feelings understood by all of the children: happy, sad, mad, and scared.

TEMPORAL RELATIONSHIP

For all four emotions, there was a general linear trend with age indicating that those children unable to conceptualize two emotions as co-occurring under any circumstances were the youngest. The mean age at which children can give acceptable responses to the *sequential* occurrence of two emotions was between 6½ and 7½ years, and the average age by which children in this sample could conceptualize the simultaneity of two emotions was 9.

All subjects who could successfully answer the simultaneous question also gave a satisfactory answer to the question involving the sequentiality of two feelings.

THE INTERACTION OF TEMPORAL RELATIONSHIP
AND AFFECTIVE VALENCE

Next, for the sequential and the simultaneous question separately, we examined the frequency and the ages of children generating same-valence and different-valence responses.

In examining responses to the *sequential* question, the same pattern was obtained for three of the four emotions, happy, sad, and scared, where these were the first emotions in the pair; *more* children reported an emotion pair of *different* valence than the same valence, and the mean age of the children describing an emotion of a different valence was 1 to 2½ years lower than those supplying an emotion of the same valence. (When mad is the first emotion in the pair, the differences in the frequencies of children reporting same and different valences for the second emotion are negligible, and the age trend is the converse of the effect found for the other three emotions.)

When one examines the children's responses to the *simultaneous* question, the general pattern for the frequency data is the opposite of that obtained in response to the sequential question. When forced to deal with the issue of simultaneity, *more* children give *same-valence* replies than give different-valence responses.

THE INTERACTION OF TEMPORAL RELATIONSHIP
AND OBJECT OF EMOTION

We then examined the frequency and ages of children generating same-object and different-object responses to the sequential questions and to the simultaneous question, separately. In first considering the *sequential* question, for all four emotions the pattern is very similar. More children spontaneously make reference to the *different* objects of the two emotions than to the same object. In addition, the children generating different-object responses were younger than those who focused on the same object as the target of both feelings.

The pattern for the *simultaneous* question is the reverse, for three of the four emotions. When asked about the simultaneity of two emotions, children are more likely to attach these two feelings to the *same* object than to a different object.

Summary of Findings

When one considers responses to the question requiring children to place two emotions in temporal *sequence*, more children are likely to describe emotions of a different valence and to attach the two feelings to different objects. Additionally, children who focus on differences for both of these dimensions tend to be younger than those who generate emotions of the same valence and emotions directed toward the same object. The opposite pattern was obtained in response to our question requiring that two emotions be conceptualized as co-occurring *simultaneously*. Of those children who could give an adequate response to this question, more made reference to emotions of the same valence, and more attached the emotion pair to the same object. The frequency of different-valence and different-object responses to this questions was extremely small.

Interpretations and Implications for Further Research

From a developmental perspective, we were tempted to cautiously interpret those categories with higher frequencies and lower ages as representing potentially "easier" responses. Thus, when asked to supply an emotion which follows the first in *time* or *sequence*, it appears easier for children to generate an emotion of a different valence and attach it to a different event, person, or situation. When we ask sequential questions, why do children tend to shift both the valence and the object? In examining the responses where *happy* is the first emotion in the pair, by far the most common second emotion mentioned was *sad*. When *sad* was the first emotion in the pair, *happy* was typically the second feeling described. Is it possible that these tend to be "natural opposites," that children learn to conceptualize happy and sad as a dichotomous pair at a relatively early age?

This explanation does not explain a similar pattern when scared is the first emotion in the pair. We have speculated on a possible "psychodynamic" interpretation here: When the question provides an opportunity to think of another feeling after you were scared, children may attempt to conceptually "escape" from the scary situation by generating a positive emotion attached to a quite different event. However, the affect of anger does not follow the pattern for the other three emotions. For the sequential question we found that the younger the child, the greater the tendency to supply an emotion of the *same* valence, another negative feeling, which is attached to a different object. This has caused us to wonder whether there is something unique about the emotion of anger that makes it more difficult to switch one's set to a positive feeling. Are the data consistent with the expression "consumed with anger" and its implication that this particular emotion mobilizes one to remain within the bailiwick of negative affects? Does the fact that the second negative feeling is typically directed toward a different object have any implications for the "displacement of anger"? These interpretations are merely speculative at this point.

What are the conceptual demands put on the child when we ask that one supply two emotion labels that can *simultaneously* co-occur?

Why does it appear "easier" for children to generate emotions of the *same* valence and to attach the second emotion to the *same* situation, event, or object? When forced to consider another feeling which one could experience at the very same time, is it more difficult to conceptually shift moods and situational targets? Intuitively this seems plausible. In fact, the combination that appears to be the most difficult involves simultaneously acknowledging that one can have different-valence feelings, both a positive and a negative emotion, toward the same target. The finding is consistent with our clinical observations. Consider the difficulty of feeling both loving and angry toward a parent at the same time.

The data point to intriguing trends. However, there remains considerable room for thoughtful interpretation. We cannot be content with explanations couched in terms of "conceptual shifts," "natural opposites," and "psychodynamic interpretations." We need to be much more precise. Answers to these questions must necessarily involve a consideration of cognitive-developmental principles as well as more psychodynamic factors.

Furthermore, we must explain why certain emotions such as mad do not follow the same pattern as other feelings (e.g., happy, sad, and scared). Why do we find what constitutes a form of décalage or developmental unevenness here? We could sweep such findings under the empirical "rug" and choose to highlight global patterns of ontogenetic change; however, we have not opted for this choice. We feel that such a strategy not only obscures an important theoretical consideration for developmentalists but places blinders on our efforts to understand how and why particular emotion labels differ from one another. Such an understanding has practical implications for our educational and clinical efforts with children as well.

The Limitations of Dimensions Derived from Spontaneously Generated Responses

When we delineated the eight possible combinations of our three dimensions, it may have been implied that we could specify a developmental sequence. The interview questions that were asked did not permit this type of analysis. Recall that the only dimension we inquired about directly was the temporal relationship between the two emotions. We required that the child demonstrate his/her ability to produce a sequential as well as a simultaneous emotion pair. We did not specifically ask children to give us both same-valence and different-valence responses, nor did we require that they deal with both same and different targets or objects of the emotion pairs. That is, we did not systematically probe for a child's understanding of those eight possible combinations. We did not test for the cognitive *ability* to conceptualize each of these possible relationships among the three dimensions.

Thus, at present, we must be cautious in our inferences about which combinations are "easier," since this term implies an ability component for which we have not tested directly. Based upon both the frequency of children generating a particular response, as well as the ages of those children, we can merely *hypothesize* that the ability to specify how emotions of *different* valence can occur in *temporal* sequence precedes the ability to specify how emotions of similar emotions occur sequentially. Conversely, we can hypothesize that the ability to conceptualize the *simultaneous* occurrence of emotions with a similar valence developmentally precedes the ability to apply such a conceptualization to two feelings of different valences. Analogous predictions can be made with regard to the object dimension.

However, our present data cannot speak to the question of a scalable sequence involving all eight combinations. An adequate test of such a progression requires that we formulate interview questions or tasks which specifically ask about *each* of the eight combinations of the three dimensions. These data can then be analyzed utilizing scalogram techniques. We can determine whether the combinations we have identified, or some subset of them, can be cast into a meaningful acquisition of sequence in which particular combinations of these dimensions systematically precede and follow other combinations. We can also examine the ages at which each of these combinations is manifested, as a second approach to the demonstration of a developmental progression in the understanding of multiple emotions.

CURRENT RESEARCH

We are presently attempting to pilot procedures which would permit such a determination. Two types of tasks look promising. Our goal is to concretize the procedure, since a verbal interview procedure tapping each of these eight combinations would be formidable for our young subjects.

In one task we will use a series of photographs of children's facial expressions drawn from a large pool that we have now taken. These will represent a range of positive and negative emotions. The child will be

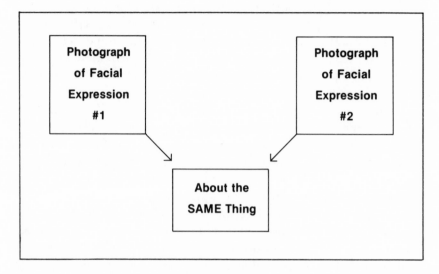

FIG. 1-1. *Schematic of photographic task designed to elicit responses about multiple emotions.*

presented with a separate sheet, like Figure 1-1, for each of the eight combinations. The one reproduced here will be used for simultaneous, same-target combinations.

The child will be asked to pick two pictures from the sample of photographs and place them on the sheet. He/she will then be asked to describe how one could have both of these feelings at the same time, about the same thing. If the feelings selected were of the *same* valence, the child will next be asked to choose one positive and one negative feeling. Our pretesting has indicated that even the 4-year-olds can sort the faces into "good" feelings and "bad" feelings, quite reliably. We will initially have each child sort them into these two categories, to facilitate his/her later choice of two that are the same valence or different.

For simultaneous–different targets, the sheet will have a separate box for each emotion with each inquiry. We will either write in a word or sketch in the content of the child's response, to further concretize the examples provided. For sequential items we will utilize a folded sheet where the first picture will be placed on the outside; then the "page" will be turned to the second fold, concretizing a second point in time, such that the first picture will be out of view.

Our second approach to the determination of a sequence will be modeled after a procedure employed by Kathy Purcell (1978) in an Honors Thesis. Purcell was struck by the fact that in most children's stories and fairy tales, the characters are viewed as emotionally unidimensional. Thus, she wrote some stories in which the characters expressed only one feeling, and others where the characters expressed more than one feeling. In presenting these to young children, utilizing a recall paradigm, she found that her young subjects would continue to relate single-emotion stories, even though they had heard stories in which the character expressed multiple emotions. We would like to expand on this paradigm, generating stories which represent all eight combinations. We would also like to incorporate the methodology of Hand (1980), who has tested a sequence of children's understanding of the co-occurrence of "nice" and "mean" characteristics (derived from Fischer's [1980] theory), by dramatizing stories through doll play. We anticipate that the construction of such a series of enacted stories will require considerable pilot work. However, we also feel it is essential that we converge on this interesting developmental phenomenon utilizing a variety of methodologies.

Through such procedures, we hope to determine whether a sequence of emotional understanding unfolds. Utlimately, we plan to relate such a sequence to the cognitive-developmental levels postulated by Fischer (1980), in his theory of cognitive skill development. Building upon Piaget's model, Fischer has constructed a theory which identifies a greater number of stage-like structures and defines them more precisely. In his research with Hand (1980), Fischer utilized these levels of cognitive development to predict an acquisition sequence involving the children's understanding of how the characteristics "nice" and "mean" could co-occur. There are obvious convergences between the operational definitions of these levels and the combinations which have emerged in our own data. Thus, we plan to pursue this convergence between Fischer's theoretically derived levels and our empirically derived dimensions in the hope of better understanding how children conceptualize co-occurrence of two or more emotions.

Children's Understanding of Parental Emotions

More recently we have also become interested in children's understanding of their *parents'* emotions. This question is intriguing in its own right. However, we also sought to assess the relationship between the child's level of understanding of his/her *own* emotions and the level at which he/she could describe parental feelings. Does the child come to comprehend his/her own affective life first and subsequently apply this understanding to others, perhaps incorrectly? A Piagetian emphasis on egocentrism would predict such an outcome during the early years. Or do parents, as models, display affects which the child first comes to appreciate in adults, after which he/she applies these labels to his/her own behavior? Such an expectation would be more consonant with a social learning theory orientation.

As with most such questions, the answer is undoubtedly both, to some degree. Obviously, the child must learn the meaning of particular emotion labels from others within a social context, and he/she must come to recognize the emotion experiences to which these verbal labels apply in others as well as him/herself. A social learning theory framework in the spirit of Bem's (1978) self-perception theory can best explain the acquisition and application of a vocabulary of emotions to one's own feelings.

How does the child apply these labels to the feelings of others, notably parents? At a very early age, he/she learns to identify and later to verbally label happiness or anger in Mommy and Daddy. But then how does the child interpret the source or *cause* of a particular parental emotion? Can the child accurately predict the cause of the parents' feelings from his/her observations, or does the child egocentrically project his/her own emotions and their causes onto the parent? These were the type of attributional questions which Rebecca Barnes and I sought to answer within a cognitive-developmental framework.

PROCEDURE

Our procedure utilizes a photographic task in conjunction with interview questions. We first obtained two sets of four photographs from two adult models, one set depicting a mother and the other a father. Each series portrays the basic four emotions, happy, sad, mad, and scared. The facial expressions are realistic, without being exaggerated, and when asked to label each, children's judgments are extremely reliable. Our stimulus materials also include two additional series of child photographs, one of a boy and one of a girl, depicting these same four emotions. To date we have asked children about single emotions only. Our procedure is as follows: We first show the subject the child series appropriate to his/her gender. We ask the child to tell us what would make him/her experience each of these four feelings and why.

We then introduce the parent pictures, one parent at a time, counter-balancing the order in which mother and father pictures are presented across subjects. After ensuring that each child can accurately identify the four emotions in each parent, we ask the child to tell us what would make each parent experience each of those feelings, and why. Thus, we can compare the child's responses about his/her own emotions to responses concerning parental emotions.

FINDINGS

The verbal data generated by such an interview procedure are extremely rich. Examination of these data indicated that the responses given for the sources of parental emotions fell into three general categories:

1. Responses which the child had given as the cause for his/her *own* emotions, or responses which were clearly child-appropriate. Examples were: "Daddy would be happy if he got to play with his toy giraffe"; "Mommy would be scared if a monster came into her room"; "Daddy would be mad if the kids made fun of him"; and "Mommy would be sad if she couldn't go out and play." (Freudian colleagues would have an interpretive field day with these responses, needless to say!)

2. Responses in which the parental emotion is adult-appropriate; however, the *child* is the *target* of that feeling. Typical comments in this category were: "Mom gets mad when I break something"; "Dad is happy if I take out the garbage"; "Mom is sad when me and my brothers fight"; and "Dad was scared when me and my sister got lost."

3. Responses in which not only is the parental emotion appropriate, but the target is something of relevance to the adult's life which does not involve the *child*. "Mom is happy when Dad takes her to dinner"; "Dad gets mad when he has to grade a lot of papers"; "Mom was sad when her car got wrecked in an accident"; "Dad was kind of scared when someone broke into his office and damaged his chiropractor's table."

We interviewed 60 children, 10 boys and 10 girls, at three age levels: 4 to 5, 6 to 8, and 9 to 11. We anticipated a developmental trend in which the youngest children would primarily utilize the self- or child-appropriate category, the 6- to 8-year-olds' responses would fall in the child-target category, and the 9- to 11-year-olds would demonstrate the ability to produce responses in which the responses were oriented toward adult concerns not involving the child subject.

The results supported this developmental pattern which we interpreted in terms of the child's increasing ability to decenter. While this general sequence was expected, we had no specific predictions concerning differences associated with the particular emotion. However, the results revealed that children do not interpret the causes of the four parental emotions—happy, sad, mad, and scared—in a uniform fashion. Their interpretations are a function of the emotion in question. Such differences highlight the need to consider developing cognitive structures in relation to the particular content domain to which they are applied, rather than viewing emotional understanding as a synchronous developmental process.

The emotion of parental anger provides the most dramatic example. Across all four emotions, the majority of responses for each age group fell in the child-target category. However, for the emotion "mad," 83% of the entire sample indicated that they were the cause of parental anger. In contrast, for the emotion "scared," only 41% of the sample felt that they were responsible for this parental affect. Falling within these extremes, 65% gave illustrations of how they were the cause of parental happiness, and for the emotion "sad," this value was 49%.

How are these findings to be interpreted? The preponderance of responses revealing that the children perceive themselves as the cause of parental affect is certainly consistent with both Piagetian and psychoanalytic observations which indicate that often the child makes erroneous cause-and-effect inferences. Typically, these involve the perception that he/she has been responsible for a negative event which often has moral overtones. We see this in Piaget's (1932) descriptions of the moral judgment of the child. Psychoanalytic theory has also alerted us to the problem of the Oedipal child whose momentary angry death wish toward the father may be interpreted by the young boy as a *cause*, should some misfortune subsequently befall the parent.

Within this context, it becomes more understandable why our child subjects feel particularly responsible for parental anger, as well as happiness. Their examples, however, tend to portray *realistic* causes of anger or happiness on the part of the parent; they are not illogical. Our subjects told us that parents get angry when the child fights with a sibling or breaks things, and that parents are happy if the child does his/her chores without being told or "is good." How is this to be reconciled with the assumption that often such judgments are erroneous?

It would seem that we must first acknowledge the potential egocentrism reflected in such responses. It is of a qualitatively different nature, though, than the egocentrism of the earliest stage in which the young child assumes that the very same events which make him/her angry or happy also cause his/her parents to experience those emotions. The egocentrism of the child-target responses, in contrast, implies that the child is the center of the *parental* universe. The realistic nature of their examples may well reflect the very fact that children do provoke parental anger and often are a source of parental joy and happiness. However, to the extent that these attributions generalize to *every* source of parental affect, this egocentric perception will result in inaccurate cause-and-effect judgments of the type described in Piaget and the psychoanalysts. Thus, the child may take responsibility for every expression of parental anger or misfortune, and be unable to discriminate between situations in which he/she is a realistic cause and those for which factors external to the child are the source of the parents' emotion or experience. An attribution linking one's bad behavior to parental divorce is a familiar example.

FUTURE RESEARCH DIRECTIONS

Our current data do not speak to the issue of erroneous generalizations. In part, this may be due to the fact that we only requested one response for each parental emotion. Although the large majority of responses for all three age groups fell into the "child as cause of parental emotions" category, one would predict qualitative developmental differences in the degree to which such attributions are realistic if a larger pool of judgments were available. Thus, if children were required to make judgments about a wide variety of events in their parents' affective life, developmental differences would undoubtedly emerge. We plan to pursue this question in future research.

We also plan to address the child's understanding of *multiple* emotions in the parents. While we will be open to novel dimensions which might possibly emerge, we will be interested in how the dimensions of temporal contiguity, valence, and object are manifest. Additionally, we will be able to determine whether children utilize these dimensions differently for the four emotions, and whether their description of parental feelings are consistent with the description of their own affective life.

An integration of these data with our findings indicating that children view themselves as a cause of parental affect will have intriguing practical implications as well. Consider our youngest subjects, who can only entertain the possibility that they can have one feeling at any given point in time. To the extent that this is the only manner in which the child can perceive his/her *own* emotional experience, one would predict that such a child can only view parental emotions from the same unidimensional perspective. Thus, when a parent is mad, he/she must be "all mad," and the child is undoubtedly unable to interpret parental anger against a backdrop of emotional concepts which simultaneously includes feelings of love and concern. This all-or-none conceptualization, coupled with the attribution that he/she is also the *cause* of this anger, must also have implications for the child's *affective* reaction to the perceived parental emotion. The fact that mommy must be "all mad" and "I'm responsible" may evoke considerably more fear, anxiety, shame, or guilt in a child than if one perceived mommy as both angry *and* loving (or caring), and if one could envisage sources of this anger other than oneself.

There are numerous questions to be pursued within this context. How does the child construct an understanding that he/she is responsible for a complex emotional state in the parent? What cognitive-developmental as well as experiential factors are involved in the child's socialization history to determine these attributions? What emotions do these attributions evoke in the child? What does it imply for the child's understanding of not only what causes an emotion to occur in the first place but what makes an affect go away? What do I do to make mommy happy when she is mad? How does this particular "set" influence the child's own affective state? What is the child's understanding of what makes his/her own emotions come and go, and how does this change with development? These are types of questions which must ultimately be addressed in pursuing the interaction between a child's developing understanding of his/her emotions and the emotions of the significant others in one's life.

The Use of Trait Labels and
Development of the Self-Concept

The clinical context from which this research evolved pointed to conceptual difficulties in acknowledging not only the co-occurrence of different emotions but different polar *attributes* such as smart and dumb. Conceptually we have treated these two classes of response very similarly in our cognitive-developmental analysis. However, it may be fruitful to distinguish between them. To date, we have confined our normative-developmental research to emotional constructs. Currently we are beginning to extend our inquiry to the domain of attributes or trait labels.

We will address some of the same issues. Does the child's perception of him/herself as smart or dumb, bad or good, athletic or uncoordinated, popular or unpopular, attractive or unattractive follow a developmental progression similar to the one emerging for emotions? Are these trait labels first applied to the self in a unidimensional fashion such that one is all smart or all dumb, all bad or all good? If so, what form do subsequent differentiations over the cause of development assume? More specifically, are the dimensions of temporal relationship, valence, and object relevant to this class of judgments, and to a similar degree?

The dimensions involving both affective valence and temporal relationship are both certainly relevant to such trait labels. The polar opposites cited earlier definitely have a positive and negative valence. Temporally, one can envisage sequential attributions—for example, the perception that one did a stupid thing yesterday, but today, one's experience leads one to feel very smart. However, can one be both smart and dumb simultaneously? And what is the counterpoint of the dimension which revealed itself as the "object or target of the emotion"?

Children do talk about having "smart parts" and "dumb parts" which coexist at the same time. The counterpart of the object dimension would seem to be the situation in which the particular characteristic is manifest. This would then dictate an examination of the extent to which attributions were situation-specific. If the child perceives that he/she has both smart and dumb parts simultaneously, at one point in time, does he/she view him/herself as smart in one situation or domain and less intellectually adequate or even stupid in a different domain? Consider the street-savvy child who is failing in school. Does he/she view him/herself as smart when he/she is outside the confines of school but cognitively inept within the school domain? Does another child perceive him/herself as smart in social studies and language arts but dumb when it comes to science and to math?

Clinical observations of child clients in play therapy (Harter, 1977) suggest that young children are "trait" theorists by dint of their cognitive limitations, and that with development they shift to a more differentiated self-perspective. Given such a perspective, one would expect that trait labels would no longer be applied to the self in a unidimensional fashion but would be attached to one's performance in particular situations. While it has been cogently argued (see Mischel, 1973) that adults treat trait labels as situation-specific, particularly when they describe themselves, we know little about how children utilize such descriptors.

The topic of traits also involves a consideration of the degree to which these characteristics are relatively stable or enduring over time as well. Herein lies a critical difference between our investigation of attributes and of emotions, since affects seem to be perceived as more transitory in nature. We would like to explore the hypothesis that attributes are viewed as more stable and as more central to one's self-definition. However, our primary focus is on the child's perception of both stability and change over time in those characteristics which define his/her own theory of self (see Harter, in press-b).

This general line of inquiry converges with our research on children's perception of their competence (Harter, 1978, 1981, 1982). In that work we have demonstrated one form of situation specificity in that children clearly do not view themselves as equally competent across the three skill domains we have tapped—cognitive, social, and physical competence. A fourth subscale taps the child's feelings of overall self-worth. However, we have not addressed the question of whether *within* a particular domain (e.g., cognitive) children can feel smart in one context and "dumb" or inadequate intellectually in another. The particular question structure devised for the Perceived Competence Scale does not permit that type of response in that we ask children to make a single judgment about their relative competence in a given domain. Thus, we would now like to address the issue of the differentiations a child makes within each domain in order to determine whether there is a developmental progression in children's appreciation of attributional dichotomies such as smart–dumb.

METHODOLOGY

We are currently piloting a task which follows from a play-therapy technique I found useful in helping children understand that they could be both smart and dumb (described in Harter, 1977). My very simple technique began with the 6½-year-old client who was having learning problems at school and felt she was "all dumb." I introduced a circle, with a line down the middle of it, marked by an S on one side and a D on the other. Not only was she able to utilize this drawing as a graphic metaphor symbolizing the smart and dumb parts of her person-

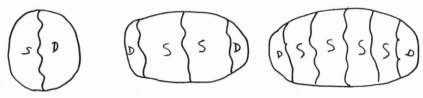

FIG. 1-2. *Sequence of child client's drawings representing herself as smart and dumb.*

ality, but her drawings became more differentiated, depicting more smart parts, as she herself received remedial help and began to improve in school. One sequence of her actual drawings is presented in Figure 1-2.

In our task, we are literally going to ask children to "slice up the behavioral pie" that defines them and their characteristics, beginning with cognitive, social, physical, and general self-worth domains. The child is presented with a circle labeled "This is ME." For the cognitive domain this is followed by "And how I do in school." The task materials involve six yellow carboard, pie-shaped slices, each labeled "smart," which will form an entire circle; and six brown, pie-shaped pieces, each labeled "dumb," which can also be made into a full circle. The child is first shown an all-yellow circle, depicting a child that might be "all smart," and an all-brown circle, depicting someone "all dumb"; and the suggestion is made that there are children who are part smart and part dumb, in varying degrees.

There are separate "This is ME" circles for the social, physical, and general self-worth domains, each with different pairs of colors. For the social domain the contrast is between having "a lot of friends" versus "not having a lot of friends." For the physical domain it is "good at sports" versus "not good at sports." For the general self-worth judgment, we based our contrast on a particularly good item from the self-worth subscale of the Perceived Competence Scale: "like the way I am" versus "wish I were different."

The child is shown the first "This is ME" circle involving how smart or dumb he/she feels at school. In our piloting we have first given a brief description of the task and have then taken a picture of the child with a Polaroid camera. This is placed above the circle to concretize the fact that this task is about "me." We then proceed as follows:

1. Self-perception of attributes: The child first chooses from among the six yellow-smart pieces and the six brown-dumb pieces the

six which best describes him/her, and then places these to form a circle. Thus, the child has the option of portraying him/herself as all smart, all dumb, or some combination of these.

2. Source of information on which the judgment is based: In order to determine the "data base," as it were, for these judgments, we ask the child to describe for each of the six parts his/her reasons, how he/she knows that he/she is smart and/or dumb.

3. Affect associated with that perception: To assess the child's emotional reaction to the self-attribution, we next ask how this judgment makes the child feel.

4. Continuity or change from the past: To learn about the children's theory of the change or stability in these self-perceptions, we next ask them to describe how they were when they were younger. They fashion their former self with the pie pieces. This is followed by an inquiry regarding their view of how they got that way and what was responsible for any change. These questions will illuminate each child's source of control over the events that occur to the self; does the child perceive him/herself as responsible, or are there people or forces beyond his/her control that result in changes in his/her personal characteristics?

5. Continuity and change in the future: We next ask the child to project into the future and indicate whether he/she feels he/she will be the same or different. The child constructs this future self and we question him/her concerning the causes of these changes.

6. Ideal self: Finally, we ask the children what they would prefer to be like, and they make this ideal self with the pie pieces. This is followed by a series of questions which probe into what would have to happen for them to be like that. Here we ascertain each child's perceptions of the sources for change, as well as how realistic his/her ideal self might be.

This same line of inquiry is then pursued with the other three content areas. The four domains—cognitive, social, physical, and general self-worth—are counterbalanced across subjects.

PILOT STUDIES

What does such a procedure yield in terms of information about the child's perceptions of self? Some sample protocols from fifth and sixth graders give a flavor for the type of verbal inquiry data which we will have to systematize. All three of these responses were perceptions of cognitive ability.

Subject 1: This sixth-grade girl first depicted herself as having five dumb parts and one smart part. In describing the dumb part, she gave the following reasons: "I get my spelling words wrong, I flunk every science test, in math everyone is ahead of me, I feel dumb because everyone calls me names like 'stupid,' and my sister, who is only seven, is even smarter than me. But I am smart in sports." When asked how this made her feel, she replied, "I feel bad because I'm real stupid compared to my friends; sports makes me feel good though cause I can do stuff." In response to the question "How were you when you were younger?" she replied, "Then I was all dumb, I never studied; I was just too interested in sports." When asked "What about how you'll be when you're older?" she responded, "In about two years I'll be like this," and she put together three smart pieces and three dumb pieces. To the question "How will you get that way?" she said, "I'll just have to study a lot and not think so much about sports, I guess." When asked "How would you most like to be?" her response was, "All smart, so I'd never have to feel stupid again! But I don't think I could ever study hard enough to get that way."

Subject 2: This sixth grader depicted herself as three parts smart and three parts dumb. She attributed her smartness to the following: "I get straight As sometimes in math, I made it into the band, I play the flute; and I don't *constantly* get in trouble." Her awareness of dumb parts was based on the following considerations: "I answer the question wrong sometimes in reading, sometimes I don't complete a project on time because I wasn't listening or paying attention, and sometimes I get sent home because of an incident at recess." When asked "How does this make you feel?" she replied, "I feel good, I feel proud of myself when I am smart at school and my mom isn't mad at me, too! I feel real yukky, though, when I'm dumb. I feel really bad if I do something wrong, and my mom gets mad at me, too." In response to the question "How were you when you were younger?" she depicted her former self as having four smart parts and two dumb parts, smarter than her current self: "I paid more attention then, I didn't have as many good friends. Now I talk to them too much and don't do my work." In answer to the question "How will you be in the future?" she said, "I think I'll stay the same, I don't really think I'll change unless I move away from my friends. Then I might get smarter!" When asked "How would you most like to be?" she replied, "The way I am now. I don't want to be oversmart or undersmart. If you're too smart, well, then you get conceited, and if you're too dumb, then you feel sorry for yourself. I don't want to be like either of those."

Subject 3: This sixth-grade boy depicted his current self as three parts smart and three parts dumb. His attributions of smartness were based on the following: "I pay attention in class and take notes, I get the answers right in school, and I do well at science; usually I get good grades." When asked "How about the dumb parts?" he answered, "Mostly its dumb things I do if you know what I mean. I act weird in class and make noises; sometimes I hit the girls 'cause they pinch me, and sometimes I de-pants girls on the soccer field and then I ask myself 'why did I do that!'" To the question "How does that make you feel?" he replied, "When I'm smart I feel happy and I have more energy. I'm not down. When I do stupid things I feel down, I'm not as active as when I'm smart." When asked "How smart or dumb do the other kids think you are?" he depicted four dumb parts and two smart parts, indicating that they think he is less bright than he does: "They think I'm dumb 'cause I act strange and weird. It's natural. I was just born weird!" To the question "How were you when you were younger?" he replied, "I was smarter then," and he put together four smart pieces and two dumb pieces—"I got better grades then in reading and math. After that I got into poor study habits. I don't like to study so hard." When asked "How will you be in the future?" he chose five smart pieces and one dumb piece: "There's just one subject I'll probably have trouble with in junior high, language. But by the time I get to high school, I'll be all smart. I'll study more and work harder." In answer to "What would you most like to be like?" he said, "All smart! Then people wouldn't think of me as dumb."

These three protocols are very typical for the fifth- and sixth-grade subjects we interviewed. They not only suggest certain dimensions of relevance to an understanding of self-perceptions, but they point to the individual differences as well. Subject 1, for example, perceives herself to be very dumb, with only one redeeming smart part, and her justification is a combination of inadequate performance, social comparison, and peer feedback. She perceives herself to have been even dumber in the past but holds out some hope for the future. Personal effort appears to be the route to such a change, to reach her ideal of being all smart.

Subject 2 currently sees herself as having an equal number of smart and dumb parts for which she seems to take responsibility. Unlike Subject 1, she views herself as slightly dumber now than when she was younger, largely because her present social life interferes with her studying. She doesn't think she will change in the future, unless an event such as moving away would remove her from the distraction of friends. Nor does she want to change. She is happy the way she is, and she verbalized her theory of the evils of being either too smart or too dumb.

Subject 3 also portrays himself as three parts smart and three parts dumb, currently, although his "stupidity" reflects behavioral misdeeds rather than cognitive limitations. In describing his affective reactions, he articulates a child's theory of depression, as it were: When he is smart, he feels active and has more energy; whereas when he acts stupid, he feels down and not as active. He views his stupidity as a rather enduring trait in that he was "born weird." He considers himself to have been smarter in the past than the present, and he believes he will become even smarter in the future, all smart in fact, if he studies hard. All smart is what ideally he would like to be.

These very rich verbal data take us far beyond our initial interest in a developmental progression from a unidimensional view of one's attributes to a more differentiated picture of the characteristics which define the self. By fifth and sixth grades, children clearly have a very differentiated conceptualization of themselves within a domain such as their cognitive skills. This pattern is the same in the other domains we have sampled. In addition, they can describe the sources of information on which they base these judgments. In the cognitive domain these include social comparison, direct peer feedback, evaluative adult feedback in the form of grades and marks (as well as comments), and personal effort. We have not yet extended this technique to younger and older children. However, there are intriguing developmental hypotheses to pursue with regard to how children at other age levels slice up the attribute pie, and upon what bases they form such a self-depiction.

The verbal data also suggest that children in the fifth and sixth grades have definite theories about the stability of their characteristics. For the most part, they hold the belief that they have changed from when they were younger and can change in the future, primarily in response to personal effort or environmental circumstance. Here, too, a developmental approach would allow us to determine whether this general orientation to the attributes of the self holds for both younger and older ages.

These issues are not merely of theoretical interest but of practical import as well. We have gone through a period of educational and clinical endeavors in which programs designed to change children's self-concepts have proliferated but not necessarily thrived. There are undoubtedly many reasons why. However, in any such effort it would seem critical to first ascertain the child's theoretical construction of how he/she developed the characteristics he/she perceives as him/herself, how he/she feels about it, the extent to which he/she wants to change, and what steps would be necessary to effect such a change. In certain cases an intervention may be aimed at altering a child's theory, whereas in other situations treatment programs may need to be individually tailored to coincide with the child's theory of change. In the absence of any knowledge of the theories on which the child's actions are based, general programs designed to enhance the child's "global self-esteem" will in all likelihood meet with minimal success. As I have recently discussed elsewhere (Harter, in press-b), we need not abandon the thought that children, as well as adults, carry with them a notion of their general self-worth. However, we must begin to give more thoughtful attention to the possible underlying dimensions which define a construct such as self-esteem or self-worth.

Summary and Conclusions

We began our empirical journey in an attempt to investigate the cognitive-developmental parameters of our clinical observations which revealed that children have difficulty acknowledging that two seemingly conflicting emotions or personal attributes can coexist simultaneously. We have now seen how the range of questions broadened when we addressed this question empirically. There are a number of new lines of inquiry. The potential sequence of several stages which define children's understanding of the co-occurrence of two emotions has yet to be determined. The investigation of children's understanding of parental emotions leads to another set of issues involving the conceptualization of affect within the social milieu. The fruitfulness of distinguishing between the experience of polar emotions and the acknowledgment of polar attributes which define the self has recently been borne out in our exploratory studies on children's use of trait labels. To date, we have only begun to scratch the surface, focusing on children's understanding of a limited number of traits which are applied to the self. In the future, we hope to extend these studies to a determination of how children apply these labels to others. Do they view others as being as differentiated as the self? In the adult social psychological literature there is now evidence that one tends to utilize trait labels in describing others but views one's own behavior as situation-specific. We plan to pursue this question developmentally.

The ontogenetic study of trait labels and how they are applied goes beyond the issue of differentiation. In both our emotion research and our pilot studies on attribute usage, it appears that with age such concepts do indeed become more differentiated. However, we must take our Wernerian zeal further and demonstrate how such concepts become hierarchically organized and integrated. We cannot be content to merely catalog the increasing number of personal concepts or labels that are utilized. As cognitive-developmentalists, we must take seriously our insistence that the child is constructing a theory of self and others which undergoes change in both content and structure (see Harter, in press-b).

There are an unlimited number of questions which can be asked in this arena of children's usage of emotion and trait labels. Part of me feels excited and encouraged that we have begun to answer a few, but another part of me feels frustrated and impatient that we haven't gone farther. The part of me that feels smart about getting a toehold on some of the issues also feels a little dumb, sometimes, when we can't see our way clear to figure out the next best step. But, in my own self-theory, there is room for change, and we think we are getting a little smarter with each step along this fascinating conceptual path.

ACKNOWLEDGMENTS

The research described in this chapter represents a collaborative effort with two colleagues, Christian Miner, currently at New York University, and Jim Connell, at the University of Denver. They have been an integral part of this program of research and have contributed richly toward every phase of this project, including its conceptualization, design, data collection, modification of our procedure, data analysis, and interpretation. The data described in this chapter were presented in a paper which I co-authored with Christian Miner and J. P. Connell, given at the biennial meetings of the Society for Research in Child Development, San Francisco, March 1979.

I would like to thank Rayma Skeen for her dedicated and successful efforts with adult models to obtain the photographic stimuli used in the study of children's understanding of parents' emotions.

REFERENCES

Bem, D. J. Self-perception theory. In L. Berkowitz (Ed.), *Cognitive theories in social psychology*. New York: Academic Press, 1978.

Fischer, K. W. A theory of cognitive development: The control and construction of a hierarchy of skill. *Psychological Review*, 1980, *87*, 477–531.

Fischer, K. W. *Understanding understanding: Piaget, learning, and cognitive development*. Unpublished manuscript, University of Denver, 1981.

Flavell, J. H. *The developmental psychology of Jean Piaget*. New York: D. Van Nostrand, 1963.

Hand, H. *The development of children's understanding of opposites in their behavior:*

How children develop the capacity to rationalize their niceness and meanness. Unpublished doctoral dissertation, University of Denver, 1980.

Harter, S. A cognitive-developmental approach to children's expressions of conflicting feelings and a technique to facilitate such expressions in play therapy. *Journal of Consulting and Clinical Psychology,* 1977, *45,* 417–432.

Harter, S. Effectance motivation reconsidered: Toward a developmental model. *Human Development,* 1978, *21,* 34–64.

Harter, S. A model of intrinsic mastery motivation in children: Individual differences and developmental change. In *Minnesota Symposia on Child Psychology* (Vol. 14). Hillsdale, N.J.: Erlbaum, 1981.

Harter, S. The perceived competence scale for children. *Child Development,* 1982, *53,* 87–97.

Harter, S. Children's understanding of multiple emotions: A cognitive-developmental approach. In A. Collins (Ed.), *Proceedings of the Piaget Society, June 1979.* Hillsdale, N.J.: Erlbaum, in press. (a)

Harter, S. Developmental perspectives on the self and self-systems. In M. Hetherington (Ed.), *Carmichael's manual of child psychology* (Volume on social development). New York: Wiley, in press. (b)

Mischel, W. Toward a cognitive social learning reconceptualization of personality. *Psychological Review,* 1973, *80,* 252–283.

Piaget, J. *The moral judgment of the child.* New York: Harcourt, Brace & World, 1932.

Purcell, K. *Children's understanding of the emotions of storybook characters.* Unpublished honors thesis, Swarthmore College, 1978.

2

Troubled Children's Use of Self-Reflection

ROBERT L. SELMAN

DEBRA REDMAN LAVIN

STEVEN BRION-MEISELS

> CHILD: I went up to the top of the John Hancock Building and looked over the ledge. Everybody else was scared, but I wasn't scared.
> THERAPIST: Gee, well, I would be kind of frightened looking down from way up there, wouldn't you?
> CHILD: Well . . . if I were a therapist and I was trying to get a kid to see that it was all right to admit that he feels frightened about some things, I might say that I would feel afraid to show him that it was okay to show that you were scared. . . . But I'm not a therapist and I'm also not afraid of anything.
>
> *Excerpt from a therapy session with a 12-year-old boy previously diagnosed at age 6 as manifesting autistic symptoms*

Introduction

Troubled children are often characterized as having extraordinary difficulty looking "inside" themselves and understanding relationships among their own feelings and motivations. Their problems are said to increase when they are expected to understand the further relationships between their feelings and motivations and their actions. From one clinical perspective these difficulties interfere with the child's ability to self-regulate or control the active expression of internal experiences and reactions, making necessary an increase in external controls or structure.

ROBERT L. SELMAN, DEBRA REDMAN LAVIN, AND STEVEN BRION-MEISELS. Laboratory of Human Development, Harvard University, Cambridge, Massachusetts, and Judge Baker Guidance Center, Boston, Massachusetts. Present address for Debra Redman Lavin: Cornell University Medical Center, Valhalla, New York.

In addition, troubled children are often said to have difficulty reflecting upon their own actions as they might be viewed from another person's perspective, to consider the effects of their actions on others and how others might view them as a result of their actions. However, clinicians such as Redl and Wineman (1952) have noted that the troubled child's ability to reflect upon his/her own feelings and motivations, rather than simply being retarded, actually varies greatly across different situations. As the excerpt that introduces this chapter indicates, in the calm of a psychotherapy session or a supportive individual interview, even a very troubled child can exhibit a highly sophisticated understanding of the reciprocal coordination of his/her own perceptions of social events and psychological reactions to those of a significant other. This ability can be demonstrated even when, as in this excerpt, the function of the expressed attitude is hostile or defensive.

To the developmental–clinical child psychologist these are particularly intriguing problems. Research with normative samples of children (Broughton, 1978; Flavell, Fry, Wright, & Jarvis, 1968; Shantz, 1975) attests to the validity of the theoretical claims of H. S. Sullivan (1953), G. H. Mead (1934), J. M. Baldwin (1906), and others that during the middle-childhood and preadolescent periods, the child's conceptual understanding of self and social relations goes through a period of rapid growth. Research in social perspective taking, for example, indicates that this growth can be characterized by three major advances in self- and social understanding (Selman, 1976; Shantz, 1975). At approximately age 4 to 6, most children begin to clearly understand on a reflective plane of understanding the difference between intentional and nonintentional social interactions (on a nonreflective plane, behavior indicative of this understanding may appear at a much earlier age). At about age 6 to 10, most children begin to understand the capacity of the individual to look inward in a self-reflective manner, to be able to reflect upon not only what the self does but to a limited extent why the self does it and how the self feels about it. At around age 10 to 14, most children understand the human capacity to inwardly examine not only *specific* thoughts, feelings, and motives, but *general* attitudes, traits, and values: what most adults mean when they speak of "personality."

This natural progression in children's understanding of self and social relations has important implications for professionals who ask children to reflect upon their own behavior and its consequences. When working with any child across this age range, it helps to know to what extent difficulty in looking at his/her own behavior (if there is

such difficulty) is a function of the natural level of social understanding common to all children at the given age period, or to what
extent there are specific pathological processes involved. Furthermore,
if disturbances in inward-looking abilities do exist, it helps to know
the extent to which they may be a function of developmental *lags* in
social-cognitive capacity and to what extent they may represent defensive *distortions* of otherwise age-appropriate *conceptions*.

In this chapter we describe exploratory research designed to help
clarify these questions and concerns. First we briefly review the theoretical framework of our own developmental–descriptive research in
self- and social conceptions. Next we describe in some detail a specific
example of the natural developmental shifts we find occurring in the
child's social understanding. This example deals with one issue in our
system which is especially pertinent to the theme of this chapter—
children's developing conceptions of the human capacity for self-
awareness. In focusing on this particular concept, our intent is to
examine how developmental research using interview methods for
studying children's social conceptions—for example, *about* the issue of
self-awareness, which is an example of what we call reflective understanding—can help us when we devise other research methods to
understand children's actual developing self-reflective capacity and
functioning, a practical understanding that appears to consolidate in
middle childhood and preadolescence. In the third and final section of
this chapter we describe a process as developed by members of our
research team for coding these naturally expressed conceptions in
group discussion data from a small sample of troubled children, and
we examine the implications of some preliminary findings on how,
when, and why these self-reflective capacities are used.

Reflective Social Understanding:
Formulating Developmental Analyses

For the past several years members of the Harvard–Judge Baker Social
Reasoning Project have been studying the child's developing interpersonal understanding. The research has gone through three phases:
initial descriptive model building, construct validation, and application
to other modes of social functioning. As is traditional in structural-
developmental research, in the initial phase a developmental analysis
was used to describe observed patterns in children's reflective knowledge. On the basis of extensive clinical interviewing and a theo-

retical model of social perspective-taking levels which grew from the seminal work of Mead (1934) and Piaget (1955), we outlined a series of five stages in children's conceptions of individuals, friendships, peer groups, and parent–child relations. In the second, or construct-validation, phase, our research is designed to evaluate formally whether these developing stage analyses of social reasoning satisfy the essential criteria of structured wholeness, invariant developmental sequence, and universality. Finally, in the third phase, these stage descriptions of reflective social understanding and reasoning are applied to an analysis of the spontaneous social comments and social interactions of individual children (Selman, 1980).[1]

Social conceptions and perspective taking are not, of course, new areas of study. Social psychologists in the areas of attribution theory, person perception, and role playing have long been interested in these processes in adults (cf. Heider, 1958; Kelley, 1973) and, occasionally, in children (cf. Shaw & Sulzer, 1964). As conceptualized in cognitive-developmental theory, however, social perspective-taking levels and social conceptual stages have special meanings which differ considerably from many previous uses. Here, *social perspective-taking* development refers to growth in a child's ability to mentally *coordinate* the perspective of another with his/her own. Developmentally, social perspective taking is viewed as beginning at a level of failure to distinguish social viewpoints of self and others. It then proceeds to develop in a series of regular steps, first to distinguish these perspectives and then to relate them to each other in progressively more complex ways. (Table 2-1 provides a synopsis of the social perspective-taking levels used in our research.) The goal of the first phase of research, then, is to develop a formal model which reflects both our empirical data about a variety of children's developing social conceptions and a logical analysis of how levels of social perspective taking underlie them.

The first task in this model is to define the specific concepts to be studied. These were chosen with both practical and theoretical considerations in mind. From a theoretical perspective, we wanted to concentrate on issues generally recognized as important in the study of interpersonal relations (Brown, 1965; Hartup, 1970). From a practical point of view, we then selected from these sources the issues which seemed most relevant to the special interpersonal concerns of children— particularly children experiencing interpersonal difficulties.

1. In our work we use the term "levels" to refer to the different hierarchical organizations of social perspective taking and "stages" to refer to the formal characteristics of each of the four relationship domains (e.g., friendship). The rationale for this nomenclature is discussed more fully elsewhere (Selman, 1980).

TABLE 2-1. *Levels of Social Perspective Taking: Relation between Perspectives of Self and Other(s)*

Level 0: Egocentric or undifferentiated perspectives

Although the child can recognize the reality of subjective perspectives (e.g., thoughts and feelings) within the self and within other, because he/she does not clearly distinguish his/her own perspective from that of other, he/she does not recognize that another may interpret similarly perceived social experiences or courses of action differently from the way he/she does. Similarly, there is still some confusion between the subjective (or psychological) and objective (or physical) aspects of the social world—for example, between feelings and overt acts or between intentional and unintentional acts.

Level 1: Subjective or differentiated perspectives

The child understands that even under similarly perceived social circumstances the self's and other's perspective may be either the same or different. Similarly, the child realizes that the self and other may view similarly perceived actions as reflections of disparate or distinct individual reasons or motives. Of particular importance, the child at Stage 1 is newly concerned with the uniqueness of the covert, psychological life of each person.

Level 2: Self-reflective or reciprocal perspectives

The child is able to reflect on his/her own thoughts and feelings from another's perspective—to put him/herself in the other's shoes and to see the self as a subject to other. This new awareness of the relation between self and other's perspective also allows the child to consider his/her own conceptions and evaluations of other's thoughts and actions. In other words, the child is able to take a second-person perspective which leads to an awareness of a new form of reciprocity, a reciprocity of thoughts and feelings (I know that he likes me; he knows that I like him) rather than a reciprocity of action (He does for me—I do for him).

Level 3: Third-person or mutual perspectives

The subject at Stage 3, aware of the infinite regress potential of the chaining of reciprocal perspectives, moves to a qualitatively new level of awareness, the awareness of a person's ability to abstractly step outside of an interpersonal interaction and coordinate simultaneously the perspectives of each party in the interaction. This ability to take the third-person perspective leads to the awareness of the mutuality of human perspectives and hence of the self–other relationship.

Level 4: Societal or in-depth perspectives

The subject conceptualizes subjective perspectives of persons toward one another (mutuality) to exist not only on the plane of common expectations or awareness but also simultaneously at multidimensional or deeper levels of communication. For example, perspectives between two persons can be shared at the level of superficial information, at the level of common interests, or at the level of deeper and unverbalized feelings. Also, perspectives among persons are seen as forming a network or system. These perspectives become generalized—for example, into the concept of society's perspective, or the legal or moral point of view.

As a result, to date we have focused our study of interpersonal understanding on four main domains: conceptions of individuals, conceptions of close dyadic friendships, conceptions of peer group relations (Jaquette, 1976), and parent–child conceptions (Bruss-Saunders, 1979). Furthermore, within each of these a more refined set of issues was defined. Included in the area of individuals, for instance, are issues of subjectivity, self-awareness, personality, and personality change. Under friendship are formation, closeness, trust, jealousy, conflict resolution, and termination. The issues within peer group relations include formation, cohesion–loyalty, conformity, rules–norms, decision making, leadership, and termination. Finally, in the parent–child domain the issues are motivation for having children, children's need, love and affection, obedience–punishment, conflict, and separation.

We begin by looking at reflective understanding. As noted, this refers to the carefully probed, reflective responses a child verbalizes about his/her interpersonal understanding in response to an interviewer's questions about hypothetical or real interpersonal situations. It is this kind of hypothetical, interview reasoning that is tapped in our initial model development (Phases I and II), and that is commonly gathered and studied by other social-cognitive researchers as well (cf. Broughton, 1978; Damon, 1977; Kohlberg, 1969; Turiel, 1975).

The nature of this understanding will be clarified by looking more closely at the methods used to evaluate it. Although a variety of procedures have been used, most involved presenting the child with an interpersonal problem or dilemma and probing his/her reasoning about it. For instance, the child's developing conceptions about individuals have frequently been evaluated with the following dilemma:

> Eight-year-old Tom is trying to decide what to buy his friend Mike for his birthday party. By chance, he meets Mike on the street and learns that Mike is extremely upset because his dog, Pepper, has been lost for two weeks. In fact, Mike is so upset that he tells Tom, "I miss Pepper so much I never want to look at another dog again." Tom goes off, only to pass a store with a sale on puppies; only two are left and these will soon be gone.

The dilemma, then, is whether to buy the puppy for Mike, and how this will affect Mike, psychologically.

As is typical in our structural-developmental research, the interview using this dilemma[2] covers a range of related issues basic to the child's developing conceptions of psychological processes within in-

---

2. A second filmstrip (or story) using older actors is oriented toward older children; in it a boy or girl finally wins a Ping-Pong game against an older child who has defeated him/her many times in the past, and then he/she finds out that the older opponent may have "thrown the game." The erstwhile winner claims that he/she did not really care about winning anyway; the interviewer probes the child's speculations about the validity of that statement, using questions similar in structure to those used for the Lost Puppy Dilemma.

dividuals. Each issue has a basic orienting question designed to elicit further explanation and clarification of the child's reasoning. For example, to explore the issue of self-awareness, we start with a general question such as: "Mike said he never wants to see another puppy again. Why did he say that?" Depending, in part, on the child's initial level of response, the experienced interviewer might choose from a range of "stage-related" follow-up questions such as: "Can someone say something and not mean it?"; "Is it possible that Mike doesn't know how he feels?"; "Can you ever fool yourself into thinking you feel one way when you really feel another?"; and so on. In addition to providing the stimuli for the child's discussion of issues raised in the dilemma, these questions act as a springboard for further probing of the child's general understanding of the issues.

Using this approach, we have interviewed subjects from preschool age through adolescence and into adulthood. From these interview data, in conjunction with the use of social perspective-taking levels as tools of developmental analyses, we have outlined five stages of development in each of 22 issues of interpersonal understanding. The result is a stage-by-issue model of developing interpersonal conceptions. This model both describes the separate development of each of the issues and domains, and suggests logical or structural parallels across the various issues, allowing stage comparison of the child's reasoning on one issue with another. (See Table 2-2 for an outline of the basic characteristics of conceptions of individual, friendship, peer group, and parent–child relations at each stage.) Table 2-3 presents a more detailed developmental synopsis of one of the four domains: conceptions of individuals.

The Growth of Children's Understanding of Self-Awareness

As an example, in this section we describe a social perspective-taking analysis of one of the issues in Table 2-3: conceptions of self-awareness. First we provide a brief description of each of five stages in developing cognitions of this intrapsychic phenomenon. Then we provide a more detailed description of the themes and aspects of self-awareness that emerge at Stage 2. In so doing, we provide a bridge to the final section of the chapter, where we attempt to identify the way Stage 2 is expressed under natural conditions of group discussion.

TABLE 2-2. *Sequence of Stages across Domains of Interpersonal Relations and Social Perspective Taking*

	Interpersonal relations				Social perspective taking	
Stage	Individual	Peer group[a]	Parent-child[b]	Friendship	Level	Characteristics
0	Physical entity	Physical connections	Boss–servant relation	Momentary physical playmate	0	Undifferentiated/egocentric
1	Intentional subject	Unilateral relations	Caretaker–helper relation	One-way assistance	1	Subjective/differentiated
2	Introspective self	Bilateral partnerships	Guidance counselor–need satisfier relation	Fair-weather cooperation	2	Reciprocal/self-reflective
3	Stable personality	Homogeneous community	Tolerance–respect relation	Intimate–mutual sharing	3	Mutual/third person
4	Complex self-systems	Pluralistic organization	Communicative system	Autonomous interdependence	4	In-depth/societal

[a]Descriptive research undertaken by Jaquette (1976).
[b]Descriptive research undertaken by Bruss-Saunders (1979).

TABLE 2-3. *Concepts of Individuals: Issues at Each Developmental Stage*

Stage	Subjectivity	Self-awareness	Personality	Personality change
0	All categories of intrapsychic phenomena undifferentiated from physicalistic (nonpsychological) phenomena.			
1	Differentiation of subjective (inner) experiences from objective (outer) experiences.	Actions will reveal intentions.	Personality as a particular motive.	Growth as change in likes or dislikes.
2	Differing subjective responses (e.g., feelings) to one object or event can occur, but only in sequence.	Differentiation of inner experience from reflection on that experience.	Personality as context-specific mood.	Growth as change through trying hard.
3	Conflicting feelings about the same object or event can be simultaneous.	Self is aware of the interaction between self as subject and self as object.	Differentiation of generalized personality traits from specific inner states.	Personality change; a stable system, difficult to change in part.
4	Conflicting subjective experiences can yield new qualitatively subjective states.	Self understands certain aspects of self's behavior are unavailable to self-awareness (unconscious).	Personality as integration of complementary and conflicting systems.	Differentiation of personality change as a restructuring of system, but maintaining identity.

Five Brief Stages

STAGE 0: PHYSICALISTIC CONCEPTS OF SELF

There are two aspects of young children's (about age 3 to 5) responses that characterize the earliest reflective conceptions of self-awareness. First, when asked questions about the inner self, the child does not appear to view the nature of inner or psychological experience as different from the material nature of outer experiences. Second, although very young children can articulate a sense of being aware of self, the nature of that self seems to have a quasiphysical quality. For instance, children will often report that their mouths tell their hands what to do or that ideas come from their tongues.

STAGE 1: RECOGNIZING DIFFERENCES BETWEEN INNER AND OUTER STATES

At Stage 1, children from about 5 to 11 years of age make several interesting discoveries. First, there seems to be a sense that what one is aware of in subjective experience is indeed a factual report of that experience—that is, what one says is what one means. While we are cognizant that even very young children are aware of the capacity to misrepresent factors or to deny the facts of situations, our interviews suggest these children do not seem to understand that one can also intentionally misrepresent one's inner reality (thoughts, feelings, motives) to either another or to the self.

A second, and related, aspect of self-awareness interpreted as Stage 1 is that although now covert attitudes and their overt representations are seen as separable (Baldwin, 1906), children limited to this level of understanding still seem to believe that a person's overt actions will eventually belie his/her inner attitude—that is, if one is a careful observer of another's outside, then one can begin to make a good guess about how that person feels inside. While there is validity to this assertion—indeed, we do know something of an individual's inner feeling from observation of his/her behavior—when the child's conception appears to go no further than this, we feel justified in coding it at Stage 1.

Finally, the assumption that in a sense the self can fool itself appears essentially synonymous at Stage 1 with the idea of changing a decision or making a shift in one's subjective concerns, rather than with any true awareness of the process of self-deception. When asked what it meant to fool the self, Jack, age 8, said, "You do something, and then you disagree with it; you find out you didn't want to do it."

STAGE 2: THE EMERGENCE OF AN INTROSPECTIVE SELF

As children in roughly the 7- to 14-year-old range move into Stage 2, they develop the capacity to assume the perspective of a second person and look back toward the self's inner states. The ability to take a second-person social perspective leads the child to theorize that inner experience acts as reality and that outer actions represent only one manifestation of that reality.

In addition, youngsters at this stage begin to reflectively understand that the self is capable of: (1) constantly monitoring its own thoughts and actions, (2) consciously and often deceptively presenting a facade to others, and (3) gaining inner strengths by having confidence in its own abilities.

STAGE 3: CONCEPTIONS OF THE SELF AS OBSERVED AND OBSERVER

George Herbert Mead (1934) hypothesized that a mature concept of self emerges from the child's (cognitive) capacity to take the perspective of another toward his/her own actions (our Stage 2). According to Mead, out of this self-as-action ideology there later emerges a self-as-entity phase that requires a second-order understanding of the simultaneity of the self as observer as well as observed. In this sense, the Stage 2 conception of subjective duality—the inner, or true, versus the outer, or apparent ("He says he doesn't want a puppy, but really he does; he is hiding how he feels.")—is transformed at Stage 3 into a deeper, more dynamic, and simultaneous understanding of the relations between self as subject and self as object ("He is trying to think about how he really feels.").

Perhaps the most striking difference between Stage 2 and Stage 3 conceptions of self-awareness is a shift from viewing the self as a passive observer (a keeper of secrets, a hider of ideas, a forgetter of unpleasant feelings) to an active psychological manipulator of inner life (a forceful remover of painful ideas). What appears new and striking at Stage 3 is a belief in the observing ego—that is, the self-aware self as an active agent. This concept of active agency strikes us as a development in the child's own theory that is critical if the child is to have a feeling of some control over his/her own thoughts and feelings. For the Stage 3 child, the mind (or ego) is now seen as playing an active moderating role between inner feelings and outer actions.

STAGE 4: THE UNCONSCIOUS AS A
NATURAL EXPLANATORY CONCEPT

Coded as Stage 4 is the realization that no matter how hard it works, there are still internal experiences not readily available to conscious awareness. At this stage, an adolescent sees that individuals can and do have thoughts, feelings, and motivations that are resistant to self-analysis even by the most introspectively functioning mind. There are two aspects to this discovery not often articulated until well into adolescence. First, there is the understanding of the existence of unconscious processes—the focus here being on the child's own growing natural theory of psychic phenomena, such as coping and defending as automatic processes. Second, there is the discovery of the concept of unconscious psychological causes of behavior—that is, that below inner reality there may be an even deeper reality. The development of the concept-in-theory of the unconscious emerges out of a need to explain observed aspects of social behavior and experience that previous conceptions of intrapsychic phenomena were inadequately structured to explain. However, it is not necessary for the adolescent to use psychological terminology and jargon to demonstrate that he/she holds a reflective awareness of these psychological processes. An understanding that people can behave on the basis of motives or needs of which they themselves are not aware, and that no purposive act of conscious effort or will can yield a total understanding of certain self-actions can be expressed without ever using the word "unconscious."

*A Closer Look at Stage 2: The Emergence of a
Self-Reflective Self and the Second-Person Perspective*

Conceptions coded as Stage 2 incorporate the further understanding that the individual can take a clear perspective on the inner life that was distinguished from outer experiences at the previous stage. In social perspective-taking terms, the self is now seen as able to put itself in the place of a second person and look back toward the self's inner states. At least four manifestations of this important developmental shift in awareness are the consequences for the child's understanding of the nature of self-awareness.

First, the ability to take a "second-person" social perspective allows the child to rethink the relative importance of outer appearance and inner reality. Whereas at Stage 1 the child responds as if he/she believes that the inner can be ascertained from the outer (and in a sense this is a valid insight maintained through life), at Stage 2 the child favors the theory that inner experience acts as reality and outer actions are only an appearance or one manifestation of that reality. In other words, there appears tó develop an articulated sense of the *priority* of inner experience (how one "really feels" about social events or interactions) over outer appearance.

INTERVIEWER: How is it you can hide the way you feel?
CHILD: If he felt real sad and stuff, you put a smile on your face and you go with everyone else and try to be regular, but sometimes you can really be sad.
INTERVIEWER: Is there a kind of inside and outside to a person?
CHILD: Yes.
INTERVIEWER: What would that mean?
CHILD: If there was a brother and a sister, like the brother always says I can't stand you, but really inside, he really likes her.
INTERVIEWER: Really deep inside. What is that inside? Can you describe it?
CHILD: Yah, I guess so, really what you really feel about something.

Second, Level 2 perspective taking marks the emergence of a working belief in the self's ability to constantly monitor the self's thoughts and actions. How does the shift manifest itself in beliefs about the ways in which the self can fool the self? How is it different from Stage 1, "changing one's opinion"? The following interview excerpts may give us some ideas.

INTERVIEWER: Is it possible to fool yourself?
CHILD: Yes, sometimes.
INTERVIEWER: How can you fool yourself?
CHILD: You can say to yourself, I didn't really care and keep on saying you didn't care, and when someone brings up the subject, you say I didn't really care and sometimes it works, and you really don't care about it.

INTERVIEWER: Do you think deep down inside you think you really don't care, or do you think you actually do care deep down inside?

CHILD: You really care.

INTERVIEWER: When you say that, can you try to fool yourself inside?

CHILD: No.

INTERVIEWER: Why not?

CHILD: If you are really upset about something you don't really forget about it that easy.

INTERVIEWER: Why not? Why is it hard to forget about things that upset you?

CHILD: It is hard, you are thinking about that thing most of the time. So it is real hard to forget about it.

INTERVIEWER: So you thought it isn't possible to fool yourself?

CHILD: No. . . .

INTERVIEWER: Could Jerry fool himself into thinking that he didn't care about the game?

CHILD: Yes.

INTERVIEWER: How is that possible to fool yourself?

CHILD: If you really talk about it and talk about it and you think you do.

INTERVIEWER: Why does talking about it make you think you do?

CHILD: Well, if you think about it, you think it is not really true, but if you really talk about it a lot and you start getting tired of talking, you don't think it anymore.

While at the previous level, self-deception was seen to occur due to external events or forces, at Level 2 we repeatedly see a new theme; through mechanistic force of habit, or by repetition, a belief can be changed by the self's effort.

There is another way that "fooling the self" is apparently understood in a Stage 2 framework—in the manner of "forgetting." By forgetting, the average 10-year-old usually means that the "observing ego" has had a lapse in vigilance or is attending to other matters at the time and cannot be bothered to review the particular issue at hand.

INTERVIEWER: Can you think outside you know how you feel, but you inside feels a different way?

CHILD: Yes.

INTERVIEWER: How is that possible?

CHILD: Because you fool yourself.

INTERVIEWER: You think you can fool yourself?

CHILD: Yah.

INTERVIEWER: How can you fool yourself?

CHILD: By forgetting something.

INTERVIEWER: How can you forget something?

CHILD: You don't remember it. . . .

INTERVIEWER: What's the difference between fooling yourself and fooling someone else?

CHILD: When you fool yourself, you kind of don't know that you fooled yourself sometimes, but when you are fooling another person, you know that you are doing it.

INTERVIEWER: Why is it you don't know you are fooling yourself when you are fooling yourself, how is that possible? Doesn't your mind always know what is going on?

CHILD: Yah, but sometimes you forget you are thinking about a different thing when you are fooling yourself. And you are thinking you are not fooling yourself.

Although this form of self-deception is still somewhat passive in nature, it is seen, apparently, as being to a greater extent under the self's control; to restore the state of "accurate awareness," all that is needed is to reattend to or refocus on the particular problem at hand.

Third, at Stage 2 the child becomes reflectively aware that the individual, the self included, can consciously and often deceptively put on a facade which is meant to mislead other individuals with respect to what he/she believes is "really" going on internally. The idea of "fronting," or putting on an appearance, is understood by the child as a useful way for people to cover up their inner feelings—for example, to save the self from embarrassment or ridicule.

INTERVIEWER: Suppose that Jerry finds out Keith let him win and he says to Keith I really never cared about Ping-Pong anyway. Why would he say something like that?

CHILD: Because he wants to make it like he didn't really care if he lost or not, it doesn't matter to him.

INTERVIEWER: Why would he try to do that?

CHILD: To cover up his feelings.

INTERVIEWER: What kind of feelings is he covering up?

CHILD: Sad ones. . . .

INTERVIEWER: Do you think there is a difference between fooling yourself and fooling someone else?

CHILD: Yes.

INTERVIEWER: What is the difference?

CHILD: It is easier to fool them because they don't have your mind.

A fourth aspect identified as related to the development of a conception of self-reflective (Stage 2) self-awareness is the child's belief that one can gain an inner strength by having confidence in one's own abilities. This new belief demonstrates how the structure of self-awareness concept can be related to the content of self-esteem. Inner awareness itself is now seen as a tool to be used as a confidence builder. Simply put, there is a newly minted belief that knowing you can do it helps you do it.

INTERVIEWER: Do you think there are any other reasons that Keith might have had for letting Jerry win?

CHILD: Well, because he didn't want him to go off and start being a poor sport about it.

INTERVIEWER: How would letting Jerry win stop him from being a poor sport?

CHILD: Because it would make him think that Jerry did it by himself and so he is improving in playing Ping-Pong, so he will start playing a lot.

INTERVIEWER: Why would he start playing a lot if he thought he won the game?

CHILD: Because if he won the game he would think he would start getting better and start playing Ping-Pong more.

INTERVIEWER: Do you think he might be trying to build up Jerry's confidence?

CHILD: Yah, he lets him win so he can make him think, "I am really better now. I can play better and sometimes win with Keith. . . ."

INTERVIEWER: What does confidence mean, what does having confidence in yourself mean?

CHILD: To know that you can really do something good.

INTERVIEWER: But how would he feel if he found out that Keith let him win?

CHILD: I would just forget it, because I would think he was doing it just to encourage you to make you think that you can play better.

INTERVIEWER: How does letting them win encourage them?

CHILD: It makes them think that they can play better, say I can play better now and I can go and play all kinds of Ping-Pong games. . . .

INTERVIEWER: If Jerry wins but finds out that Keith let him win, how is Jerry going to feel?

CHILD: I don't think he will feel too good. He wanted to win by himself.

INTERVIEWER: Why is it better to win by yourself?

CHILD: That means that you did it by yourself and the other person did not let you win, you have confidence in yourself.

INTERVIEWER: What does that mean, to have confidence in yourself?

CHILD: It means you think you can do things by yourself.

INTERVIEWER: Why would it help to have confidence?

CHILD: If you have confidence in yourself, then you can do more things better.

INTERVIEWER: Which is better, confidence in yourself or someone else having confidence in you?

CHILD: I think you having confidence in yourself is better.

INTERVIEWER: Why?

CHILD: Because when someone else has confidence in you it means they trust you. When you have confidence in yourself it means that you trust yourself and you can do other things like that.

INTERVIEWER: How does a person build confidence in himself?

CHILD: He keeps on thinking that he can do things, trying to build confidence.

Although the emergence of this attitude plays a major role in the social development of the preadolescent child, still, as within any developmental construction, the Stage 2 orientation has both new strengths and remaining limitations. For example, in the two preceding excerpts, the interviewer is interested in eliciting the child's understanding of the concept of "self-confidence." Rather than directly asking the child what self-confidence is, the interviewer uses the concept in the context of the particular dilemma and observes how the child interprets it. The emerging (Stage 2) idea of self-confidence as a mode of behavioral control is an example of how at this stage, in comparison to the previous one, the psychological aspect of self is seen by the child to have greater control over action. However, conceptions of self-awareness coded as Stage 2 still tend to be focused on a self composed of relatively concrete actions. One gains "strength" or "self-confidence" by knowing and being assured of one's physical abilities— to think one can *do* something is an action orientation. At higher levels, self-confidence will be understood as an awareness that the self can *be* something or someone; higher-level thinking implies an additional understanding of feeling good about the self as a psychological whole.

Summary

To study developing reflective social understanding we start with a developmental model of how children process or coordinate the self's and others' perspectives, and use the model to analyze the developmental meaning that social concepts such as self-awareness have for the child at each level. In addition, it also needs to be noted at this juncture that the analysis is not one way (from structure to conceptions) but reciprocal between the two. The developmental study of issues (like self-awareness) helps to illuminate and identity the various ways each deeper structural level of social perspective taking may operate in the child's mind. For this chapter, our focus is on how Level 2 perspective taking offers an important new set of concepts about the self's ability to reflect upon its own psychological processes, as well as to make inferences about others' internal states. One may conjecture about a range of effects this development may produce—for example, a new awareness of the possibilities for self-control, new levels of empathy, and advances in communication and problem-solving skills (Brion-Meisels, 1977). Speculations about the behavioral effects of changes in reflective social understanding (like those already described) are problematic, however, until we know more about how children *use* these perspective-taking levels and social conceptions in their everyday social interactions. The following section describes a method for beginning to look at how troubled children *use* their social cognition in a small group setting.

Observing Practical Expressions of Social Understanding Stages: Toward a Naturalistic Method

The result of the first, or constructive, phase of research, then, is a formal stage-by-issue model of interpersonal reasoning derived from both empirical research and structural analysis. The goal of the second phase is to evaluate whether developing interpersonal conceptions actually fit this developmental perspective-taking model. To do this, data are more formally gathered and evaluated to determine whether or how well children's interpersonal reasoning meets criteria such as structured wholeness, invariant sequence, and universality. Initial results of our work in this area (Selman, 1976, 1980; Selman & Jaquette, 1978) have been generally supportive. Nevertheless, we believe that this model remains limited in that it deals only with general developmental patterns in the child's *reflective* social understanding (conceptions-in-theory). The purpose of this final section is to suggest the potential value of going beyond development and validation of this reflective model to a third phase of research which utilizes these findings for the analysis of how children, both typical and troubled, might actually *apply* their understanding in the context of their natural social functioning.

It is important to keep in mind the developmental shifts in social understanding that the use of in-depth interview procedures has clarified. These shifts might not be apparent from either direct observation of children or less intensive discussion with them. For instance, the excerpts of responses in the previous section we coded as Level 0 or Level 1 demonstrate that while young children may initially sound like they are capable of being self-reflective at age 4 or 5, an in-depth probing of the meaning of the words they use indicates that they do not have the same level of understanding as do older children or adults. However, when most practitioners speak of a child's ability to look at his/her own behavior and feelings, they usually *assume* a level of understanding on the part of the child which is minimally Level 2 in the developmental sequence.

One specific question we ask then in the third phase of our research is this: What level of understanding might we expect to find in the naturally occurring statements and verbal interactions of troubled children whose reflective understanding sometimes lags behind those of their better-adjusted peers? In particular, we want to know whether children who do (or do not) clearly and consistently manifest what we call Level 2, or self-reflective, understanding under interview conditions can do so under natural conditions. Or, on the other hand, do these children demonstrate even less use of self-reflective awareness in naturalistic discussions? We are trying to explore these questions in an ongoing series of naturalistic studies undertaken in normal afterschool settings (Selman, Schorin, Stone, & Phelps, in press) as well as in a child psychiatric setting, the Judge Baker Guidance Center. This chapter focuses on the latter research.

The Classroom and Therapeutic Context of the Research

For several years we have been able to work and undertake research each year with several groups of children between the ages of 7 and 15 who manifest interpersonal difficulties severe enough to warrant their placement in a therapeutic day school, the Manville School of the Judge Baker Guidance Center. While intellectually these children fall predominantly within the normal range, they often do poorly in academic areas, sometimes manifest physical or somatic difficulties, and invariably evidence either very isolated and/or aggressive social behavior. Some of the children occasionally manifest behavior psychiatrically characterized as borderline psychotic. Upon admission, a child is placed with a teacher in a small class of six to eight children, participates in a structured social and physical activity program run by members of the counseling staff, and usually is assigned to a psychologist for psychotherapy (once or twice weekly).

The research component of the school is designed to be socially and educationally helpful to the students as well as to take a scientific attitude that can alternately be characterized as ethological, anthropological, ethnomethodological, and/or formative. Doctoral students in developmental psychology from the Harvard Graduate School of Education have participated in the work of the school in various roles—doing crisis counseling, working on activities and overnights, and designing and conducting research in which their role is clearly "participant-observer" in nature and which examines natural and "quasinatural" interactions with implications for developmental theory.

This naturalistic research format is useful for training developmental psychologists interested in working with and understanding troubled children: Even more importantly, it is essential to the ecological validity of our research. Children in general, and particularly troubled children, need to know the role and function of each adult who works with them. Established relationships and long-term commitments also create trust in the children, which is vital to their comfort and freedom to behave naturally. Research of the kind we are interested in cannot be done unobtrusively by "strangers" or "outsiders," and we make every attempt to incorporate the research and researchers into the school.

Within this context, we recently have been studying children's naturally expressed social understanding in two settings: (1) a weekly classroom, interpersonal problem-solving session in which children evaluate their week's performance along such issues as cooperation, conflict resolution, and decision making (Jaquette, 1978; Lavin, 1979); and (2) individual psychotherapy with staff psychologists and supervised psychology trainees (Jurkovic & Selman, 1980).

For example, for his doctoral research, Jaquette (1978) developed a "class meeting" procedure which has become a natural part of the school week. It has also allowed us to look at a number of facets of preadolescent social development from a social-cognitive perspective. Meetings generally take place on Friday so that the unit of time to be reviewed is the week just ending. The meeting usually lasts from 30 minutes to 1 hour. Both the teacher and counselor (researcher) participate in the meeting. By having the adults responsible for a large part of the child's daily school experience present at each meeting, the children's ability to examine social relations is facilitated, not just relations in the classroom but in all aspects of the milieu. Each week a different child is elected as class meeting leader on a regularly rotating basis. The order is determined early in the year and posted so the students will know when it is their turn.

The class leader has two responsibilities: to begin the meeting, he/she is asked to poll the class to let each child "rate the week." In this structured activity, each child responds on a five-point scale (excellent, good, fair, poor, terrible) and gives his/her reason for the rating. The children are encouraged to think about and evaluate their own behavior and that of their classmates, both in educational work and in the interpersonal problems that may have come up during the week. Then the class leader reads suggestions from the "suggestion and complaint box." The purpose of the suggestion box is for students to write down comments or complaints about any problem which may have arisen with peers or staff (e.g., something the student thinks is unfair), or to make suggestions about activities. The students are encouraged to write down a suggestion whenever it happens to occur, and occasionally the teacher prompts this behavior during the week or may even raise a problem. Further details of the class meeting procedure can be found elsewhere (Jaquette, 1980).

For the type of research described here, several kinds of data are gathered. First, the class meeting discussions are tape-recorded and transcribed. Second, the participating children are individually interviewed once before the beginning of a given series of class meetings, using the hypothetical interview described previously, to determine their competence in a reflective one-to-one interview.

Eventually, we expect these data to provide information in several areas related to the developmental stability and instability of naturally expressed social conceptions. These data will include: (1) a comparison of the individual's level of conception on reflective interviews and in a natural context about the same issues, (2) comparisons of the level of social conceptions in small-group discussions with children differing in age or level of social competence, and (3) a developmental flowchart or time-series analysis of the interpersonal reasoning level of individuals and groups at regular intervals over a period of time (e.g., weekly over the school year).

Coding Conceptions in Use:
Social Perspective Taking at Level 2

In this section we focus on describing a method developed by the authors to look specifically at the existence, function, and quantity of self-reflective (Level 2) communication in one class in the Manville School over a series of 12 class meetings. The class consisted of a core of five students plus several others who entered and left during the school year. In applying this particular method to the 12 class meetings held from mid-November to mid-April of the school year, the following questions were explored:

1. Which children make self-reflective (Level 2) statements during class meetings and under what circumstances?
2. What is the relation between the child's developmental level as ascertained through the hypothetical individual interview and the quantity and type of self-reflective statements and communications used during the 12-meeting observation period?
3. What functions do these communications serve? Are they used prosocially, antisocially, instrumentally, or defensively?

The first step in this process is the construction of a system for coding verbal expressions developmentally. To define categories of statements indicative of Level 2, we rely heavily on information gathered during the interview phase of the research but apply it in this significantly different context.

In practice we have found it useful to designate self-reflective conceptions into one of three categories:

1. Self-reflective statements that specifically have the self as a referent (coded as self-referent, or SR).
2. Statements that make use of the self-reflective process to reflect on another person's thoughts (coded as other-referent, or OR).
3. Statements which reflectively link the points of view or thoughts of self and other (coded as SR-OR).

The unit of analysis for this coding system is each complete expression of an individual's idea; usually this is represented by the uninterrupted expression of a thought by a class member. It is also possible that the idea might be expressed across an interruption by another child (or adult) or that in one monologue a child could provide multiple self-reflective "Level 2" statements. However, these latter possibilities have not occurred in our data.

The crucial element in coding a statement at Level 2 is that it clearly demonstrates the speaker's explicit capability to step back and view the self as a psychological object. Simple assertions of opinion or preference such as "I think X" or "I want Y" do not qualify.

Self-referent statements (SR) at Level 2 include the following categories:

1. Reflectively constructed statements about the self's (as object) past or present *feelings*—for example, "You ask stupid questions. That's what gets me mad."
2. Statements which indicate that the speaker can imagine him/ herself in a hypothetical situation and predict what his/her *psychological reactions* would be—for example, "I know that if it were my turn to get snacks and you didn't let me, I would be angry."
3. Reflections on the self in psychological terms—for example, traits or personality constructs where these terms clearly represent or refer to internal constructs (e.g., "I wouldn't give my money to anybody, even if they were poor. See I'm one of those greedy money lovers.") rather than to overtly behavioristic attributes or labels (e.g., "I'm nice."). This code always requires some conceptual interpretations and inference.

4. Reflective statements that distinguish (or link) the self's actions as they are overtly observed and the self's underlying motives—for example, "Hey, don't get all upset, I was just teasing you."
5. Statements demonstrating the ability to consider two or more possible psychological reactions either to the same event or at the same time—for example, "Well, I would have voted (rated the week) excellent because I'm *happy to be getting discharged*, but *I'm going to miss* everybody, so I only give it good."

Other-referent statements (OR) at Level 2 include the following:

1. Statements of inferences from another person's actions to their feelings or motives; or the reverse, from their motives or feelings to their overt actions—for example, "The teacher's *angry* at us today for making a lot of noise. That's why he's so *crabby* today."
2. Statements that predict another person's *psychological reaction* to a hypothetical situation—for example, "If the counselor were here *you* would be plenty scared."
3. Statements that attempt to clarify another child's intention or explain the meaning underlying his/her observed action or communication—for example, "He didn't mean you were gay. He only said that so he wouldn't have to go to the back of the room."
4. Statements which request or demand that another person take a different perspective on a situation and imagine how he/she would feel or what he/she would do in that situation—for example, "Well, what do you think, the other person that you were throwing snowballs at their window, what do you think they wanted you to do?"

Self–other-referent statements (SR-OR) at Level 2 include:

1. Explicit statements of the coordination of the self's perspective with that of another person—for example, "*I knew* that the *counselor knew* I did it. So I might as well admit it."
2. Statements of the coordination of *intentions* and/or *expectations* between self (selves) and other(s)—for example, "If you want to *act like* a dog, then we'll *treat* you like a dog."

3. Active statements indicating an agreement of mental operations (e.g., opinions, feelings, expectations) between two parties—for example, "I agree with teach[er] on that one." However, for a statement to be included here, the speaker must explicitly acknowledge a "meeting of minds" rather than just "going along" with a previous statement ("I agree," or "Me, too.").

Reliability at this point is more accurately described as collaborative coding. Each author codes the transcribed tape, and points of disagreement are discussed. Often the meaning, and therefore the developmental level, of a child's comment appears ambiguous or unclear. Here both teacher and counselor annotate the response, giving their recollection of the specific meeting, its context, and what each thought the child meant at the time. Where agreement is not possible, or where statements are too ambiguous, the alternatives are noted. These instances are uncommon. Clearly, our knowledge of the children in the context of the meeting is certainly a factor that influences coding. However, scorers can agree on meaning-in-context, as the agreement on assignment to a category is over 90%.

An Interpretive Analysis of a Discussion

To demonstrate the content of our data and the process of coding and analyses, let us look at excerpts from one typical midyear meeting. The meeting begins with a discussion of problems from the suggestion box.

Meeting 8, January 1978. Participants include two adults (the teacher and the counselor), the class leader for the meeting (Carl), and the other five children in the class: Dennis, Bill, Frank, George, and Alice (a girl who stayed in this class for about 10 weeks). All children's names have been changed to protect their right to privacy.

Excerpt 1

1. TEACHER: It's time for the suggestions.
2. DENNIS: You know, Carl, that's why I don't trust you. [Dennis had brought $20 into school and was showing the money to his classmates with much grandeur and bravado. Carl had come along and swiped the money in front of Dennis in a teasing action.]
3. CARL: I was just playing around with you, Dennis.

4. GEORGE: Dennis! Never bring your money out like that because if someone take it, they're never going to give it back to you.
5. CARL: I'd give it back.
6. ALICE: I wouldn't.
7. CARL (*as leader*): Hey, Debbie [counselor], is the tape on? I'm starting [the meeting]. (*Carl then reads the first suggestion from the box.*) "What about the problem that happened with Dennis's money?" Man! That just happened! [*implying*—How did that suggestion get into the box so quickly?]
8. COUNSELOR: I wrote it.
9. CARL: We was just kidding around.
10. COUNSELOR: But I still think it's a problem.
11. DENNIS: But I still don't trust you (*to Carl*).
12. TEACHER: I think the problem is, Why did Dennis bring it out of his pocket?
13. DENNIS: Well, he [Bill] asked me was it my money and I told him yes, and he asked me to let him see it.
14. CARL: So you should have showed it to him underneath the desk.
15. COUNSELOR: That's a good suggestion. Maybe not underneath the desk, but not out in front of everyone. Dennis, can I ask you a question? How come you are carrying around so much money? That's an awful lot of money.
16. BILL: I know. [*means*—I know it is a lot of money.]
17. CARL: Shoot, I don't know anybody with that much money around. You know something? If they seen Dennis with all that money around my house—if they seen Dennis with all that money, they beat your head in.
18. COUNSELOR: It is a lot of money.
19. CARL: They beat your head in for a five. Man, you let them see you with money, you be in trouble.
20. DENNIS: I wouldn't give my money to anybody, even if they were poor. See, I'm one of those greedy money lovers.
21. GEORGE: And homely looking too!

Excerpt 2 (approximately 5 minutes later)

1. CARL: Okay George, give me that one (*refers to another piece of paper from the suggestion box*). "Why does Dennis act like a dog?"
2. DENNIS: Who wrote that!
3. GEORGE: It looks like Frank's writing! Yup. It was Frank's writing.
4. ALICE: Because he is a dog; going around woof, woof, woof.

5. TEACHER: Okay, Frank. Would you sit down please?
6. CARL: One at a time. Raise your hand. Mr. Brion. [As class leader, Carl asserts his class leader role. Frank, the accused suggestion writer, had gotten out of his chair and in an anxious manner had feigned a defensive–fighting posture.]
7. DENNIS: Well, I really am a dog.
8. CARL: Dennis, be quiet. Wait your turn.
9. DENNIS: Well, I am a dog.
10. CARL: I'm tired of that, too.
11. GEORGE: Okay. If you want to act like a dog, we'll treat you like a dog. We'll crush your cookies and put them on the floor, and you have to eat them like that.
12. ALICE: We'll give you Purina Dog Chow.
13. CARL: Come on. Hold it. All right, now cut the crap. [There has been a lot of talking and joking about Dennis.] One at a time. Anbody here got anything to say about Dennis? Debbie, you had your hand up.
14. COUNSELOR: I wanted to say that if Frank would specify his complaints, it would be better—rather than just say he acts like a dog.
15. FRANK: Could you say that in English?
16. COUNSELOR: Well, it would be better to talk about what kinds of things get you mad.
17. FRANK: Okay, okay. Yesterday he said something about this is a rocket ship and I'm gonna put rocket fuel in it. [*interpretation*: Dennis tends to verbalize certain fantasies in class and then defend them to the point that it is often upsetting to the rest of the class, particularly Frank, who also has some difficulty maintaining for himself the distinction between fantasy and fact.]
18. BILL (*defending Dennis*): What's wrong with that?
19. FRANK: But that made me mad.

Excerpt 3 (approximately 3 minutes later)

1. CARL (*as class leader, reading suggestion*): "What should we do about swearing in the classroom?" Who wrote that?
2. TEACHER: I did.
3. CARL: I knew you did. All right (*to Alice*), go ahead.
4. ALICE: We should make them put their hands in the cage and let the gerbils bite their fingers.
5. GEORGE: He doesn't bite.
6. CARL: Three warnings and you're out [present rule].

7. COUNSELOR: Before you do that, let me make a suggestion. How about cutting down to a two-warning rule. Could kids handle that, do you think?

8. BILL: No!

9. DENNIS: I wouldn't want that. I think a three-warning rule would be better. Three in the morning, three in the afternoon.

10. TEACHER: Frank's got something to say.

11. FRANK: You might break my head for saying this, but the person who gets three warnings in the morning and three in the afternoon should be kept after school.

12. DENNIS: Frank—that's a dumb thought, mentally retarded you know!

13. FRANK: That's how you are! [A general confusion ensues with lots of insults and name calling within the group.]

14. TEACHER: You don't have to call names, you just say you disagree.

15. CARL (to counselor, who has hand raised): Go ahead.

16. COUNSELOR: How do people feel when someone says something like that about them?

17. CARL: Frank, you made some stupid ones, too, and I made some, too.

18. FRANK: But I didn't say things like cutting their throats off or stuff. [Dennis often describes gorey actions such as the one Frank notes.]

19. DENNIS: Yeh, well people say my ideas are stupid so if they say my ideas are stupid, I can say their ideas are stupid.

20. CARL: Okay, Brion. [The teacher has raised his hand.]

21. TEACHER: I have a suggestion. How about if an idea comes up that you think is wrong, instead of saying it is a stupid idea, say that you disagree.

22. CARL: Yeah, that sounds good.

23. DENNIS: Or you can say, well, that idea really ain't the *smartest* idea.

The first comment coded as SR/Level 2, indicating that a child is using his/her understanding of self-reflection, is found in Excerpt 1, line 3, Carl's comment: "I was just playing around with you." Inferred from this statement is Carl's awareness that he knows his actions have an effect on Dennis, that Dennis does not know Carl's true motives (i.e., that he, Carl, does not intend to keep the money), and that Carl himself realizes there is a discrepancy between his overt actions and his covert intentions. In other words, not only does Carl's statement indicate that he differentiates inner and outer experiences, but he can coordinate the two—a statement coded as a self-reflective, or "Level 2," structure.

Line 14 of Excerpt 1 exemplifies a comment that probably reflects another active use of a self-reflective structure, but the language does not permit us to code it as OR/Level 2. When Carl says to Dennis, "So you should have shown it to him under the desk," the sophistication of that statement is naturally appreciated by the counselor, as indicated by her response. One could expand Carl's statement to mean, "I realize that the class will get interested in Dennis's money, and if Dennis does not want this to happen he should keep the money out of sight." In other words, Carl is suggesting that Dennis be self-reflective, that he look at what he (Dennis) is doing and why. However, the expansion or explication necessary for this interpretation goes beyond the level of inference we feel comfortable making.

Dennis's response, (Excerpt 1, line 20) "I wouldn't give my money to anybody," may be expressing his intentions but not necessarily in a "self-reflective" or "second-person" mode. However, his added comment, "See, I'm one of those greedy money lovers," indicates two important dimensions: It not only refers to the self as an object as well as a subject, but in addition, the reflected-on self (object) is attributed certain psychological traits and dispositions (e.g., money *lover*). Therefore, in the case of Dennis's later statement, (Excerpt 2, line 6) "Well, I really am a dog," the SR/Level 2 coding is not given. Here, the three scorers agreed, Dennis was referring to his own fantasies rather than making a figurative comment about his own personality through the use of a simile or metaphor.

Another response coded as SR/Level 2 is found at the end of Excerpt 2, when Frank talks about how Dennis's insistence on maintaining fantasies even when challenged "made [him] mad." Not only is Frank referring to an observed psychological reaction in the self, he is also talking about the self's reaction which occurred in the past. This is different from the self's present attitude because it requires the self to view his past feelings as an object. While it is likely that the counselor's earlier question played an important part in eliciting this verbal response (perhaps even its form) from Frank, as social-cognitive naturalists, our interest here is primarily in describing instances of observed behavior, not in explaining their cause.[3]

---

3. From a clinical point of view, it is worthwhile noting that this form of "tuned in" communication has been extremely rare for Frank in the past. When clinician, teacher,

Coded as SR-OR/Level 2 is George's comment, (Excerpt 2, line 11) "If you want to act like a dog, we'll treat you like a dog." Here George's statement can be read to mean that he is aware of the reciprocal relation between the expectations of one party (the class) and the intentions of the other (Dennis)—for example, that the self (in this case, "we," the class) will act in accordance with its understanding of the way other (Dennis) wishes to be treated.

On the other hand, Dennis's statement in Excerpt 3, (line 19) "If my people say my ideas are dumb, I can say their ideas are stupid," is not coded as SR-OR/Level 2. Even though Dennis is talking about "ideas," he is referring only to a "reciprocity of *actions*"—that is, the reciprocity of insults rather than actually evaluating intentions and expectations, as in George's comment.

In essence, we are looking at children's natural language and attempting to develop reliable codes for inferring underlying social-cognitive structures. The absence of observed Level 2 statements does not necessarily mean that a child "lacks" the capacity to conceptualize at that level; there is no existing way to show absence of a given level. But our choice of an analysis heavily reliant on language is significant and important nonetheless. It rests upon three important assumptions: (1) that discussions during class meetings are real and meaningful interactions for the children, (2) that the language children use to communicate with each other and with adults is a critical part of how they are judged by peers and adults with respect to their social competence, and (3) that the individual child's social competence (both actual and perceived) affects his/her social interactions and general

---

and counselor would try to substantiate their claim that Frank's social competence had improved greatly, it was just this kind of comment (and Excerpt 3, line 11) that they would point to as indicative. Frank's verbalization "You might break my head for saying this," addressed appropriately in the context of the discussion, might not seem significant to someone unfamiliar with Frank. However, for Frank, an extremely isolated and fragile child with an intensive fantasy-like preoccupation with physical power (e.g., various superheroes), it was an indication of a relatively new way in which he was making use of language to make connections between himself and others, to communicate to the class that he understood that his suggestion might generate displeasure in others toward him. Of course, context and interpretation must be considered here. If Frank meant he thought other class members would simply react physically and literally break his head, the comment would not be coded as self-reflective or "Stage 2"—it would be a simple prediction of other's actions, not a judgment about other's attitude or opinion about the self. However, the counselor and teacher agreed that Frank was speaking figuratively and not literally; hence the response was included. Frank's case is a good example of how knowledge of a child's social cognition can augment a broader clinical perspective and understanding of a child.

social development. In its use of natural language as an important vehicle for inferring levels of social cognition, the analysis bears a marked similarity to the earliest natural studies undertaken by Piaget (1955) in his study of thought and language. However, the problem in this case is made more complicated, and hence to us more fascinating, because of hypotheses we have formed from observation of the children. These are children who may, as a group, lag behind peers in their conceptions-in-use—just as we have found them to lag behind in reflective understanding (Selman, 1980).

Generating Exploratory Hypotheses from Clinical Data

Table 2-4 presents the numbers of "Level 2" communications across the 12 weekly class meetings. The table provides not only a picture of who is communicating at this level, but also when. Using these data together with information found in the transcripts, we may speculate about the situational factors that function as facilitators or impediments to the expressed Level 2 conceptions. Inspection of the table with the transcripts also shows the functions of these self-reflective concepts for the children in this class.

For example, in 3 of the 12 meetings, no comments were coded at Level 2. Meetings 6 and 11 were largely focused on pragmatic class plans (school fair, school newspaper), indicating that amount of self-reflective communication in part may be a function of the topic of discussion. In Meeting 5, however, the primary situational variable appears to have been the teacher's absence from the meeting. The quality of this meeting's communications were quite unfocused and superficial, and although the children looked at a number of interpersonal difficulties in that meeting, they did not use any higher-level communication to do so. In most meetings, the adults' participation often serves as a stimulus to think seriously about issues, which tends to lead to higher-level reasoning and self-reflection. When an interpersonal issue is raised, the adults' task is to interject probing questions or point out contradictions which stimulate the discussion. The two adults in the class work best as a team, to keep discussion focused and at the same time deal with disruptive behavior. In this case, the single adult had to focus on managing behavior. Therefore, many relevant statements (which might have led to more sophisticated self-reflection) were not probed.

TABLE 2-4. *Self-Reflective (Level 2) Perspective-Taking Statements Coded at Each Class Meeting*

Subject	Meeting number												Number of statements			
	1	2	3	4	5	6	7	8	9	10	11	12	Total	SR	OR	SR-OR
Bill				OR(2)									2	—	2	—
George												OR	1	—	1	—
Frank			SR					SR OR				SR-OR	4	2	1	1
Dennis	OR(2)	SR-OR					OR(3) SR	SR(2) OR SR-OR	SR(4) SR-OR	SR SR-OR		SR-OR	19	8	6	5
Carl	SR	SR					SR	SR(2)				SR-OR OR	7	5	1	1
Other	OR(2) SR	SR(2)	SR					SR				SR-OR	8	5	2	1

Another factor that may influence the amount of reflective communication observed in individual children is the degree to which the child is involved in or is the focus of discussion. For example, Dennis is frequently "in the limelight" because his interpersonal behavior is often so provocative. Many of the reflective statements made by Dennis (e.g., in Meetings 8 and 9) function as means by which he attempts to defend his actions or opinions to the rest of the class.

Given this picture of the "natural usage" of Level 2 self-reflection, what can be said about its relation to the assessed conceptions-in-theory of each child in the group? Table 2-5 presents some information of relevance. In the first column of this table is each child's average reflective interpersonal understanding level (across 17 issues), as ascertained through an interview procedure administered prior to the observation of class meetings. The second column reports the *range* of levels used by the child across the interview procedure. Columns three through six summarize the quantity and type (SR, OR, SR-OR) of self-reflective comments made across the 12 weeks.

While it is obvious that this small sample does not allow for the statistical *testing* of previously formulated hypotheses, a number of hypotheses can be formulated from the data available. For example, Bill's reflective interview scores showed that he made fairly consistent use of Level 1 in his hypothetical interpersonal reasoning. Yet over the course of the class meetings, he did demonstrate the capacity for Level 2 conceptions-in-use as well, indicating that the hypothetical interview does not necessarily tap the child's highest capability. In this case, Bill was not comfortable in the individual interview situation, making it difficult for anything but the sparsest responses to be obtained. He

TABLE 2-5. *Reflective and Practical Understanding: A Summary of Level, Range, and Quantity*

Child	Reflective social understanding[a]		Practical understanding[c]			
	Interview score[b]	Range of levels in interview	SR	OR	OR-SR	Total
Bill	1.00	1	0	2	0	2
George	1.30	1–2	0	1	0	1
Frank	1.56	1–2	2	1	1	4
Dennis	1.56	0–2	8	6	5	19
Carl	1.81	1–2	5	1	1	7

[a]From premeeting interviews.
[b]Average across 17 issues.
[c]Type and number of Level 2 statements in class meetings.

avoided direct contact with the interviewer by playing with toys, barely seeming to pay attention.

For most children, though, the individual interview allows the child to take the time to thoroughly consider his/her responses, aided by the interviewer's follow-up probes, without fear of what impressions his/her responses will make on his/her peers. Because the one-to-one setting seemed to evoke anxiety from Bill rather than comfort, we found it helpful to look to the available clinical information, which revealed that one of Bill's "clinical issues" is difficulty in relationships with females. As the interviewer was female, we hypothesized that it might be Bill's discomfort at being in a one-to-one situation with a woman which made the interview session so difficult, and the resulting anxiety perhaps interferred with his demonstrating his highest social-cognitive capacity.

It is also interesting to explore under what conditions in the group discussions Bill was able to utilize Level 2 self-reflection. Bill made two reflective statements over the 12 meetings, both of which were "other-referential," not focusing on his own feelings or motives. Two aspects of the conditions surrounding these statements are of interest. First, both statements occurred during the meeting where Bill was the class leader. Perhaps being put in this position of responsibility helped Bill to have confidence to utilize his highest capabilities. Second, both statements could be construed to have a semicritical tone. Again, looking to supporting information, it becomes clear that this child is quick to react defensively when anyone contradicts his view of a situation. It appears to be easier for Bill to be critical of others than to be critical of himself. Perhaps there is some intrapsychic issue which makes it difficult for Bill to look inward and reflect on or evaluate himself; therefore, Bill is only comfortable using his self-reflective capacities to reflect on other people. One may speculate that this reluctance to reflect on his own thinking may be related to his reacting to disagreements as if they were personal criticism.

Dennis, on the other hand, showed extreme oscillation in his reflective interview scores. He is the only child to have interview responses coded at three levels (0–2). This same pattern of oscillation, characteristic of what we call the "disequilibrated child"—that is, one with a high level of social-cognitive capacity but variable functioning—is evident in the class meeting as well. Although he provides the greatest number of Level 2 communications, he also generates a solid number of lower-level responses as well (e.g., "If they say my ideas are stupid, I can say their ideas are stupid"), particularly when he feels attacked or challenged. In addition, Dennis also appears to use higher-level social-cognitive abilities in a defensive or hostile way a significant portion of the time ("I'm a greedy money lover").

For example, Meeting 9 is largely focused on discussing a punishment for Dennis after he stole a staff member's keys. Ironically, here Dennis receives social-cognitive "credit" for his statement—"I'd rate the week bad, but it's not because I feel guilty about stealing the keys. It's because I got caught." Here we see a situation similar to the one that led Piaget, in his study of socialized communication of younger children (1955), to differentiate between use of socialized thought in the service of "collaborative" goals and such use in the service of "quarreling."

The functions of Dennis's reflective statements vary. Many statements do serve a prosocial or "collaborative" goal, such as giving support to a peer through recognizing the peer's feelings, or guiding decision making by predicting responses of peers to possible actions. However, many of Dennis's reflective statements do serve a negative function, showing defensiveness or hostility. It could be hypothesized that Dennis is trying to get a "rise" out of his peers, to stir up negative reaction, in order to draw attention to himself. This analysis of Dennis's reflective comments serves to corroborate conclusions based on other clinical evidence. Dennis has an elaborate fantasy life which often involves aggression and mutilation. He parades these fantasies in front of all newcomers and often seems to utilize them to gain attention, albeit negative, from peers. Dennis's use of self-reflective statements appears to follow a similar pattern. Both from his individual interview and the class meetings, Dennis has demonstrated the capacity for higher-level reasoning and self-reflection; however, he either cannot or chooses not to use this capability consistently in his interactions. This detailed clinical example brings home, in a way which would augment and complement any findings from a study with a large sample size and better controls, the point that higher-level social understanding, while it may be a necessary condition, is itself not equivalent to social competence or maturity of interpersonal relating.

In addition, these data also suggest that (Level 2) self-reflection is a level of social cognition which can be applied across different communicative functions in children. For example, the statements coded as Level 2 (self-reflective) here function to: (1) provide feedback to a peer (Carl's statement, Excerpt 1) and (2) defend the self against criticism from a peer (Dennis's statement, Excerpt 2). Other meanings have produced self-reflective statements which have functioned to: (3) support or encourage a peer, (4) assess a peer's inner states, (5) contribute to a group solution to a classroom problem, and (6) to explain the intent behind one child's actions to another. In other words, this mode of social cognition (Level 2 self-reflection) may have application in different social situations, and it may affect behavior as well as interpersonal awareness. One hypothesis generated by such an analysis, which could be tested with a sample of better-adjusted children, might be that troubled children have relatively greater difficulty in applying their self-reflective understanding toward constructive (prosocial) goals, or that troubled children have a restricted or inconsistent ability to transform reflective social conceptions to practical conceptions and are not able to integrate these into their more general social functioning.

In sum, in keeping with the spirit of the workshop for which it was originally prepared, this chapter provides a vehicle for us to describe research in progress. Our aim has been to draw attention to two important contextual questions in the field of children's social-cognitive development. One major question is how to study the relation between level of social perspective taking applied to reflective social conceptions and applied to statements made in real-life contexts such as class meetings. The second question is how developmental social-cognitive constructs can be usefully employed in the description of the social behavior of both troubled children and their better-adjusted peers. It was suggested that the role of social-cognitive naturalist would be useful for gaining a better understanding of when, where, and by whom each social-cognitive level was employed, as well as for determining the function which each level served.

Suggestions for Future Research

The kind of field research described in this chapter needs to be extended in several directions. First, and most obvious, the verbal manifestations of various levels of social understanding need to be extended to the examination of the discussion skills in normal children at different ages. Second, research needs to look at children in interaction with one another, in work and play, in competitive as well as cooperative contexts, to see how social-cognitive levels are used. Third, field research needs to be extended beyond the still relatively short period of 12 weeks reported here. Frequent, unobtrusive observations over 1-, 2-, or 3-year periods, where feasible, are needed to gain a more accurate and richly descriptive picture of what the development of social understanding as expressed in practice actually looks like. Through the use of natural observation at frequent intervals over a long period of time, there will emerge a clearer picture of the relation between long-term, large-scale, and qualitative shifts in developmental levels of social understanding and the day-to-day growth in social and communicative competence.

ACKNOWLEDGMENTS

Preparation of this chapter was supported in part by a Research Scientist Development Award, KO2-MH00157-2, from the National Institute of Mental Health. The research described in this chapter was supported in part by a grant from the Spencer Foundation, Chicago, Illinois.

REFERENCES

Baldwin, J. M. *Social and ethical interpretations of mental development.* New York: Macmillan, 1906.
Brion-Meisels, S. *Helping, sharing and cooperation: An intervention study of middle childhood.* Unpublished doctoral dissertation, University of Utah, 1977.
Broughton, J. The development of concepts of self, mind, reality and knowledge. In W. Damon (Ed.), *New directions for child development* (Vol. 1). San Francisco: Jossey-Bass, 1978.
Brown, R. *Social psychology.* New York: Free Press, 1965.
Bruss-Saunders, E. *The development of children's understanding of the parent–child relation.* Unpublished doctoral dissertation, Harvard University, 1979.
Damon, W. *The social world of the child.* San Francisco: Jossey-Bass, 1977.
Flavell, J. H., Fry, C., Wright, J., & Jarvis, P. *The development of role-taking and communication skills in children.* New York: Wiley, 1968.
Hartup, W. W. Peer interaction and social organization. In P. Mussen (Ed.), *Carmichael's manual of child psychology* (Vol. 2). New York: Wiley, 1970.
Heider, F. *The psychology of interpersonal relations.* New York: Wiley, 1958.
Jaquette, D. *Developmental stages in peer group organization: A cognitive-developmental analysis of peer group concepts in childhood and adolescence.* Unpublished qualifying paper, Harvard University, 1976.
Jaquette, D. *Longitudinal analysis of social-cognitive functioning in a group of disturbed preadolescents.* Unpublished doctoral dissertation, Harvard University, 1978.
Jaquette, D. A case study of social-cognitive development in a naturalistic setting. In R. Selman (Ed.), *The growth of interpersonal understanding: Developmental and clinical analyses.* New York: Academic Press, 1980.
Jurkovic, G., & Selman, R. A developmental analyses of intrapsychic understanding: Treating emotional disturbances in children. In R. Selman & R. Yando (Eds.), *New directions for child development: Clinical developmental psychology* (Vol. 7). San Francisco: Jossey-Bass, 1980.
Kelley, H. H. The processes of causal attribution. *American Psychologist,* 1973, *28,* 107–128.
Kohlberg, L. Stage and sequence: The cognitive developmental approach to socialization. In D. Goslin (Ed.), *Handbook of socialization theory and research.* New York: Rand McNally, 1969.

Lavin, D. *A study of patterns of social reasoning in emotionally disturbed children under varying social contexts.* Unpublished doctoral dissertation, Harvard University, 1979.

Mead, G. H. *Mind, self and society.* Chicago: University of Chicago Press, 1934.

Piaget, J. *Language and thought in the child.* New York: New American Library, 1955.

Redl, F., & Wineman, D. *Controls from within: Techniques for the treatment of the aggressive child.* New York: Free Press, 1952.

Selman, R. Toward a structural analysis of developing interpersonal relations concepts: Research with normal and disturbed preadolescent boys. In A. Pick (Ed.), *Minnesota Symposia on Child Psychology* (Vol. 10). Minneapolis: University of Minnesota Press, 1976.

Selman, R. (Ed.). *The growth of interpersonal understanding: Developmental and clinical analyses.* New York: Academic Press, 1980.

Selman, R., & Jaquette, D. Stability and oscillation in interpersonal awareness: A clinical-developmental approach. In C. B. Keasey (Ed.), *Nebraska Symposium on Motivation* (Vol. 25). Lincoln: University of Nebraska Press, 1978.

Selman, R. L., Schorin, M. Z., Stone, C., & Phelps, E. A naturalistic study of children's social understanding as expressed in reflective interviews, group discussions, and group task negotiations. *Developmental Psychology,* in press.

Shantz, C. The development of social cognition. In M. Hetherington (Ed.), *Review of child development research* (Vol. 5). Chicago: University of Chicago Press, 1975.

Shaw, M., & Sulzer, J. An empirical test of Heider's levels in attribution of responsibility. *Journal of Abnormal and Social Psychology,* 1964, *69,* 39–46.

Sullivan, H. S. *The interpersonal theory of psychiatry.* New York: Norton, 1953.

Turiel, E. The development of social concepts. In D. DePalma & J. Foley (Eds.), *Moral development.* Hillsdale, N.J.: Erlbaum, 1975.

3

Conceptions of Friendship and Interaction between Friends: An Organismic–Developmental Perspective

FELICISIMA C. SERAFICA

Introduction

The importance of peer relations in psychological development has both theoretical and empirical bases. Both Adler (1930) and Sullivan (1953) assigned a critical role to peer relations in personality development, in contrast to Freud (1909/1959), who emphasized the parent–child relationship. According to Adler, positive relations with peers enhance a child's intrinsic social feelings and are essential if the greatest personal growth is to be achieved by the individual. Similarly, Sullivan (1953) believed that the infant's transformation from a biological organism into a human being is brought about through interpersonal relations, particularly with peers.

Some empirical evidence supports the theoretical propositions advanced by Adler and Sullivan. Sociability with peers has been found to be related to a child's personal–social effectance (Baumrind, 1972; Bronson, 1975). Peer contacts also contribute to the socialization of aggression (e.g., Hetherington & Deur, 1972; Patterson & Cobb, 1971) and sexual socialization (Kobasigawa, 1968). Significant linkages between peer relations during childhood and psychological adjustment in adolescence and adulthood have been demonstrated in several major predictive studies (Cowen, Pedersen, Babigian, Izzo, & Trost, 1973; Roff, 1963; Roff, Sells, & Golden, 1972). According to Hartup (1976), much evidence supports the contention that peer relations are crucial to a child's development, and no evidence refutes it.

FELICISIMA C. SERAFICA. Department of Psychology, The Ohio State University, Columbus, Ohio.

In sum, both theory and research suggest that peer relations occupy a central role in a child's life and contribute uniquely to his/her development. This importance of the peer system rests in part on its appropriateness as a context for the development of mutuality, a characteristic considered by many (e.g., Sullivan, 1953) to be the hallmark of mature love. Elaborating on this particular contribution of the peer system, Wenar (1971) asserted that the vast gulf between the child's world and the adult's world, as well as the "vertical" nature of the parent–child relationship, militates against the emergence of mutuality. In contrast, the relatively equal, or "horizontal" nature of peer relations facilitates its development. Nowhere is this more apparent than in that special relationship between two peers known as friendship.

The study of friendship has long been of interest to developmental psychologists. Previous research in this area, relying heavily on naturalistic observations, was concerned mainly with interactions between friends (e.g., Green, 1933; McCandless & Marshall, 1957). Only recently have investigators started examining the development of children's ideas about friendship (e.g., Selman, 1976). Today, there continues to be an active interest in both these facets of friendship, but they are still being studied independently. Not only are the questions asked and the methods used different, but the world views guiding these two lines of research also differ. In this chapter, contemporary research on conceptions of friendship and friendship interaction are reviewed selectively in order to delineate conceptual and methodological issues, identify possible links between these two lines of research, and suggest new directions for future investigation.

Conceptions of Friendship

Developmental Trends

What is friendship? This is a question that has intrigued philosophers and writers over the centuries, starting with Aristotle (ca. 300 B.C./1962). Now, it is being asked by developmental psychologists from people of different ages in order to ascertain whether the concept undergoes systematic, sequentially ordered changes and, if so, to describe their nature.

In approaching a relatively unexplored domain, an investigator frequently turns to an existing theory about the phenomenon or set of phenomena in question for insights and hypotheses. To date, however, there is no comprehensive, well-articulated formal theory of friendship and its development comparable to available theoretical formulations of the infant–mother relationship (Ainsworth, 1969) which have generated a rich stream of empirical studies. Thus, the research in this area has been largely atheoretical, and the questions asked are determined primarily by a particular investigator's values and perspective on the study of development in general, with some rare exceptions. One of these is the study of children's conceptions of friendship.

Studies of how ideas about friendship evolve are classifiable into structural and content-oriented approaches. The methods used in these two approaches overlap somewhat in that both use, in conjunction with story dilemmas, the clinical method or semistructured interview whose heuristic value for research was convincingly demonstrated by Piaget (1967). The differences lie in their theoretical underpinnings and, consequently, in their analyses and interpretation of the data.

STRUCTURAL APPROACHES

The work of investigators using this approach is conducted in the Piagetian tradition which focuses on delineating the distinctions between children's and adults' conceptions of both internal and external phenomena, and demonstrating that children's concepts change in a manner which can be represented by a sequence of stages or levels of organization constituting successive approximations to adult modes of thought. The structural approach is exemplified best by Selman's (1976) work on friendship, which itself is part of a broader research program on the development of social reasoning as manifest in reflections about the self, dyadic, and group relations. From a general structural theory of social-cognitive development, he has proposed that the development of friendship can be indexed through sequential changes in the individual's reflections on six critical issues: formation, closeness and intimacy, trust and reciprocity, jealousy and exclusion, conflict resolution, and friendship termination. Based on a dilemma-interview procedure conducted with 93 male and female subjects ranging in age from 3 to 4 years, the following description of the developmental progression was formulated (Selman, 1981).

At Stage 0, friendship is viewed as momentary, physicalistic interactions. Emphasis is placed on physicalistic parameters (e.g., propinquity and proximity) as the bases of friendship. At this stage, friendship is highly unstable in that it rarely extends beyond actual interaction. A close friend is one's playmate at a given moment of interaction. Issues such as jealousy or the intrusion of a third party into a play situation are construed at this stage as specific fights over specific toys or space, not as fights involving personal feelings. At Stage 1, friendship is viewed as one-way assistance. A friend is someone who performs specific activities to meet one's goals or who abides by one's standards. Also, a friend is no longer just a person with whom one interacts but rather someone whose likes and dislikes are known. At Stage 2, friendship is viewed as fair-weather cooperation. It is now seen as a two-way, or reciprocal, relationship, involving the coordination and approximation through adjustment by both parties of their respective likes and dislikes, instead of matching one's actions to the other's expectations. However, the relationship is fair-weather, easily broken by specific arguments. At Stage 3, friendship is defined as an intimate and mutually shared relationship, characterized by an enduring affective tie between the involved parties. Friendship is viewed as a context within which mutual intimacy and mutual support can emerge, and it now transcends specific and minor conflicts. The limitation of Stage 3 arises from the overemphasis of the two-person clique and the possessiveness that arises out of the realization that close relations are difficult to form and maintain in that they take constant effort. At Stage 4, friendship is conceptualized as autonomous interdependence. It is not construed as an open relational system based on a delicate balance between dependence and interdependence of the partners. Close friends rely on each other for psychological support, draw strength from one another, and enhance their respective self-identities through identification with each other; but there is also recognition and acceptance of the fact that each partner has complex and sometimes conflicting needs which require other kinds of relationships for their satisfaction.

A similar, but not identical, sequence has been proposed by Damon (1977), based on some work done by Weinstock (1976). This sequence is as follows:

At Level 1, friends are associates with whom one plays or comes in frequent contact; those who make the best playmates at any one time are the most valued, and those who "act nice" and are fun to be with are preferred. There is as yet no sense of liking or disliking the stable personality traits of another. Friendship is affirmed by the material act of goodwill and the sharing of valued resources. It can be terminated by a negative material and/or act, such as taking away a toy or hitting. At this level, a friendship is quickly formed and just as quickly dissolved, and it is not considered to have long-term or permanent status.

At Level 2, friends are persons who assist one another, spontaneously or upon request by one of them. Friendship is now viewed as a reciprocal exchange between two parties, and each party must respond to the other's needs or desires. Friendship is affirmed by demonstrating, through concrete or material acts of kindness, that one can be relied on to help when needed, and conversely, that one can be counted on not to harm or take advantage of the other. Reciprocal trust now constitutes a defining attribute of friendship. Friendship can be terminated by an action that is incongruous with the self-interest of the partner, such as a refusal to help, the ignoring of a need, or the commission of an act that is considered harmful or untrustworthy. At this level, there is a realization that friendship is subjective, in the sense that like or dislike of another person may be based on his/her dispositions and traits. The basis of friendship has shifted from frequent play contact to subjective evaluations of a person's personal characteristics.

At Level 3, friends are persons who understand one another and share with each other their innermost thoughts, feelings, and secrets. Friends are people to whom one can turn for help regarding psychological problems. Friendship is based on compatibility of interests and psychological makeup, rather than on the objective "goodness" or general worth of the individual. Friendship is affirmed over a period of time, through the mutual sharing of personal interests, private thoughts, and psychological comfort ("getting to know" someone). Since friends are capable of mutual understanding and forgiveness, only a continual display of disaffection and/or bad faith is considered enough to terminate a true friendship. Thus, friendship is seen as a relatively long-term relation, distinct from mere acquaintance.

Also from a structuralist position, Youniss and Volpe (1978) have investigated children's definitions of friendship and the actions or operations that govern relations between friends. They found that around ages 6 and 7, children depict friends as interacting according to shared rules of conduct (e.g., sharing or playing together). Being nice to each other is the essence of these rules because they have minimal reference to the personal characteristics or states of the friends. At ages 9 to 10 years, the same rules prevail but are now based on particular characteristics, states, or needs of the persons involved (e.g., sharing is a sign of friendship when one child gives something the other needs). Hence, they are referred to as rules conditioned on persons. Also at this same period, friendships are characterized by equality or reciprocity (e.g., friends have similar interests). Around early adolescence, these same rules still hold. Little substantive change was observed among 12- and 13-year-olds.

The actions or operations involved in the establishment or termination of friendship were also studied by Youniss and Volpe (1978), through interviews in which the child was first asked to tell a story in which one friend did something that the other did not like or was bothered by, then to describe what the offended party would do, followed by what the offender might do, and so on until "things were made better and they were friends again." At ages 6 to 7 years, children cited violations which were unconditioned, rule-like acts (e.g., hitting, taking a toy, name calling). In contrast, 12- to 13-year-olds generated violations in the context of a stated principle (e.g., breaking a promise, revealing secrets). Children at ages 10 and 11 years generated both types of violations about equally.

Three general patterns which children use to repair disrupted friendships were identified. Each of these occurred in response to unprovoked (i.e., no mention of a possible impetus) or unequal (i.e., mention of unequality between friends in some relevant aspect) violations. According to Youniss and Volpe (1978), these different patterns suggest that at ages 6 to 7, a violation can be replaced by a rule-abiding procedure. Rules are viewed as having functional equality and reciprocity, not as part of an integrated system. For example, an unprovoked violation is simply ignored, and the friends go on playing. From age 10 on, rules are regarded as subordinated to a system wherein one interaction can compensate for another. Some sort of acknowledgment that a violation has been made is required before the relationship is repaired. The specific nature of repair action varies with the type of inequality in the friendship or the nature of the provocation.

CONTENT-ORIENTED APPROACHES

One's concept of or knowledge about a phenomenon or set of phenomena permits identification, classification, and organization of informational input from the environment. It also operates in a mediational capacity and thereby influences behavior. Several investigators, influenced by this view and using a paradigm borrowed from person-perception research, have investigated age-related changes in the concept of friendship through an examination of what children at different ages expect in their friends.

A pioneering study in this area was conducted by Bigelow and LaGaipa (1975), who asked teachers in grades 1 through 8 to instruct their pupils to think about their best friends of the same sex and to write an essay about what they expected in their best friends that was different from other acquaintances. These essays were then rated along 21 friendship expectation dimensions. Reciprocity of liking, ego reinforcement, and sharing-friend as giver were dimensions which remained stable across grades. Two dimensions, sharing-friend as receiver and general play, decreased as grade advanced. Significant increases were found to be associated with advances in grade status in the following dimensions: help/friend as giver, common activities, propinquity, stimulation value, organized play, demographic similarity, evaluation, acceptance, admiration, incremental prior interaction, loyalty and commitment, genuineness, help/friend as receiver, intimacy, common interests, and similarity in attitudes.

Bigelow (1977) cross-validated his earlier results in a sample of 480 Scottish children. An increase with age for 11 of the 21 friendship expectations was also found in this sample. Furthermore, 9 of the 11 friendship expectations which showed developmental trends were found to have relatively high concordance. A cluster analysis applied to the data yielded support for a hypothesized invariant sequence characterizing the evolution of friendship expectations. The three stages are: (1) a situational stage (grades 2–3), when reward–cost is salient, and common activities as well as propinquity are important bases of friendship; (2) a contractual stage (grades 4–5), when the sharing of norms, values, rules, and sanctions is emphasized, and character admiration is largely the basis of friendship; and (3) an internal psychological stage (grades 6–7), when friendships provide empathy, understanding, and opportunities for self-disclosure as well as the experiences of intimacy. At this last stage, dispositional personality factors play a crucial role in determining friendship choice. To date, empirical support for the hypothesized invariance of this sequence has not yet been presented. Bigelow's data have yet to be subjected to an appropriate test of invariance such as a scalogram analysis.

Developmental trends in children's expectations of friendship were clearly demonstrated by Bigelow's research. However, the use of written essays to elicit children's expectations has been questioned. Nevertheless, a study employing an interview method (Reisman & Shorr, 1978a) yielded a developmental progression for four dimensions in Bigelow and LaGaipa's system. It was found that intimacy potential, common activities, and loyalty–commitment significantly increased with age up to about the eighth grade but were cited less often in adulthood. Play, on the other hand, decreased with increasing age.

A more specific issue regarding the possible bias introduced into the results by Bigelow's data collection procedure was raised by Gamer (1977). She wondered whether the open-ended instructions biased the children to write only about those behaviors which were most salient and easiest to express. She suggested that, if this were the case, Bigelow's results may underestimate the prosocial expectations of younger children as well as the more abstract commitments of older respondents. To explore this issue further, she employed a three-part interview to assess children's criteria for friendship and prosocial expectations (i.e., support, loyalty, trust, unselfishness, and reciprocity). The interview schedule consisted of five open-ended questions about friendship, a set of ten stories written to illustrate the presence or absence of prosocial qualities, and a set of eight statements about friends. The results showed that children as young as 6 and 7 do have prosocial expectations of their friends—that is, that the latter should not tease or tattle on one another and should keep secrets told to them. At ages 9 and 10, children emphasize that a friend should lend assistance in a fight, even if one's safety is placed in jeopardy, and that he/she be reliable as well as supportive. By ages 12 to 13, the dominant expectations are that a friend will delay or give up something for the sake of a friend, share confidences and intimacies, and interact positively. Both older groups also significantly expect a friend to be "someone who understands your feelings." In sum, the study showed that prosocial criteria for friendship are held by children as young as 6 years old and become elaborated with age.

The hypothesis that psychological attributes, particularly those labeled "prosocial" by Gamer (1977), acquire more salience as defining criteria of friendship received further confirmation in a study by Campbell, Gluck, Lamparski, Romano, and Schultz (1979). A structured-interview approach was used to elicit ideas about friendship from 134 children ranging in age from 5 years to 14 years, classified into three groups: primary, intermediate, and junior high. The results showed that children's spontaneous definitions of friendship change with increasing age in the direction of emphasizing psychological attributes (trustworthiness and keeping secrets) and similarity of interests and attributes. The percentage of children who described a friend as someone who helps and is a companion also increased with age. It is interesting to note that although the percentage of children who described a friend as a playmate was significantly lower among junior high pupils, a significantly high percentage of this group defined a friend as someone who shared specific leisure activities. Thus, the difference may be more apparent than real since such activities may be the functional equivalent of the younger child's play.

These different content-oriented studies, employing varied procedures to elicit descriptions of a friend and a wide variety of categories to code the verbal responses, have yielded remarkably similar results. Further replication of these studies is, of course, still needed in order to obtain more solid normative data. Nonetheless, the results thus far indicate that there are systematic changes with increasing age in children's ideas about the defining attributes of a friend, the functions of friendship, and how friendships are formed, maintained, and terminated. These age-related shifts appear to be of sufficient magnitude as to be consistently evident in different eliciting conditions including a written essay, open-ended questions, stories, and pictures. Clearly, the concept of friendship is a developmental variable (Wohlwill, 1973).

To summarize, both content-oriented and structural approaches have revealed that the concept of friendship undergoes developmental changes. These two approaches, however, seem to be measuring different aspects. What is being measured by the content-oriented approach appears to be the individual's representation of a friend as social object. Its concern with the defining attributes of a friend suggests that the target of scientific inquiry is the acquisition of knowledge about social object properties. The structural approach, on the other hand, although also concerned with attributes, might be more appropriately characterized as the study of friendship (i.e., of relations between social objects). Given this distinction, one might expect different organizing principles to account for the observed developmental trends. The capacity for abstraction underlies the representation of a friend, while the ability to coordinate perspectives is the basis of one's reasoning about relations between friends.

Organizing Principles

What accounts for the observed developmental trends in the concept of friendship? Selman has repeatedly asserted (Selman, 1976, 1981; Selman & Jaquette, 1977a) that perspective taking, or "coordination of perspective" structures, underlies the sequential changes noted. In his view, transformations in the child's conceptualization of relations between friends are based on developmental changes in the child's ability to mentally coordinate social perspectives, his/her own and those of others. The changing patterns of relations between friends reflect the child's progression from an initial state wherein he/she is unable to differentiate his/her own viewpoint from that of another (Level 0), then realize that other individuals' subjective thoughts and feelings are different from his/her own (Level 1), that one's subjective attitudes can be grasped by another (Level 2), that both self and another can consider each other's viewpoints mutually and simultaneously (Level 3), and finally, that there is a general perspective which transcends, both in depth and scope, the understanding which emerges between two people. Correlational data in support of this hypothesized relationship between perspective taking and the concept of friendship have been presented by Selman (1976).

In a recent paper, Selman (1981) has criticized investigators using a content-oriented approach for failing to articulate the organizing principle that underlies the developmental trends in the concept of friendship which they have reported. We submit that the capacity for abstraction is the organizing principle where representations of a friend are concerned. Age-related changes in children's descriptions of a friend's attributes are surface manifestations of the child's increasing ability to infer generalizations and abstractions from different behaviors exhibited by an individual in varied contexts. In a recent study, we investigated the hypothesis that children's descriptions or representations of a friend would show a progression from global or vague descriptions, to concrete, and thence to abstract categories. It was predicted that this progression would characterize age-related changes in the attributes or properties ascribed to a friend. The possibility was also explored that a similar sequence characterizes the development of children's thinking about the functions of a friend and about the means whereby friendships are formed, maintained, and terminated. Another aim of this study was to specify what children at different ages take to be the defining properties and functions of friendship, and the means employed in its formation, maintenance, and termination. Thus, the study was an attempt to elucidate both the form and content of conceptions about the friendship, although only the results pertaining to alterations in the form of a child's representation of a friend are presented here.

The sample consisted of 15 male and 15 female children at each of five age groups (5, 7, 9, 11, and 13 years). All subjects were Caucasian, middle-class youngsters of at least average intelligence, drawn from a suburban school. Their ideas about a friend and friendship were elicited through a Friendship Questionnaire administered individually in the classic clinical method—that is, the initial questions were standardized, but further inquiry was conducted when needed to clarify a subject's response or to probe the range and depth of his/her knowledge. Responses were written during the interview by the interviewer; an audio recording of the session was also made so that the completeness of the interviewer's record could be verified.

The verbal responses were examined to identify descriptive statements, then each statement was coded twice, initially for its form and then again for its content. In regard to form, responses were classified as global, concrete, or abstract. "Global responses" were descriptions that were vague or undifferentiated, and which the child was unable to explicate further during the inquiry. "Concrete responses" were descriptions which referred to specific observable characteristics and behaviors. These were classified further into physical or demographic characteristics and observable behavioral regularities. "Abstract responses" were descriptions which referred to psychological states or qualities that were not limited to specific individuals or contexts. These fell into three subcategories: internal states such as feelings or cognitions, inferences about behavioral dispositions, and traits. The responses were coded independently by two trained raters who were unfamiliar with the study's hypothesis. Interrater reliability ranged from 94% for physical or demographic characteristics to 100% for traits.

Preliminary analysis of the data showed that, as expected, the number of different attributes used to describe a friend increases with age. In order to equate for these age differences in output, proportion scores were used to test for the main hypothesis. A child's proportion score for a given category was obtained by dividing the number of responses which fell into that category by the total number of descriptive statements given by that particular child. The results show that, with increasing age, there is a shift in the form of children's descriptions of a friend's attributes. This shift is evidenced by an age-related decrement in the proportion of concrete descriptions and a concomitant increase in the proportion of abstract responses. These developmental trends are most marked for behavioral regularities and inferential statements about the dispositional characteristics of a friend. Parenthetically, it should be noted that in this sample, by age 5 global attribute responses were practically nonexistent, so this category was excluded from the analysis. A decrease with age in the use of concrete responses and an age-related increase in the use of abstract responses also characterized children's descriptions of the means used to form, maintain, and terminate friendships. Thus, there is some tentative support for the hypothesis that the capacity for abstraction underlies at least the representation of a friend. It can account for the similarities observed across different studies. The next step would be to examine the relationship between the form of the attribute and measures of abstract thinking. We plan to do this in a subsequent study.

The coding procedure described earlier also allowed us to explore quantitative changes characterizing the concept of friendship. Previous studies have focused on what behaviors or traits are ascribed to a friend. Although these are not precisely qualitative changes in the sense that structural changes are, they nonetheless represent changes in kind rather than quantity. However, only statements about the order of change have been made. Little attention has been paid toward specifying the direction of change or the shape of the developmental function. With our coding procedures an approximation of the form of development can be obtained—for instance, by plotting the incidence of responses signifying different degrees of abstraction at each age period assessed. It can yield a curve depicting the increase or decrease of particular types of constructs at different age periods. The kind of data obtained can even be used to show age-related shifts in the relative incidence of a particular defining attribute. The main point to be made here is that our approach allows both qualitative and quantitative descriptions of developmental changes. The latter provides information about the general form of development which can be useful in the study of individual differences and in understanding the role of certain determinants. For example, knowledge about the rate of change can provide insight into the timing of developmental processes and permits identification of major discontinuities which may be important for our understanding of individual differences.

Levels of Friendship

The developmental trends described earlier emerged from studies which differed in regard to the stimulus used in eliciting children's ideas about friendship. In some (e.g., Bigelow, 1977), children were asked to describe a "best friend," while in others (e.g., Reisman & Shorr, 1978a), they were encouraged to talk about a "friend." These differences imply an assumption that there are different levels of friendship.

The idea that there are hierarchically ordered levels of friendship can be traced as far back as Aristotle (300 B.C./1962). He proposed that there are three levels of friendship—utility, pleasure, and ideal—which can be differentiated on the basis of their essential functions. At the lowest level is a friendship based on the provision of material assistance (utility), a higher level is represented by one which offers friendly social intercourse (pleasure), and highest of all is that which is founded on love for the other and not for oneself (ideal). Conceivably, each of these levels emphasizes different defining attributes and ways of establishing, maintaining, and terminating the relationship. Reisman and Shorr (1978a) found evidence to support Aristotle's hypothesis of an age shift from utility to pleasure in the function of friendship.

Both Bigelow (Bigelow, 1977; Bigelow & LaGaipa, 1975) and Berndt (1978) asked their subjects to describe a best friend, but since a description of another level of friendship was not elicited, the spontaneous descriptions they obtained do not permit any comparisons between levels of friendship. Information bearing on this issue is provided, however, by data from children's responses to cartoons depicting behavior of best friends or acquaintances—that is, children who go to the same school but don't know each other very well (Berndt, 1978). Kindergarten, third-grade, and sixth-grade children alike expected less quarreling and more sharing from friends than acquaintances. This finding, however, was qualified by another finding that more positive behavior was expected from friends only if one friend had not seriously offended the other.

In Berndt's study, an acquaintance was really operationally defined as a familiar child, not as a friend. A more clear-cut distinction between levels of friendship was made by Gamer (1977), who asked children to judge the level of friendship between story characters, then to state their criteria. Children ages 12 to 13 years (compared to 6- to 7-year-olds and 9- to 10-year-olds) were significantly more likely to differentiate best friends from friends on the basis of prosocial criteria, particularly the willingness to delay self-gratification and to act in the best interests of a friend. The finding that the ability to draw distinctions between levels of friendship increases with age was confirmed by Campbell *et al.* (1979). In their sample, junior high school children were significantly more likely to report considering a best friend as trustworthy, someone they could confide in and talk to easily. Although the distinctions between best friend and just a friend were drawn most sharply by junior high school pupils, all subjects studied understood the notion of "best friend." Moreover, best friends were described as better liked by 42% of the sample and as seen more often by 19%. These findings were interpreted by Campbell *et al.* as indicating that differences between a best friend and a friend were quantitative rather than qualitative, and that, in general, definitions of a best friend closely parallel the definition of a friend.

In our own program of research, variation in young adults' conceptions of same-sex friendship as a function of friendship level were examined in one study (Rose & Serafica, 1979a, 1979b) which also assessed the effects of life stage, sex, and hypothetical–actual friendship status. The subjects were 30 single undergraduates (mean age = 21.2 years); 30 single, employed college graduates (mean age = 25.2 years); and 30 married, employed college graduates (mean age = 25.1 years). Both sexes were equally represented in each age group. Each subject was individually interviewed to elicit his/her ideas about friendship in general and about three levels of friendship—best, close, and casual.

Speaking of hypothetical same-sex friendships, subjects attributed the characteristics "honest," "accepting," "dependable," and "similar" to oneself proportionately more often than other characteristics to both best and close friends. Furthermore, both best and close friends were described as having these characteristics proportionately more often than were casual friends. In contrast, the latter were significantly more likely than best or close friends to be described as stimulating—that is, as having traits or engaging in behaviors which were novel, interesting, and enjoyable.

The functions of friendship also varied significantly with level. Best and close friendships were described as having essentially similar functions; they provide both material and psychological support, contribute to an individual's sense of self-identity, and serve as a context wherein intimacy may be experienced. Close and casual, in comparison to best, friendships were significantly more often perceived as bringing intellectual stimulation and companionship, thereby enriching the lives of the individuals involved.

The formation of a best friendship was described as involving the development of positive feelings between two people, significantly more so than in the case of a close friendship—although both best and close friendships were said to be established proportionately more often than casual friendships, through the development of positive feelings, continued interaction, and sharing. Casual friendships were more often said to be formed through the parties being in proximity to one another (e.g., living in the same apartment building) or through circumstances (e.g., a class project).

The maintenance of friendship also varied somewhat with level. Both best and close friendships were described proportionately more often than casual friendships as having to be maintained through continued but not necessarily proximal interaction. It was deemed important to keep in touch, even if it was only by phone or correspondence. In contrast, casual friendships were more likely to be sustained through the friends continuing to remain in the vicinity of one another (e.g., living in the same dorm); it was strictly a case of out of sight, out of mind. The maintenance of best friendships was seen, significantly more often than in casual friendships, as requiring that positive feelings for one another continue to exist; this requirement was mentioned proportionately more often for close friendships in contrast to casual ones, but less often in comparison to best friendships. Interestingly, continued interaction was cited proportionately more often as being important for the maintenance of close than best friendships. This finding is perhaps related to the fact that only best friendships were described as self-maintaining—that is, one does not have to do anything to maintain such a relationship, once a best friend, always a best friend. For some interviewees, the best friend was someone they met in high school or in college and had not seen in years, but the interviewees *just knew* they were still best friends.

The termination of best friendships differed from that of close and casual friendships in that it sometimes occurred because one of the friends got married or entered into a romantic heterosexual relationship. Both best and close friendships were alike, however, in that they ended due to a decrement in frequency of interaction or in sharing, significantly more so than casual friendships. The latter, not surprisingly, ended because of a resultant lack of proximity between the partners. If one moved away or changed jobs, the friendship ceased. The exact nature of the termination process was described with less specificity for casual friendships, whereas this was well differentiated for best and close friendships. This suggests that casual friendships tend to end alike, whereas there are diverse routes to the demise of a close or best friendship.

The results of this study indicate that although there are commonalities across levels of friendships, there are also differences. Young adults emphasize different patterns of attributes for best and close as compared to casual friendships; they perceive these relationships as serving different functions and in some ways, as formed, maintained, and terminated differently. These results also suggest that qualitative differences between levels of friendship might be better understood through an examination of patterns of attributes or means.

Other results from this study showed that when subjects are asked to describe a hypothetical friend, they respond with a composite drawn from their descriptions of best, close, and casual. It is important, therefore, to keep these distinctions in mind when doing research on conceptions of friendship. The level of friendship of interest to the investigator should be specified to the subject, and the results can be expected to generalize only to friendships at that level. We cannot solicit descriptions of best friends and infer that they reflect peoples' ideas about friends in general.

Individual Differences

SEX DIFFERENCES

Studies of social cognition have typically not yielded sex differences (Selman, 1975; Campbell *et al.*, 1979). However, some sex differences do seem to characterize the concept of friendship. Gamer (1977) found that when stories and statements were used to elicit criteria for friendship, there were no sex differences. However, in response to open-ended questions, girls were more likely to assert that positive interaction was an essential ingredient of friendship and best friendship. Girls, particularly older girls, were also more likely than boys to differentiate between best friendships and regular friendships, the former being based on prosocial attributes and the latter on shared activity.

Our own research (Rose & Serafica, 1979c) on same-sex friendships of young adults has yielded some sex differences. Although sex was found to have a significant impact on only one attribute—namely, honesty (a characteristic emphasized more by women)—it did influence three of the four functions: intimacy, identity, and life enhancement. Women were significantly more likely than men to mention intimacy as a function of actual best friendships; men were significantly more apt than women to say that actual best friendships contributed to one's sense of identity; and married women, compared to married men, reported that friendships, irrespective of level, provided intellectual stimulation and enhanced the quality of their lives. These differences probably reflect socialization influences. For instance, women are socialized to engage in self-disclosure and seek intimacy in interpersonal relations with members of both sexes, whereas men are less so. Parenthetically, a number of men perceived intimacy as a function of cross-sex but not same-sex friendships. Last, sex also had an effect on the termination of friendship. Women were significantly more likely than men to say that a friendship ended because it was no longer meeting their needs or because it was disrupted by their own or the friend's other relationships (e.g., lovers or spouses).

PEER STATUS DIFFERENCES

Groups that differ in status among their peers have been found to differ somewhat in their ideas about friendship. Campbell *et al.* (1979) tested the hypothesis that more popular children (based on peer ratings and peer nominations) would exhibit more mature responses. Their specific prediction that the more popular children would include mutual liking in their definitions of a friend was confirmed. However, another prediction that emotional support and assistance would likewise be cited by the more popular children received support only among the intermediate group. This type of response did not differentiate the popular from the less popular children in the primary group because it occurred so infrequently, nor in the junior high group where it showed up too often. Campbell *et al.* (1979) also hypothesized that more popular children would give higher-level responses to questions about friendship termination following a fight and when a friend moves away. Again, the data yielded only partial support. Only in the youngest group were the more popular children less likely to respond that they would not be friends after a fight. In addition, the prediction that peer popularity would be associated with more advanced responses to a question about a friend moving away was confirmed only in the primary and intermediate groups.

Additional evidence of an association between peer status and slow development in concept of interpersonal relations comes from a study by Selman (1976) which showed that although positive sociometric status was not significantly correlated with any of the reasoning domains, high negative sociometric rating was significantly and negatively correlated with interpersonal reasoning stage.

Gottman, Gonso, and Rasmussen (1975) have also presented evidence relating popularity to concept of friendship (i.e., knowledge of making friends). High-friends children (identified through a sociometric measure) received significantly higher scores on measures of referential communication accuracy than did low-friends children. In the classroom, high-friends distributed more positive reinforcement than did low-friends children, a difference which increased from third to fourth grade. Gottman *et al.* concluded that their results suggest relationships between knowledge of friendship and social interaction.

The data just presented indicate that children who differ in the degree to which they are accepted, liked, and sought out by their peers may also differ significantly in their knowledge about friendship, but only sometimes. The discrepancy does not appear at all ages but instead is most apparent during periods of transition. The data suggest that the more popular children are ahead of their less popular peers in their grasp of certain aspects of friendship. It is tempting to say that their more advanced knowledge contributes to their popularity, but it is also possible that the social experiences engendered by their greater popularity provide opportunities for cognitive restructuring, thereby facilitating advancement in friendship concept development. A training study can provide information which could clarify this issue.

CLINICAL STATUS DIFFERENCES

Selman (1976) has presented evidence indicating that children with interpersonal problems lag behind a matched sample in interpersonal reasoning (i.e., concepts of persons and dyadic relations) around ages 7 to 9 and also at ages 10 to 13. Also, when the synchrony across domains of reasoning (logicophysical reasoning, perspective taking, interpersonal reasoning, and moral judgment) was examined, the matched sample showed a relatively greater synchrony across logicophysical and social domains, whereas the clinic group lagged further behind in the social areas. Finally, the data also indicated that if a child was at an extremely low level of interpersonal reasoning in comparison with his/her peers, chances were extremely high that he/she would also be in the clinic group. These results suggest that children who differ in their interpersonal functioning also differ in their level of friendship concept development. Some corroborative evidence of emotionally disturbed children's showing a deficit relative to their nondisturbed peers in their knowledge of how to respond to friends comes from a study by Reisman and Shorr (1978).

In summary, studies dealing with both the form and content of friendship have revealed systematic sequential changes with increasing age. These developmental trends appear to be associated with improvements in the ability to coordinate social perspectives and the capacity for abstraction. Studies of both children and adults suggest that there are hierarchically ordered levels of friendships which are characterized by different patterns of attributes, functions, and modes of formations, maintenance, and termination. Last, some studies (Gamer, 1977; Rose & Serafica, 1979c) have yielded sex differences. Since these sex differences seem more pronounced in young adults than in children, one wonders whether sex differences characterizing friendship become more sharply delineated as people grow older and, in traditional societies, assume more clearly differentiated roles. Other individual differences, associated with peer status and psychopathology, have also been found. Additional research on individual differences is needed to further clarify the nature of the relationship between friendship concept and peer popularity or impaired interpersonal functioning.

Conceptions of Friendship and Friendship Interaction

The problem of understanding the nature of the relationship between thought and action can be approached in several ways. First, the problem can be construed as a search for consistency in level of social reasoning across situations. Second, one might look for correspondences between level of concept development and behavioral interaction between friends. Third, one could examine the influence of interactions with friends on concept development and vice versa.

Consistency

The consistency issue deals with the generality of one's level of representation or reasoning about friendship. Evidence pertaining to this issue comes from two types of studies, those which compare the individual's ideas about hypothetical and actual friendships, and those which compare an individual's reflections about friendship in hypothetical and real-life situations.

HYPOTHETICAL AND ACTUAL FRIENDS

In the study of young adults cited earlier (Rose & Serafica, 1979b), descriptions of hypothetical and actual friendships were elicited and compared. It was found that the pattern of attributes ascribed to a hypothetical friend differed somewhat from that described in regard to an actual friend. Actual best friends were described significantly more often than hypothetical ones as accepting and stimulating. Actual close and casual friends were also characterized as stimulating, significantly more so than their hypothetical counterparts. The hypothetical–actual status also influenced the functions of friendship somewhat. Across group and sex, an actual casual friendship was significantly less likely to be seen as serving a life-enhancing function when compared to a hypothetical casual friendship. Comparisons of means employed in friendship formation, maintenance, and termination also revealed some differences associated with the hypothetical–actual distinction. First, although hypothetical best friendships were perceived as being established significantly more often through the development of positive feelings toward one another, this was not true for actual friendships. Second, proximity and interaction are important ways of establishing all levels of friendship. In regard to maintenance, hypothetical friendships differed in some instances from actual friendships, at the same level. First, hypothetical best friendships were more often described as being self-maintaining than were actual best friendships. Second, the maintenance of hypothetical casual friendships, as compared to actual ones, was more likely to be described as requiring continued geographical proximity, though not necessarily involving continued interaction. As for termination, comparisons of hypothetical and actual friendships at the same level indicated that subjects mentioned loss of feelings and decrease in interaction more often as ways of terminating hypothetical as compared to actual best friendships. When describing actual best friendships, subjects were more likely to say that the friendship just faded away or that it ended abruptly than they were for hypothetical best friendships. For close friendships, decrement in interaction was mentioned proportionately more often as a cause of a hypothetical friendship being terminated than an actual friendship; however, interference from other relationships was significantly more likely to be given as a reason for actual close friendships ending than for hypothetical ones.

The results of this study show that in a representative sample of young adults, there are differences as well as similarities between descriptions of hypothetical and actual friends. Descriptions of a hypothetical friend are more complex and at the same time more highly differentiated.

At the other end of the age continuum, two studies of preschoolers provide some indirect support for consistency in the criteria used to define hypothetical and actual friends. Hayes (1978) asked 3-year-olds why they liked an actual best friend. Propinquity, common activities, general play, evaluation, and physical possessions were the most frequent explanations. He also asked them whom they disliked (and by implication would not want to be friends with). This turned out to be the child who violates rules, behaves aggressively, or exhibits aberrant behavior. A recent observational study by Masters and Furman (1981) yielded some empirical support for these hypothetical criteria in that preschool children selected as friends the peers who exhibited high rates of reinforcing and neutral acts specifically toward them but not those who manifested a high rate of punishing behavior.

REASONING IN HYPOTHETICAL AND NATURAL CONTEXTS

Selman and Jaquette (1977a) are investigating the consistency in a child's level of interpersonal reasoning in an interview situation where the child is alone with the interviewer and in natural peer group interactions within a psychoeducational or social setting. They found that, among the eight children observed, three responded consistently at a relatively high level, one child reasoned at a consistently low level, and the remainder oscillated between high and low levels of reasoning. These individual differences were observed irrespective of whether comparisons were being made in hypothetical and natural contexts or reasoning in various natural situations over time and across contexts. The oscillations seemed to be associated with varying situational conditions, particularly with perceived status in the class and the specific content of issues being discussed. In turn, according to Selman and Jaquette, these situational factors interact with particular psychological or psychodynamic concerns of individual children.

   The studies cited here are obviously not comparable since they involved different age groups and used different methods. Taken together though, they all show both consistency and inconsistency in peoples' ideas about hypothetical and actual friendships. The question as to whether consistency increases with age remains unanswered. Additionally, observations of children with interpersonal problems show that some, but not all, children oscillate in their level of reasoning about interpersonal relations. This finding raises further questions about what underlies these inconsistencies. One possible explanation is that fluctuations in level of functioning are most likely to be exhibited by children who are in transition from one level of development to the next higher one. Another possibility is that situational conditions create the observed variations. We submit that while there may be some instances when a given situation or content will reduce the level of functioning in all children being observed, more commonly it is the child's interpretation of these variables which brings about the oscillations. In other words, cognitive and affective organismic factors interact with environmental conditions to produce inconsistencies in reasoning about relations between friends.

Correspondence between Friendship Concept and Interaction

The search for correspondence between an individual's concept of friendship and his/her behavioral interactions with friends involves at least three tasks: (1) specification of patterns of friendship interaction which reflect different levels of concept development, (2) demonstrating that these patterns differentiate interaction between friends from that of nonfriends, and (3) identification of conditions which are most likely to activate these differential patterns.

PATTERNS OF FRIENDSHIP INTERACTION

Do children's interactions with their friends accurately reflect their theorizing about relations between friends? Thus far, very little is known about the behavioral patterns of interaction which correspond to different levels of construing the defining attributes of a friend, the functions of friendship, and the ways in which friendships are formed, maintained, and terminated. Although there are abundant descriptions of how friendships are formed or terminated and of how conflicts between friends are resolved (Campbell *et al.*, 1979; Selman & Jaquette, 1977b; Stein & Goldman, 1981; Youniss & Volpe, 1978), they have not yet been validated through observations of friendship interaction in naturalistic or laboratory settings. About the only information available concerning developmental changes in children's friendship interaction patterns comes from a progress report on a study of communication between friends by Gottman and Parkhurst (1977). These investigators are currently engaged in a descriptive study of communicative sequences in the conversations of friends ranging in age between 2 and 9 years. Their preliminary findings are that the collective monologue observed in previous studies of nonfriends (Garvey & Hogan, 1973) does not occur very much at all in the conversation between friends; older best-friend dyads do not display the sequences of rapid adjustment and clarification of miscommunications which are typical of younger best-friend dyads; and the expressions of feeling by one partner are more likely to be followed by expressions of sympathy from the other partner in younger than in older dyads. These findings are interesting but not easily integrated into known sequences of friendship concept development.

Our slow progress in empirically identifying friendship interaction patterns may be due partly to the methodological considerations involved. First, there is the temporal factor to be considered. Once the child is past the point when a friend is whoever he/she happens to be playing with at the moment, identification of behavioral patterns requires repeated observations. Friendships are formed (and sometimes ended) over time, with the actors oftentimes not fully aware of what is happening nor cognizant of the markers which denote that a bond has been established or severed. Second, these patterns of interaction are not constantly displayed. In the course of a day, children interact toward their friends in much the same manner as they do toward children who are not their friends. As they grow older, their time is so structured that there are fewer and fewer opportunities to observe their interactions with friends. Also, with increasing age the relevant interactions (e.g., sharing secrets) lend themselves less to direct observations. It therefore becomes critical for the investigator to identify those conditions which activate friendship interaction.

DIFFERENTIAL RESPONSIVENESS

The hallmark of an interpersonal relationship is differential responsiveness. When two individuals have a particular relationship with one another, as in friendship, it is assumed that under certain conditions they will interact with one another in a manner different from their interactions with others. An adequate operational definition of friendship interaction therefore requires a demonstration of differential responsiveness. In addition, we need to know whether the difference is quantitative, qualitative, or both. For instance, do friends resolve conflicts more frequently than do nonfriends? Do they also resolve them differently?

There are very few studies of interaction between friends, although studies of peer interaction in general abound. The demonstration of differential responsiveness has been a major concern in most studies of friendship interaction. In a pilot study (Serafica & Destefano, 1978) comparing ten friendly male dyads with nonfriendly male dyads matched for age (7 years), sex, socioeconomic status, and ethnic membership, we found a significant difference ($p < .05$) in the frequency of collaborative activity in a 20-minute unstructured-play situation.

Friendly dyads were more likely to engage in a play activity with a common goal than nonfriendly dyads. Significant group differences in frequency of individual or identical play activities did not emerge. The frequency of talking was about equal in the two groups, but when the content of verbal statements was examined, it was found that statements directed to the partner differed significantly ($p < .05$) as a function of friendship status. Further analysis of this dependent measure revealed that the significant differences occurred mainly for suggestions and commands. More suggestions and commands were given between friends than nonfriends. Although there was a tendency for approach behaviors to occur more frequently among friends, this trend did not reach an acceptable level of significance. The frequency of either visual or contact behaviors did not vary significantly with the status of the partner. Also, nonfriendly dyads smiled and laughed just as much as friendly dyads. A similar finding emerged with respect to negative affect.

Other investigators have found differential affective responding in friendly versus nonfriendly dyads. In both studies, behavior in the presence of friends was assessed to determine the facilitative effects of friendship. Foot, Chapman, and Smith (1977) videotaped the reactions to a comedy film of pairs of 7- and 8-year-old children. The dependent variables were looking, laughing, smiling, talking, and touching. Friends and strangers were placed in same-sex or mixed-sex pairs. Friendship had an overwhelming effect in facilitating responsiveness on all the measures. The results were interpreted as supporting Patterson's (1976) arousal model of social intimacy which asserts that changes in intimacy behaviors initiated by one person (A) are reciprocated by a second person (B) if these changes produce in B positively valued arousal.

The Foot *et al.* (1977) study examined differential responsiveness by friends in a situation which made no clear demands for social interaction. Newcomb, Brady, and Hartup (1979) exposed first- and third-grade boys and girls to both competitive and cooperative conditions in order to examine the interaction between friendship and incentive condition on both performance-related outcomes and process components of the social interactions. Children were randomly paired with a same-sex, same-age friend or nonfriend based on ratings obtained in free-response and forced-choice sociometric measures, and on teacher ratings of interaction frequencies. Friends and nonfriends did not differ significantly on any of the task outcome measures, which consisted of the total number of blocks handled during a trial (total work) and the discrepancy between individual partners' work during each trial (d-work). For the social interaction measures, friends and non-friends did not differ significantly in the frequency of talking, although talking increased linearly across phases. Friends, however, made more references to issues of equity than did nonfriends ($p < .003$). Also, the frequency of affective expression was significantly higher during the interaction of friends than nonfriends. Friendship status also had an effect on both the intent of and compliance with commands. Commands of mutual intent were more likely to be given by friends, while nonfriends issued more commands of individualistic intent. Nonfriends, as compared with friends, evidenced a sharp increase in the use of individualistic commands during the competitive phase. Compliance with commands occurred more frequently between friends; nonfriends were more likely to negate commands by failing to comply or by offering countersuggestions ($p < .03$).

These three studies indicate that differential responsiveness does occur but its incidence varies with the situation and the behavioral indices. These findings further highlight the importance of identifying activating conditions.

ACTIVATING CONDITIONS

The concept of activating conditions is borrowed from Bowlby (1969), who borrowed it from ethologists. Speaking of infant attachment, Bowlby stated that attachment behavior is not always manifested; instead, it is activated only under certain subjective and objective conditions. Within a systems theory framework, Bowlby conceptualizes the infant–mother relationship as a goal-corrected system, by which he means that the system is so structured that the behavior it controls is constantly corrected by reference to whatever discrepancy exists between current state and the set goal. By set goal (henceforth referred to as "goal"), he means either a time-limited event or an ongoing condition, either of which is brought about by the action of behavioral systems that are structured to take into account discrepancies between goal and performance.

For Bowlby, maintaining proximity is the goal in the earliest form of an interpersonal relationship—namely, infant–mother attachment—but there may be other goals. Elaborating Bowlby's formulation, an interpersonal relationship may be more heuristically viewed as a multi-dimensional construct involving goals other than proximity. Because of its importance for the infant's survival, particularly in the environment of evolutionary adaptedness, proximity may be the primary goal during infancy, but other goals which also have adaptive functions may emerge, as suggested by Sroufe and Waters (1977) and Serafica (1978). The means through which these goals are attained are classes of responses or behavioral patterns of interaction which constitute indices of an interpersonal relationship.

What are the goals of friendship? Studies of proximity behavior among peers suggest that the goal of proximity initially posited by Bowlby and strongly validated by empirical studies (Ainsworth & Bell, 1970; Ainsworth & Wittig, 1969) also characterizes friendship. Lewis, Young, Brooks, and Michalson (1975) observed that infants were much more likely to maintain proximity to their friends than strangers. Contact or an experience of the other's presence achieved through sensorimotoric, perceptual, or conceptual symbolic means may be still another goal in friendship. Empirical support for the conceptual distinction between proximity and contact as goals, and between the means employed to attain them, has been presented (Serafica, 1978), based on a sample of infants ranging in age from 8 to 24 months. That infants are more likely to manifest tactual contact with friends than strangers has also been reported by Lewis *et al.* (1975).

The studies on personal space in children and adolescents (Guardo, 1969; Guardo & Meisels, 1971) suggest that the goal of proximity may also be true for friendship during childhood and adolescence. Guardo's (1969) data yielded support for the hypothesis that the distance between members of depicted (printed silhouettes) peer dyads varies with the degree of acquaintance and the degree of liking attributed to them by sixth-grade children. Silhouette peer dyads separated by shorter distances were judged by the subjects to have greater knowledge of and more liking for one another than those separated by longer distances. An inverse relationship emerged when the subjects were asked to place distances between a self-referent figure and printed peer figures variously described in terms of degree of acquaintance, liking, and threat.

To return to the subject of activating conditions, if proximity in physical or psychological terms is a goal of friendship, then discrepancies between goal and actuality will activate specific friendship interaction patterns designed to restore the desired goal between the partners. These patterns may include those described by Selman and Jaquette (1977b) for dealing with issues of jealousy–exclusion and conflict resolution as well as the modes of repairing violations observed by Youniss and Volpe (1978). Presumably, the behavioral patterns would vary with age, reflecting differences in the individual's concept of relations between friends. In sum, specifying the goals of friendship might provide insight into the conditions which are most likely to activate friendship concept and interaction patterns. Statements about the functions of friendship provide clues as to what might be the other goals of friendship and the objective or subjective conditions activating behavior toward these goals.

Within a Wernerian perspective (Werner, 1948; Werner & Kaplan, 1963), the goals of friendship would be assumed to undergo sequential changes characterized by increasing differentiation and hierarchical integration. Friendship interaction patterns would be expected to change in the same manner, resulting in hierarchically ordered levels of functioning. The specific behavioral means used to attain a particular goal may change, but continuity resides in the fact that these behaviors, although different, serve the same goal. Therefore, there is functional equivalence. Thus, parallel to the different levels of organization in children's conceptions of friendship, there would be different modes or patterns which characterize transactions between friends around a specific goal or for a particular class of situations, at different ages. Organismic–developmental theory also assumes that there are multiple levels of functioning. Applied to friendship this could mean that: (1) a child's level of reasoning about friendship may be higher than the level of friendship interaction patterns he/she manifests in a particular context, or (2) having reached a particular level of functioning in either thought or action, a child may perform at a lower level in either domain, under certain objective and subjective conditions. Thus, organismic–developmental theory lends itself to both structural and functional analyses of developmental changes in friendship goals and interaction patterns. Combined with the ethological concept of activating conditions, it could provide us with a more meaningful and valid analysis of when and how friends interact at a particular age and of the transformations these interaction patterns undergo during the life span.

Basically, what seems to be needed is a taxonomy of goals and activating conditions, subjective as well as objective. It is important to remember, however, that it is the meaning of the situation to the individuals which will really determine whether or not the friendship system will be activated. Situations which appear different can have the same meaning, and therefore both will activate friendship. Moreover, aspects of the situation will be selectively responded to by the individual, and the individual him/herself affects the character of the situation.

In attempting to determine the activating conditions for friendship interaction, better knowledge of the child's social world and the similarities and differences between this world and the adult world would be useful since the child must survive in both. Rom Harre (1974) has suggested that there may be at least two social worlds in childhood. One of these, the schoolchild's social world, is a precursor of the adult social world, but the other, an earlier one, is not. It is in the former that children acquire the ability to create and maintain the social order by ceremonial means. In this world, children learn the conventional and ritualistic ways of maintaining smooth interpersonal relations. Certain activating conditions may require just this kind of ritualistic behavior between friends; whereas others elicit more spontaneous, idiosyncratic patterns, and still others facilitate logically ordered relations.

Finally, in discussing correspondence between knowledge about friendship and interactions between friends, we should not overlook the fact that the consequences of the interaction have an effect on repeated use of a particular behavioral pattern. The reinforcing effect of consequences can be accommodated within a systems theory perspective on friendship interaction. Behavioral patterns which result in good attainment or close approximations to it are far more likely to be repeated.

Causal Relationships

UNIDIRECTIONAL VIEWS OF CAUSALITY

Content-oriented investigators (e.g., Bigelow, 1977; Reisman & Shorr, 1978b) have tended to view the concept of friendship as a possible determinant of social interaction. It is assumed that the specific attributes used to describe a friend also represent expectations about how friends will or ought to behave toward one another (Berndt, 1978). This view implies a unidirectional causal relationship between concept and action.

RECIPROCAL VIEWS OF CAUSALITY

From a social-cognitive perspective, the causal relationship between thought and action, if it exists at all, is construed as a reciprocal one. An individual's concept of friendship provides a framework within which interactions with peers may be understood and organized. Proponents of a social-cognitive perspective on friendship (Selman & Jaquette, 1977a; Youniss & Volpe, 1978) have argued strongly against making specific predictions about friendship interaction based upon the concept of friendship. As discussed earlier, other variables influence the translation of thought into action. The importance of the concept for friendship interaction, Youniss and Volpe assert, is that it enables people to understand the implications of: (1) the interactions of the friendship insofar as specific social behaviors affirm, disrupt, or mend it; and (2) following one, instead of another, interactive course and anticipating its effects on the friendship.

Of just as much, if not more, interest to investigators with a social-cognitive orientation is the influence of friendship interactions upon the development of the concept of friendship. In their view, interactions between friends provide the aliment for concept development. Social experiences, particularly those which present interpersonal dilemmas, facilitate the restructuring of ideas about friendship and, as a consequence, transitions from one level to the next. The task for the investigator is to identify the social experiences which are most likely to facilitate developmental shifts for specified groups of individuals.

Directions for Future Research

This selective review of research on conceptions of friendship and interaction between friends has shown that the concept of friendship, studied from different theoretical perspectives and through different methods, undergoes developmental changes. There have been attempts to demonstrate the organizing principles underlying these changes, but studies of the factors which facilitate transitions in development and those affecting the rate of change have yet to be done. Some studies have yielded empirical support for the hypothesis that there are hierarchically ordred levels of friendship, though just exactly when these distinctions start being made and what changes they undergo still remain unknown. Individual differences also have been noted, associated with sex, peer status, and psychopathology. However, these differences do not characterize all aspects of the concept, nor do they appear at all ages studied. Thus, more information is needed as to when and what individual differences may be expected, and their bases.

The studies reviewed revealed a hiatus between the study of the concept and the study of behavioral interactions dealing with friendship. Investigators focusing on the concept have examined its generality across stimulus (hypothetical–actual) and situation (interview–peer group meeting). Those who have studied friendship interaction have been far more concerned with demonstrating that friends behave differently from nonfriends in different situations. In these studies, the behavioral indices and situations did not seem to have been chosen with levels of friendship concept development in mind; at most, the situations might perhaps be construed as assessments of certain functions of friendship. What seems needed are studies designed to establish correspondence between levels of concept development and behavioral patterns of interaction between friends. Such studies might require repeated observations and identification of the conditions which are most likely to bring out the distinguishing patterns of friendship interaction. In this regard, it might be helpful to conceptualize friendship as a system with specifiable goals and behavioral patterns for achieving those goals which are activated under subjective or objective conditions. Age-related changes in these goals, means, and activating conditions can then be explored and related to the concept of friendship. Finally, studies which examine the effect of friendship interactions on concept development and vice versa, and the effects of affect and motives on both ideas and actions regarding friendship will add immensely to our understanding of the dynamics and development of friendship.

REFERENCES

Adler, A. *The education of children.* New York: Greenberg, 1930.

Ainsworth, M. D. S. Object relations, dependency, and attachment: A theoretical review of the infant–mother relationship. *Child Development,* 1969, *40,* 969–1026.

Ainsworth, M. D. S., & Bell, S. M. Attachment, exploration and separation: Illustrated by the behavior of one-year-olds in a strange situation. *Child Development,* 1970, *41,* 49–68.

Ainsworth, M. D. S., & Wittig, B. Attachment and exploratory behavior of one-year-olds in a strange situation. In B. M. Foss (Ed.), *Determinants of infant behavior* (Vol. 4). New York: Barnes & Noble, 1969.

Aristotle. *The Nichomachean ethics.* Cambridge: Harvard University Press, 1962. (Original ca. 300 B.C.)

Baumrind, D. Socialization and instrumental competence in young children. In W. W. Hartup (Ed.), *The young child: Reviews of research* (Vol. 2). Washington, D.C.: National Association for the Education of Young Children, 1972.

Berndt, T. J. *Children's conception of friendship and the behavior expected of friends.* Paper presented at the meeting of the American Psychological Association, Toronto, 1978.

Bigelow, B. J. Children's friendship expectations: A cognitive-developmental study. *Child Development,* 1977, *48,* 246–253.

Bigelow, B. J., & LaGaipa, J. J. Children's written descriptions of friendship: A multidimensional analysis. *Developmental Psychology,* 1975, *11,* 857–858.

Bowlby, J. *Attachment and loss* (Vol. 1). New York: Basic Books, 1969.

Bronson, W. C. Developments in behavior with age mates during the second year of life. In M. Lewis & L. A. Rosenblum (Eds.), *Friendship and peer relations*. New York: Wiley, 1975.

Campbell, S. B. G., Gluck, D. S., Lamparski, D. M., Romano, J. M., & Schultz, H. T. *A developmental study of children's ideas about friendship*. Unpublished manuscript, University of Pittsburgh, 1979.

Cowen, E. L., Pederson, A., Babigian, H., Izzo, L. D., & Trost, M. A. Long-term follow-up of early detected vulnerable children. *Journal of Consulting and Clinical Psychology*, 1973, *41*, 438–446.

Damon, W. *The social world of the child*. San Francisco: Jossey-Bass, 1977.

Foot, H. C., Chapman, A. J., & Smith, J. R. Friendship and social responsiveness in boys and girls. *Journal of Personality and Social Psychology*, 1977, *35*, 401–411.

Freud, S. Analysis of a phobia in a five-year-old boy. In *Collected papers* (Vol. 3). New York: Basic Books, 1959. (Originally published, 1909.)

Gamer, E. *Children's reports of friendship criteria*. Paper presented at the meeting of the Massachusetts Psychological Association, Boston, 1977.

Garvey, C., & Hogan, R. Social speech and social interaction: Egocentrism revisited. *Child Development*, 1973, *44*, 562–569.

Gottman, J. M., Gonso, J., & Rasmussen, B. Social interaction, social competence, and friendship in children. *Child Development*, 1975, *46*, 709–719.

Gottman, J. M., & Parkhurst, J. T. *Developing may not always be improving: A developmental study of children's best friendships*. Paper presented at the biennial meeting of the Society for Research in Child Development, New Orleans, March 1977.

Green, E. H. Friendships and quarrels among preschool children. *Child Development*, 1933, *4*, 237–252.

Guardo, C. J. Personal space in children. *Child Development*, 1969, *40*, 143–152.

Guardo, C. J., & Meisels, M. Factor structure of children's personal space schemata. *Child Development*, 1971, *42*, 1307–1312.

Harre, R. The conditions for a social psychology of childhood. In M. P. M. Richards (Ed.), *The integration of a child into a social world*. New York: Cambridge University Press, 1974.

Hartup, W. W. Peer interaction and the behavioral development of the individual child. In E. Schopler & R. J. Reichler (Eds.), *Psychopathology and child development*. New York: Plenum Press, 1976.

Hayes, D. S. Cognitive bases for liking and disliking among preschool children. *Child Development*, 1978, *49*, 906–909.

Hetherington, M., & Deur, J. The effects of father absence on child development. In W. W. Hartup (Ed.), *The young child: Reviews of research* (Vol. 2). Washington, D.C.: National Association for the Education of Young Children, 1972.

Kobasigawa, A. Inhibitory and disinhibitory effects of models on sex-inappropriate behavior in children. *Psychologia*, 1968, *11*, 86–96.

Lewis, M., Young, G., Brooks, J., & Michalson, L. The beginning of friendship. In M. Lewis & L. A. Rosenblum (Eds.), *Friendship and peer relations*. New York: Wiley, 1975.

Masters, J. C., & Furman, W. Popularity, individual friendship selection and specific peer relations among children. *Developmental Psychology*, 1981, *17*, 344–350.

McCandless, B. R., & Marshall, H. R. A picture sociometric technique for preschool children and its relation to teacher judgments of friendship. *Child Development*, 1957, *28*, 139–147.

Meisels, M., & Guardo, C. J. Development of personal space schemata. *Child Development*, 1969, *40*, 1167–1178.

Newcomb, A. F., Brady, J. E., & Hartup, W. W. Friendship and incentive condition as determinants of children's task-oriented social behavior. *Child Development,* 1979, *50,* 878–881.

Patterson, G. R., & Cobb, J. A. A dyadic analysis of "aggressive" behaviors. In J. P. Hill (Ed.), *Minnesota Symposia on Child Psychology* (Vol. 5). Minneapolis: University of Minnesota Press, 1971.

Patterson, M. L. An arousal model of interpersonal intimacy. *Psychological Review,* 1976, *83,* 235–245.

Piaget, J. *The child's conception of the world.* Totowa, N.J.: Littlefield, Adams, 1967.

Reisman, J., & Shorr, S. I. Friendship claims and expectations among children and adults. *Child Development,* 1978, *49,* 913–916. (a)

Reisman, J. M., & Shorr, S. I. Friendship claims and communications of disturbed and normal children. *Journal of Clinical Child Psychology,* 1978, 7, 142–148. (b)

Roff, M. Childhood social interaction and young adult psychosis. *Journal of Clinical Psychology,* 1963, *19,* 152–157.

Roff, M., Sells, S. B., & Golden, M. M. *Social adjustment and personality development in children.* Minneapolis: University of Minnesota Press, 1972.

Rose, S., & Serafica, F. C. *Maintenance and function of friendship in early adulthood.* Paper presented at the meeting of the Eastern Psychological Association, New York, 1979. (a)

Rose, S., & Serafica, F. C. *Young adults' close and casual friendships: Attributes, functions and means.* Paper presented at the meeting of the American Psychological Association, New York, 1979. (b)

Rose, S., & Serafica, F. C. *Women's friendships: Implications for building professional networks.* Paper presented at a Women's Studies Research Forum held at The Ohio State University, Columbus, October 1979. (c)

Selman, R. L. *Interpersonal thought in childhood, preadolescence, and adolescence: A structural analysis of developing conceptions of peer relationships.* Paper presented at the meeting of the American Psychological Association, Chicago, 1975.

Selman, R. L. Toward a structural analysis of developing interpersonal relationship concepts: Research with normal and disturbed preadolescent boys. In A. Pick (Ed.), *Minnesota Symposia on Child Psychology* (Vol. 10). Minneapolis: University of Minnesota Press, 1976.

Selman, R. L. The child as a friendship philosopher: A case study in the growth of interpersonal understanding. In S. Asher & J. Gottman (Eds.), *The development of children's friendships.* New York: Cambridge University Press, 1981.

Selman, R. L., & Jaquette, D. Interpersonal awareness: Its development and function. In C. B. Keasey (Ed.), *Nebraska Symposium on Motivation* (Vol. 23). Lincoln: University of Nebraska Press, 1977. (a)

Selman, R. L., & Jaquette, D. *The development of interpersonal awareness (a working draft): A manual constructed by the Harvard–Judge Baker Social Reasoning Project.* Boston: The Project, January 1977. (b)

Serafica, F. C. The development of attachment behaviors: An organismic–developmental perspective. *Human Development,* 1978, *21,* 119–140.

Serafica, F. C., & Destefano, T. *Children's interactions with friends versus strangers.* Unpublished manuscript, The Ohio State University, 1978.

Sroufe, L. A., & Waters, E. Attachment as an organizational construct. *Child Development,* 1977, *48,* 1184–1199.

Stein, N. L., & Goldman, S. R. Children's knowledge about social situations: From causes to consequences. In S. Asher & J. Gottman (Eds.), *The development of children's friendships.* New York: Cambridge University Press, 1981.

Sullivan, H. S. *The interpersonal theory of psychiatry.* New York: Norton, 1953.

Weinstock, B. *Children's conceptions of friendship.* Unpublished manuscript, Clark University, 1976.

Wenar, C. *Personality development.* New York: Houghton Mifflin, 1971.

Werner, H. *Comparative psychology of mental development.* Chicago: Follett, 1948.

Werner, H., & Kaplan, B. *Symbol formation.* New York: Wiley, 1963.

Wohlwill, J. *The study of behavioral development.* New York: Academic Press, 1973.

Youniss, J., & Volpe, J. A relational analysis of children's friendships. In W. Damon (Ed.), *New directions for child development: Social cognition.* San Francisco: Jossey-Bass, 1978.

4

Interpersonal Problem Solving: A Cog in the Wheel of Social Cognition

MYRNA BETH SHURE

Introduction

It might have seemed obvious when Michael Chandler asked: "What makes social cognition social?" (in Shure & Selman, 1977). Isn't an understanding of others' thoughts, feelings, and motives, by definition, social? Not necessarily. The Conversation Hour discussion provided further insights: David Bearison noted that "unless we can show that how a child understands his social environment has something to do with how he behaves in a social situation . . . perhaps all we are studying is cognition about social events," or, as Chandler added, "an understanding of people as objects, not as subjects with the same rules and developmental processes who are also organized and changing."

How can we know, however, when (and if) thought precedes behavior or the reverse? As Robert Selman proposed, might we look "not at a matching of social cognition and specific behaviors, but rather, the reciprocal relationship between children's interactions and their [general] understanding of [them]?" But, as Norma Feshbach inquired, "Should a child who shows this understanding (in, say, a test situation) be expected to behave accordingly when observed at a later time?" "We all know," replied Seymour Feshbach, "that a child (or adult) who may understand another's point of view does not always take that into account during actual conflict," adding, "We need to distinguish between children's capacity to comprehend a task . . . and their habitual modes of thinking and when they display [it]. Perhaps

MYRNA BETH SHURE. Department of Mental Health Sciences, Hahnemann Medical College and Hospital, Philadelphia, Pennsylvania.

part of the task of training is to utilize the cognitive capacity [people] may have in *various* social contexts." But John Flavell gave us pause when only half in jest he quipped, "I wonder, what makes us think in the first place?" Equally provoking, he then asked, "Once someone makes a judgment, what impels him to behave as a consequence of the thinking [he's] done?" Tantalizing us further still, he followed, "Do we [even] always think [at all]?"

It may not always seem so. But things are not always what they seem to be. As Carolyn Shantz suggested, "A child [in physical pursuit] of another may not [in his view] be displaying antisocial behavior at all; he may merely be coming to the defense of a vulnerable friend." Such a child may indeed be experiencing empathy (it hurts me to see my friend attacked), and may even be actively perspective taking (my friend is afraid of the attacker; I am not). And, as S. Feshbach noted, "It could be that the more a child understands the nature of a social injustice, the angrier he may become." We now ask, would this child consider various options and perhaps even the consequences of what to do? If so, is it reasonable to believe that *this* time, this child might have decided that physical confrontation would be the best way to save his/her friend from further harm?

Whether or not thought is exercised during an isolated interchange, it seems equally important to examine individuals' *capacity* to think, and their general patterns of behavior across a variety of social situations. Research reviewed by C. U. Shantz (1975) suggests that empathy and perspective-taking skills do relate to predominant behavior patterns. When considering options and their consequences, a person expands his/her repertoire to a third dimension of social cognition, that of interpersonal problem solving. We have learned that interpersonal problem solving also has dramatic significance for social adjustment. It has particular relevance to issues initiated and expanded at the Society for Research in Child Development (SRCD) Study Group held at The Ohio State University in June–July 1978.

One issue of concern to the Study Group was how much to examine the process of children's thinking, the content of it, or both. This, it was agreed, would depend upon one's theoretical orientation. To understand, for example, how social cognition shifts from a concrete level to an abstract one would require an interpretation of content. Our orientation, however, has led us to research strategies that examine primarily the process. In the context of interpersonal problem solving, this process involves a style of thought, including means–ends linkages, ability to generate alternative solutions to problems, appreciation of consequences, and a tendency to turn to another solution, if needed. Because a child may not necessarily do (in the natural environment) what he/she says *can* be done (when asked in an isolated test situation), our second goal was to learn how processes of problem-solving thinking may extend to behavior in natural, real-world settings. How our theoretical orientation affected the priorities of our research strategies in light of these issues form a central focus of this chapter.

Specifically, a period of early theory building led us to identify interpersonal cognitive problem-solving (ICPS) skills important to social adjustment in young children, and our intervention model helped us to understand their role as behavioral mediators. The development of ICPS skills was then examined through a key source of acquisition—the child's mother. Though most of our research has been done with young children, Platt and Spivack (1973); Platt, Spivack, Altman, Altman, and Peizer (1974); and now a number of other colleagues have investigated ICPS in a variety of age groups. Following a discussion of developmental trends in both specific interpersonal problem-solving abilities and content, and in the relationship between ICPS and behavior, this chapter presents some speculations about how social perspective taking might relate to the interpersonal problem-solving skills of the young child.

Early Theory Building

When a predelinquent adolescent boy who had run away from a residential treatment school was asked whether he had thought of other ways to make his wants known and about the consequences of his running, he insisted, "I didn't think"; "I didn't think about that." George Spivack, then research director of the school and also the boy's clinician, began to believe he was telling the truth. Perhaps the youngster really *didn't* think; possibly he didn't know how. This and other similar clinical experiences led Spivack to systematically investigate interpersonal cognitive problem-solving processes in that age group (Spivack & Levine, 1963). They learned that regardless of IQ and test verbosity, middle-class antisocial and disturbed adolescents were markedly deficient compared to normals in a variety of interpersonal thinking skills.

One of these differentiating skills is what Spivack and Levine called "means–ends" thinking. This process of thought is the ability to plan sequenced means to reach a stated goal, to consider potential obstacles that could interfere with reaching it, and to recognize that goal satisfaction may not occur immediately. Subsequent studies have confirmed their findings in both the lower and the middle class across a variety of age groups (see Spivack, Platt, & Shure, 1976).

From age 9 through adulthood, the *content* of means given to reach a goal may or may not have differed. However, the most striking relationships to adjustment revolved around the presence or absence of planning as part of the cognitive style of the respondent. How abnormal individuals more typically jumped toward immediate goal attainment is illustrated later in this chapter.

When our attention shifted to ICPS in younger children, we quickly learned that enough range could not be obtained by testing means–ends thinking. A simpler task of asking for alternative solutions to age-relevant problems (Shure & Spivack, 1974b) showed that, again, the process, not the content, was the relevant indicator of adjustment (Spivack & Shure, 1974). As early as age 4, both the adjusted and nonadjusted expressed forceful ways to obtain a toy from another child (e.g., hit the child, grab the toy). While most children also thought of some form of "ask," the difference was that the adjusted youngsters thought of a greater variety and range of nonforceful ways (e.g., "trade a toy," "be his friend"), a finding later confirmed in middle-class youngsters (especially girls) the same age (Bazar, 1976).

Chilman (1966) states that competence and impulse control as criteria for positive mental health may only reflect a middle-class value system. She suggests that the constant and overpowering frustrations of slum dwellers make them take a pragmatic, physically aggressive, impulsive, and alienated view of life. Our investigations (Shure & Spivack, 1970b) showed that indeed, more lower-class children created stories or solutions limited primarily to pragmatic, impulsive, and physically aggressive strategies than did those in the middle class. Regarding Chilman's statement, however, that in the lower class "a more goal-committed, rationalistic, involved and verbal approach might lead to higher rates of mental breakdown than now occur" (1966, p. 30), our findings suggest that among the poor, the better adjusted have available not only a greater number of options and superior capacity to plan, but also a wider range of rational, thoughtful, and nonaggressive strategies than do the disturbed (see also Shure, Spivack, & Jaeger, 1971). Thus, we are in no way claiming that *what* a person thinks is irrelevant to adjustment. But the wider repertoire of options can help one choose an effective solution after considering a variety of factors.

What might other factors be? Spivack and Levine (1963) found that while normal and nonnormal adolescents thought equally of the idea to transgress in the face of temptation, normals were more likely to think through the pros and cons of possible actions, both conforming and transgressing—adding further spice to our hypotheses about the relationship of thought process to adjustment. Also, Ojemann (1967) and his colleagues (e.g., Muuss, 1960a, 1960b) have suggested that sensitivity to causes underlying an act rather than the overt nature of it influences the quality of adjustment. Putting all these findings together, our rationale for investigating the process of interpersonal cognitive problem solving as a significant index of mental health began to stabilize.

It seemed reasonable to assume that an individual who is not adept at interpersonal thinking skills may make impulsive mistakes, become frustrated and aggressive, or evade a problem entirely by withdrawing. If one's initial need remains unsatisfied, and such failures recur, varying degrees of maladaptive behavior may follow. On the other hand, someone more capable of using these skills should more effectively evaluate and choose from several possibilities, turn to a different (more effective) solution if need be, and thus experience less frustration.

An implicit assumption has been that problem-solving thinking skills antecede adjustment. If educators and clinicians have assumed that relieving emotional tension paves the way for one to think straight, our research examines the reverse idea—that ability to think straight can pave the way for emotional relief and healthy adjustment. The next step was to put this assumption to empirical test. By enhancing ICPS skills via controlled intervention, the question would be whether children who would most improve in ICPS skills would also most improve in adjustment. Assuming that intervention at the earliest feasible age is optimal for enhancing positive mental health (and supporting cognitive growth), and with our research indicating a relationship between problem-solving capacity and behavioral adjustment at age 4, we began our intervention studies with that age group. Because lower-class youngsters, particularly behaviorally aberrant ones, were more limited in their ICPS skills than their middle-class counterparts, we designed the program for inner-city youngsters enrolled in federally funded daycare.

In our first two pilot training studies (Shure, Spivack, & Gordon, 1972; Shure, Spivack, & Powell, 1972), ICPS-trained children clearly improved their problem-solving skills, and when compared to both placebo-attention and no-treatment controls, encouraging behavioral improvement was observed as well. Most importantly, a direct linkage between improvement in the trained thinking skills and in behavior provided further support for our position of ICPS as antecedents to adjustment, and this was the backdrop for our full-scale research program.

ICPS in Young Children

A battery of tests, given to inner-city 4- and 5-year-olds has identified ICPS skills which: (1) distinguish good from poor problem solvers, (2) relate to behavior, and (3) function as mediators of social adjustment and interpersonal competence. The first two criteria were examined by correlational studies; the third, by intervention.

Correlational Research

"Alternative solution thinking" (also called "solution thinking"), as measured by the Preschool Interpersonal Problem-Solving (PIPS) test (Shure & Spivack, 1974b), clearly distinguished 4- and 5-year-olds' ability to conceptualize ways to: (1) get a chance to play with a toy another child has, and (2) avert mother's anger after having damaged property. Consistent throughout seven studies (see Shure & Spivack, 1975; Spivack et al., 1976), well-adjusted children could usually offer at least three or four solutions to each problem, while those displaying characteristics of impulsivity or inhibition more typically thought of only one or two.

Illustrating the properties of impulsivity and inhibition may help us understand the relationship between these behaviors and poor problem-solving ability. One dimension of impulsivity consists of persistent nagging and demanding of adults when denied a wish; when a desire has to be delayed, if even for a short time; or when the adult is temporarily occupied with someone or something other than the child's immediate attention. Inability to wait also includes interactions with other children. Unable to share or wait a turn, a child often grabs toys as the quickest and surest way to get it "now." Another dimension of impulsivity includes overemotional reactions to frustration—often intense distress and/or anger. Physical aggression and bossy-dominating behaviors toward peers also fall into a statistical factor we call "impulsivity."

At least among inner-city Black preschool and kindergarten children, most display some or all of these behaviors at times. It was reasonable to conclude that a child who *never* hits, who rarely shows anger or distress, or who appears to be willing to wait *forever* for a turn may be so shy, timid, or fearful that he/she cannot display even normal amounts of aggression; and/or this child may control his/her emotions to the point of maladaption. In our studies, children judged to display these kinds of behaviors were classified as "inhibited." Any child not exhibiting behaviors of either inhibition or impatience–impulsivity beyond that typically observed in the "average" child as rated by teachers on the Hahnemann Pre-School Behavior (HPSB) Rating Scale was considered to be "adjusted." (Behavior group classifications are detailed in Shure & Spivack, 1975.)

If availability of only a few options does increase the chance of failure and possible frustration, what role does thought about the consequences of acts play in the behavior of a young child? Assessed by the What Happens Next Game (WHNG; revised from that which first appeared in Shure et al., 1971), adjusted children could best anticipate the effects of: (1) one child grabbing a toy from another, and (2) a child taking something from an adult without first asking. A stepwise discriminate analysis on 257 children (Shure, Newman, & Silver, 1973) showed that those who scored low on both the PIPS and the WHNG were most likely to be inhibited. In contrast, impulsive children, though often low in solution scores, may not have been low on the WHNG. Perhaps such children, however aware of the consequences, do what they do because they have few other options from which to choose. A child who grabs a toy may insist: "I don't care [if he hits me]. I *want* the [truck!]" Inhibited children, even more unaware of solutions, and also of consequences, may have experienced failure so often that possibly they find it safest to simply withdraw from people and from problems they cannot solve. Possibly that is why they either watch others, play by themselves, or do nothing much at all.

A third ICPS skill, that of "causal thinking," distinguished 4-year-olds who did and did not spontaneously consider what led to a stated outcome. When asked, for example, what a child might be saying to a friend with whom he/she was angry, causal statements (e.g., "You broke my toy.") versus noncausal ones (e.g., "I don't like you anymore.") either did not relate to behavior (Shure et al., 1971), or (unlike solution or consequential thinking skills) any relationship that did occur appeared to depend on the child's IQ (Shure & Spivack, 1975). Five-year-olds who were specifically asked "why" an event might have occurred did show significant, predicted behavior group differences.

Regardless of Binet-IQ or test verbosity, adjusted youngsters stated the most different possible causes, and the inhibited stated the least.

Further analyses, however, diminished optimism about causal thinking as a potential mediator of adjustment. Unlike consequential thinking, the relationship between causality and behavior was attributable to solution skills (Shure & Spivack, 1975). This finding is particularly interesting in view of an action one child took. Standing near the bottom of a slide, with her back turned from it, the girl was accidentally bumped on the shoulder by an oncoming child. Without hesitation, she turned around and hit the child. When asked why she did that, her reply was "My mommy told me to hit." Remembering what her mother told her (the circumstances of which, no doubt were misunderstood), this girl did not find out what happened nor did she consider other ways to deal with it. She just impulsively did what she (thought) she was supposed to do. Any consideration of why she was "hit" or that her action might create a new problem was either absent or irrelevant to her.

A final ICPS skill studied during this period of our research was that of "interpersonal sensitivity," a spontaneous tendency to perceive a problem as interpersonal, assessed by the Sensitivity to Interpersonal Problems (SIP) test (Shure & Spivack, 1975). Shown pictures of people and asked "What's happening," or "What's wrong," some youngsters focused on the interaction between the people (e.g., a boy standing in front of a TV is "in his parents' way"); some focused on a personal problem (e.g., "He's mad 'cause his shirt is ripped."); some on an impersonal problem (e.g., "The TV set is broken."); and some on no problem at all (e.g., "The dog's behind the TV."). Although tendency to perceive problems as interpersonal did not relate to behavior, it did relate to each of the other ICPS skills in both age groups.

It appears that 4- and 5-year-olds who are deficient in solution thinking may or may not consider the effects of their actions on others, probably do not recognize the prior event(s) that led up to the present problem, and are probably not even cognizant of the real problem that exists. Children who are hit "back" often focus upon "He hit me," instead of the real problem, "He hit me because I hit him first." Thinking only of their immediate needs, what might happen next becomes only secondary, and they continue to pursue their original desire by the limited repertoire of options they have. The intercorrelations between these skills suggest that perhaps sensitivity and causal thinking may enhance solution and consequential skills, but regardless of consideration for the latter, knowing what else to do in case of failure is the cognitive skill that best prevents, or at least diminishes, continued frustration and subsequent need for impulsive behaviors or withdrawal.

Zachery, who was seen exercising his skills, may support this speculation. When Richard refused to let him have a wagon, Zachery did not create a new problem by reacting impulsively. His ability to think of other options led him to another tactic. "If you let me have the wagon, I'll give it right back." When Richard did not answer, Zachery asked him why he couldn't have it. Richard replied, "Because I need it. I'm pulling the rocks." "I'll pull them with you," shouted Zachery. Richard agreed, and they played with the wagon together. In finding out about the other child's motives, Zachery was able to incorporate them into a solution that was successful. Like other good problem solvers, he may have *thought* about hitting or pushing Richard, or just pulling the wagon away, and he also may have been able to anticipate the consequences of such acts. But most importantly, his ability to think of other options prevented Zachery from experiencing frustration and failure. We observed that good problem solvers could also better cope with frustrations when they could not have what they want. Children able to turn to different activities if their original desire could not be obtained were less nagging and demanding of others, and others were less nagging and demanding of them.

Importantly, the kind of resourcefulness displayed by Zachery also related to PIPS test scores in middle-class 4-year-olds (Schiller, 1978) and in 5-year-olds (Arend, Gove, & Sroufe, 1979), as evaluated by teacher ratings of ego resiliency (Block & Block, 1971). Regression analyses have also shown that of the ICPS skills measured to date, PIPS solutions also predict other social competencies, especially HPSB-measured concern (or at least awareness) of others in distress and how much the child is sought out and liked by peers. Of 17 other HPSB items—including need for closeness to the teacher, general language skills, and comprehension of shapes, colors, and the like—only the degree of the child's initiative and autonomy showed (with IQ controlled) significant relationships to solution and consequential thinking skills.

Given the significant independence of ICPS from impersonal cognitions and behaviors, we believe we have uncovered a unique area of thought processes that suggest important implications for social adjustment and interpersonal competence. How these cognitive processes can be extended to natural, real-world settings has special significance to our theory of mental health.

Training ICPS Skills

Because correlational studies alone cannot determine the "cart" and the "horse," we applied intervention to investigate a linkage between ICPS ability and behavioral adjustment. If experimentally altering ICPS skills could produce changes in the child's display of impulsivity and inhibition, it would be possible to offer a new approach to handling and preventing behavioral difficulties. It would also be possible to offer a new dimension of social-cognitive skills toward a theory of behavioral mediation.

A particular ICPS skill would be viewed as a mediator if increased scores on its measures correlated significantly with changes in adjustment measures (independent of IQ and general verbal skills). In combination with pretraining correlations, such a correlation of change scores would suggest evidence of a *direct link* between ICPS and adjustment. If ICPS ability does mediate such behaviors, our experimental manipulation model would also identify which ICPS skills play the most significant role in the behavioral adjustment of children 4 and 5 years of age.

TRAINING APPROACH

Our training strategies grew out of what we learned from our pretest results, from what we observed children actually do and say, and from the theoretical position which served as a springboard to our research. Because adjusted children could think of more solutions to a problem than could aberrant ones, and because forceful ways to obtain a wish were clearly part of adjusted youngsters' repertoire, we would not try to inhibit this kind of thought. Rather, we would help the more behaviorally aberrant think about what they do and recognize the possibility of other ways to solve the problem.

Because our conceptual framework proposed that the process, or style, of thought helps children generalize their problem-solving skills to new situations, no one solution would be stressed. Given this, our focus was to help children develop the habit of generating *different* ways, not adult-valued good ways, to satisfy their needs and cope with frustration. Encouraging children to think of their own solutions to problems and consequences to acts would, in our view, add to their understanding of what they do in interpersonal situations. If our theoretical position of problem solving is correct, the child's social adjustment and interpersonal competence would be guided more by *how* he/she thinks than by *what* he/she thinks.

In addition to daily 20-minute small group lessons created by Shure and Spivack (1971; presented in full in Spivack & Shure, 1974), teachers and their aides applied the techniques during the day when children were having actual problems at school. While not always possible to do so (e.g., if a child is too emotional to respond), use of the technique in the course of most problem situations can, in time, be quite effective. Here is how one teacher talked with a child who had just pushed another off a bike.

TEACHER: Steven, what happened?
STEVEN: He won't give me the bike.
TEACHER: What happened when you pushed Robert off?
STEVEN: He started fighting.
TEACHER: How did that make you feel?
STEVEN: Mad.
TEACHER: How do you think Robert felt when you pushed him?
STEVEN: Mad.
TEACHER: Pushing him off is *one* way to try to get to ride the bike. Can you think of a *different* way so he won't fight and so you won't both be mad?

What Steven would say next is not critical. What is critical is that Steven was helped to think about the problem and about what happened when he acted as he did. We have observed that children, when allowed to think, are less likely to resist than they are when suggestions are offered or demanded by the adult.

In addition to helping children develop a problem-solving style of thinking, use of such dialogues maintains a consistency in communication from the formal lessons to real-life events. Further, in reply to S. Feshbach's concern (reported at the beginning of this chapter) that children need to utilize their thinking skills in multiple contexts, dialogues guide them to *apply* their newly acquired ability when the need arises, across a variety of actual problem situations. (Further examples of the technique are illustrated in Spivack & Shure, 1974; more detailed interpretation of its benefits are described in Shure & Spivack, 1980, and Shure, 1981.)

IMPACT OF TEACHER TRAINING

Relative to controls, inner-city 4-year-olds exposed to the combination of the formal 3-month ICPS curriculum and teacher-guided problem-solving dialogues dramatically improved their ability to conceptualize solutions, consequences, and causal connections in (hypothetical) interpersonal contexts. In behavior, ratings by teachers and their aides indicated that, compared to controls, the frequency and/or intensity of both impulsive and inhibited behaviors were markedly reduced. For example, one painfully shy child who watched but did not (or could not) play with other children came forth on her own near the end of the program. To a group at the stove in the doll corner, the girl shouted, "I just cooked a cake," and a child answered, "Can we have a party?" She gleefully joined the group, an outcome quite different than before training, when teacher suggestions such as "Why don't you ask them to play" or "Tammy could feed the baby" only created further anxiety and withdrawal. (See Shure & Spivack, 1973; Spivack & Shure, 1974; and Shure, 1981, for detailed statistical analyses.)

Most importantly, our mediational theory was supported when change in the trained solution skills significantly related to change in behavior (the direct link). Somewhat less dramatically, consequential skills also improved with behavior, though causal thinking did not. With training having been equally advantageous to those previously displaying impulsivity or inhibition, and since neither ICPS or behavior gain was due to initial IQ (70–120 +) or IQ change, it was evident that a wide variety of children could benefit.

When all nursery youngsters who were still available were followed into the kindergarten year, we discovered that 6 months and 1 year later, nursery-trained children remained significantly superior in their solution and consequential skills without further ICPS exposure. In behavior, the percentage of trained youngsters rated as adjusted continued to be higher than among those never trained. Unexpected and particularly inspiring was the discovery that among children who did not show behavior problems in nursery, significantly fewer trained than controls began to show them in kindergarten—highlighting also the preventive effects of ICPS intervention (Shure, 1979; Shure & Spivack, 1979, in press).

By using an upgraded program script (Shure & Spivack, 1974a), youngsters *first trained* in kindergarten showed the same improvement as those trained in nursery. Interestingly, the linkage between improved consequential thinking and behavior change was stronger in the kindergarten than in the nursery year (Shure & Spivack, 1980), suggesting that this skill may be developmentally more suitable for children at age 5 than at age 4. But causal thinking, even with a revised measure designed to explicitly ask "why" (a child [hits] another), continued to disappoint us as a potential mediator of healthy, adaptable behavior. Finally, we learned that for the ultimate criterion goal—

behavioral adjustment—1 year, either year, was as beneficial as 2 years (Shure & Spivack, 1979); and still another year later, at the end of first grade, nearly all trained youngsters maintained that change. Though kindergarten was not too late, the preventive and holding-power evidence suggests that youngsters could begin kindergarten at a better behavioral vantage point if trained a year earlier, in nursery.

Three replications of daily 3-month intervention have shown that alternative solution thinking is not only the single most powerful predictor of behavior before training but is most enhanced by it, and that behavior improvement is most strongly related to change in this trained skill. During a study group discussion with colleagues (SRCD, 1978), Chandler challenged whether one "good" solution would suffice. Perhaps. But, we believe, it is the process of turning to another that encourages one not to give up too soon. Also, it is that very flexibility that allows one to generalize a style of thought from one problem situation to another. While in the short run it may be one "good" solution that solves a given problem, in the long run the issue for social adjustment is the ability to generate the kind of thinking that results in resiliency instead of frustration.

Nevertheless, the significance of multiple options does not imply that one needs a limitless repertoire. Empirically, as noted earlier, three to four solutions per problem appear to suffice for healthy social adjustment in young children. Increasing this skill through training of already adjusted children does, however, appear to prevent later behavior problems, as evidenced in our kindergarten study, perhaps because a *style* of thought that includes such flexibility is likely to be perpetuated.

EVALUATING TEACHER-TRAINING RESEARCH

If we have discovered two ICPS skills which mediate behavior, still it may be impossible to know exactly how much change might have been due to factors other than training. We recognize, for example, that our design of having teachers who did the training also do the ratings could be viewed as a serious methodological flaw. However, subsequent research suggests that this flaw may be less significant than it might first appear to be. First, concern about teacher bias was allayed by ratings of follow-up teachers (kindergarten and first grade), teachers unaware of the child's earlier experience or behavior. These ratings allowed at least 83% of the children to be placed into the same behavior category as did those of the nursery teacher—indicating remarkably similar judgments by completely independent raters (even after time had passed). With additional teacher bias issues addressed in Shure and Spivack (1980), our discussion of mother-training research in the next section further shows why we believe teachers did rate the children honestly and objectively.

Importantly, the validity of our approach has recently been confirmed by Wowkanech (1978). Two groups of middle-class 4-year-olds were trained, one group receiving our complete ICPS program package (including informal dialoguing); the other, a program wherein teachers suggested solutions, modeled how to carry them out, and in addition, explained why a particular solution was a good one. Observed by independent raters (research staff who were unaware of the hypotheses or which group a child was in), it is noteworthy that in actual conflict situations, ICPS-trained children spontaneously generated their own solutions to the problem and turned to a different one if the conflict was not successfully resolved. On the other hand, once training had stopped, tactics of the modeling group more often reverted back to those previously used, such as hitting, grabbing, or other similar forms of behavior. In handling conflict, the important issue is that these children less often tried more than one way to deal with it.

The data suggest that ICPS skills add to our understanding of behavior, that applying them does not generalize from being told or shown what to do, and that the quality of social adjustment can be better understood in light of our increasing knowledge about the process of interpersonal problem-solving cognition. We learned still more about ICPS functioning when we turned our attention to the home.

Development (Acquisition) of ICPS Skills

How the subtleties of ICPS skills are learned is not yet known, but we do have some insight about why young children differ in them. In addition to discipline techniques, parents can affect behavior of their children by the extent to which they encourage development of interpersonal cognitive problem-solving skills, a function, we have learned, that is somewhat dependent on their own abilities in this domain.

ICPS SKILLS OF MOTHER AND CHILD

To discover how mother's interpersonal thinking skills relate to those of her child, urban Black mothers were tested for solution, consequential, and means–ends skills about adult-related problems (e.g., a woman is having an argument with her boyfriend), and for child-related problems (e.g., a child has been saying no to his/her mother a lot lately). Also, mothers were interviewed for what we call "child-rearing style" when handling actual problems with their 4-year-olds (Shure & Spivack, 1978).

To measure childrearing style, each mother was asked to re-create her usual way of handling a problem (e.g., the child wanting something he/she cannot have) by describing what was said and done by both herself and her child. Though mothers may not always have reported exactly what happened (though that was the stated intent), their reports did represent, at least, the style in which they could *think* about it.

Of interest was the extent to which the mother helped her child to articulate the problem and to explore his/her own solutions and consequences. In examining childrearing style, methods of discipline or the content of advice would not be of concern, but rather, the *approach* the mother would take. We assert that a mother who tells her child to hit back, or not to hit back but tell the teacher instead, is offering different advice but using the same approach—thinking *for* the child. A child who says that he/she is afraid to hit back, or that his/her friend will get him/her if he/she tells the teacher, may hear: "I told you what to do!" Because the mother is likely not listening but just thinking of *her* point of view, often the child does not have to think further about *what* to do but only worry about how to do it (or how to keep his/her mother from learning that he/she hadn't). It is also possible that a child may act impulsively when told what to do, as did the previously described girl in front of the slide who gave no thought to her action at all. It is even possible that a child may use this tactic when frustrated because he/she does not, or cannot, distinguish "hit" from "hit back." Except for communication which elicits children's own ideas, and why they think they are or are not good ones, very few techniques bring children into the process of thinking about the problem and the actions they take.

Partial correlations suggested that a mother's ICPS skills for child-related problems depended on her ability to solve adult-type problems, but that how she thought about child-related problems more directly influenced her reported childrearing style. It turned out that mothers adept at hypothetical child-related means–ends thinking were, when required to handle *real* problems, more likely to offer suggestions, state the consequences, and talk to their children about feelings (which, before mothers were trained, were among the most sophisticated techniques used). But two separate studies showed that despite finding no sex differences in the child's ICPS skills, or in any measure given to mothers of boys and of girls, mothers' cognitive problem-solving skills and childrearing style correlated with ICPS skills of daughters but not of sons. Why? We are not sure, but as Hoffman (1971) has noted, boys are normally more resistant to influence than girls, and they may be even more so when they do not have fathers (the case in nearly 70% of our youngsters). If, as Hoffman has also reported, mothers are more affectionate to their fatherless girls than to boys, and if children adopt parental characteristics to the extent that the parent is an important, relatively consistent source of nurturance and reward (e.g., Mussen & Rutherford, 1963), young fatherless boys may resist modeling their mother's ICPS thinking style just as they resist other forms of influence and discipline.

Where then, do boys—no less deficient than girls—acquire their ICPS skills? It is not obvious that fathers have a significant impact on ICPS acquisition of boys. Even in intact homes, Flaherty (1978), who has confirmed our positive mother–daughter and our nonsignificant mother–son relationships, has also learned that our measure of child-rearing style of inner-city fathers has little influence on the ICPS skills of either their daughters or their sons. One possibility is that, because many of these fathers had two jobs, they were not around enough to have such impact. Another is that the amount of their paternal restrictiveness (including order giving) may overshadow that of nurturance (Radin, 1973). If too little nurturance is given by lower-class fathers to their sons, perhaps the boys resist their fathers' demands, thus leaving them with no greater ICPS modeling agents than boys who have no father at all.

For boys, might peers provide the missing link? Young boys appear to be generally more vulnerable to pressures and challenges from their peers than girls (Emmerich, 1971), and also, they are more likely to play with the same children (Clark, Wyon, & Richards, 1969). The importance of peer relations notwithstanding (e.g., Hartup, 1979), it is difficult to believe that peers would have an influence on boys' ICPS skills equal to that of mothers on their daughters. (More thorough speculations on this issue are discussed in Shure & Spivack, 1978.)

TRAINING MOTHERS AND THEIR CHILDREN

If ICPS skills are more naturally associated in mothers and daughters, could such skills of girls *and* boys be enhanced if both mother and child were trained? The question was how. Also, would a change in mother's ICPS skills and childrearing style relate to the child's ICPS skills and subsequent behavioral adjustment? Using a program script suitable for parents (Shure & Spivack, 1978), our training procedure enhanced mothers' skills above and beyond those which even the best problem solvers exhibited before training. At that time, better problem solvers offered suggestions about what to do, and perhaps they explained why—including feelings and other consequences. But when children were guided to think about what they could do and why, the ICPS of boys as well as girls improved. Compared to matched controls, trained mothers and their children improved in ICPS skills, and the children's behavioral adjustment significantly improved in school. Our data suggested that mothers' improved ability to solve hypothetical adult problems (such as how to keep a friend from being angry after showing up too late to go to a movie) *did not* relate to their childrens' improved ICPS skills, but their ability to solve hypothetical problems about children (or about children and their parents) did.

Importantly, mothers who best learned to solve hypothetical child-related problems were also most likely to apply problem-solving dialogues when real problems would arise—partly, we believe, because they learned to solve a problem one step at a time, to recognize and circumvent potential obstacles, to appreciate that problems cannot always be solved immediately (i.e., means–ends thinking), as well as to understand and, at least at times, accept their children's viewpoints. These thinking and communication skills had a significant effect on the child's ICPS skills and behavioral adjustment. Analyses of covariance revealed that it was still the child's enhanced ICPS skills, especially solution skills, which had the most direct impact on improved behavior as observed by teachers in school.

In our mother-training studies, teachers were completely unaware of the training procedures and goals. That children trained at home could improve their behavior in school as judged by completely independent raters adds credence to the earlier described validity of our teacher-training research. That children's ICPS skills did not improve as a function of mere attention given by the mothers is evidenced by this trained group having improved in ICPS skills significantly more than a previous group of mother-trained children. In the first study, mothers administered the program script to their youngsters (thus giving them the same amount of attention as the latter group) but were not given ICPS training of their own. The validity of ICPS as behavioral mediators is again supported by the direct link. That alternative solution thinking most directly related to behavioral improvement replicates results of the teacher-training research.

Mothers, then, can become effective training agents, especially when given ICPS training of their own. It is encouraging that both teachers and inner-city mothers, many of the latter ICPS-deficient at the start, could transmit these skills to children in only 3 months time. That children trained at home could improve their behavior in school is, we believe, due to our approach. If boys were more resistant to modeling ICPS skills of their mothers before training, it is possible that they were less resistant to it when guided, then freed to think for themselves.

ICPS and Behavior: Developmental Trends

One way to approach ICPS developmental trends is to identify which thinking skills emerge at what age, in what sequence, and how the overall problem-solving abilities mature. Using D'Zurilla and Gold-fried's (1971) framework, Marsh (1982) found that in suburban young-sters, the ability to define an interpersonal problem undergoes sig-nificant developmental change earlier, between second and fourth grades, than other cognitive problem-solving abilities. This change was reflected in the number of separate, relevant aspects of the problem recognized (e.g., a *friend* threw a frisbee *and* a lamp got broken). Between grades four and six, further developmental differences emerged. Not only did the number of different solutions and consequences increase, but the final solution chosen by the child began to involve a greater number of the perspectives of the relevant people in the situa-tion. In addition, the problem definitions and consequences shifted from an emphasis on the concrete, such as objects and behaviors (what people do), to the abstract, such as psychological aspects (how people think and feel) and conceptual considerations (e.g., friendship, re-sponsibility, and fairness). Feldgaier and Serafica (1980) found similar structural and content shifts, except for alternative thinking, in middle-class boys (girls were not studied). The lack of a significant increase in alternative thinking in eighth-grade boys might be related to their verbalizing fewer forceful solutions. While the ability to do so was no doubt within their repertoire of thought, this apparent screening proba-bly prevented their total solution score (number) from being signifi-cantly higher than that of younger children.

Using an adapted version of the PIPS with single-child middle-class youngsters, McGillicuddy-DeLisi (1980) discovered that even across a younger age range, other developmental advances occur. The tendency to think of conflict resolution strategies that suggest active social interchange (e.g., "trade a toy," "take turns") increases sometime between the preschool years and first grade. Interestingly, the quantity of conflict resolution strategies increases at about the same time. While no further development showed up between the first and second grade, the previously described Marsh (1982) and Feldgaier and Serafica (1980) results suggest that further quantitative and qualitative change may emerge about 2 years later.

Our approach to developmental trends focuses upon how specific cognitive problem-solving processes may differ in their significance for adjustment within different age (and socioeconomic) levels. Although designed for 4- and 5-year-olds, the PIPS test appears to be a valid indicator of social competence in somewhat older children as well: in the lower class, as measured through age 6 (Granville, McNeil, Meece, Wacker, Morris, Shelly, & Love, 1976); and in the middle class, as measured through age 8 (Johnson, Yu, & Roopnarine, 1980). In the latter study, high PIPS scores were best associated with positive, pro-social behaviors; and in our own study of middle-class 4-year-olds, with *not* being inhibited (Shure & Spivack, 1970b). The consistent predicted relationships of PIPS' solutions with impulsive, inhibited, *and* pro-social behaviors in the lower class, and primarily to more positive behaviors in the middle class, suggest the possibility that this process of problem-solving thinking has relevance to different qualities of behaviors for different social-class groups during the early childhood years.

Nearly every study described thus far (and those to follow) has investigated, and negated, the possibility of confounding effects of verbal and/or total IQ in relationships between ICPS and developmental structure, or between ICPS and behavior. One study which did find that verbal IQ affected the relationship between solution skills and social competence was that of Enright and Sutterfield (1980). In first graders (social class unstated), predicted relationships between solution skills and percentage of unsuccessful (but not successful) interpersonal outcomes remained intact. In this study, social competence focused on the *outcome* of a goal-directed interaction (success or not) and not on the means to obtain that goal. Thus "taking an object, seeking information, or commanding" (p. 157) are goal-directed behaviors which define social competence if they meet with success. While socially competent children may on occasion hit, grab, and/or command (with or without thought), what is not known is the quality of strategies predominantly used, or the variety the child employed to solve the problem.

The major difficulty in interpreting these findings, however, is that one encounter included all behaviors by two people until the interaction ended—someone interrupted, one of the children walked away, etc. Enright (1980b) explained that a child may have tried two ways to, say, obtain a toy from another before succeeding. If uninterrupted, this child received a score of one success for that interaction. However, had the child tried unsuccessfully, and had he/she been interrupted or walked away, this would have been scored as unsuccessful whether or not the child returned to try again. It may be that high-score problem solvers would not let interruption deter them from trying again, and/or that they would wait (and perhaps even think about what to do next)—in either case, displaying the very lack of impulsivity often characteristic of high-score problem solvers. Given this unit of analysis, it is reasonable, as Enright and Sutterfield (1980) found, that children with a limited repertoire of options would fail more often. However, each of the two children just described may have been successful on, say, the third try, the first receiving a score of 100% success (for a given interaction); the second, only 33%. Also not known is how many encounters, whether successful or not, were in interaction with the same child or different children, or how many times the child was successful in solving the same type of problem (with the same or different children).

If success is one way to define competence, so too is the effect that a strategy has on the recipient. As Krasnor and Rubin (1981) illustrate, another significance lies in the flexibility (different strategies) a child is willing (and able) to exercise. Thus a child who (within reason) does not give up after failure, and whose predominant behavioral strategies have a positive effect on others, is in their view (as in ours) displaying important qualities of social competence. Given the previously described Wowkanech (1978) findings, it was this very flexibility that ICPS-trained children did, in fact, acquire. Considering all these factors and the earlier expressed Chandler challenge ("Would one good solution suffice?"), the question becomes that of determining to what extent and under what conditions any one strategy is effective, from whose point of view, and how much peoples' general pattern of behavior is associated with, and generated by, their underlying capacity to think.

A new measure created by Elias (1978) has distinguished high and low problem solvers in first graders, and it has been used with third and fourth graders as well (Bensky, 1978). Called the Social Problem Situational Analysis Measure (SPSAM), it assesses (by use of cartoons) several interpersonal cognitive skills. Elias learned that both means–ends linkages and solution thinking provided "meaningful predictors of independent social problem solving behaviors as perceived by peers on sociometrics" (1978, p. 185). Elias's findings for means–ends linkages at age 6 are enlightening and important, because our pilot work showed that an age-relevant adaptation of the original Means–Ends Problem Solving (MEPS) procedure (developed for adolescents by Spivack & Levine, 1963) did not differentiate behavior groups in regular school settings until the age of 9 or 10.

In the 9- to 12-year age range, MEPS scores distinguished behavior groups within homogeneous samples of dependent–neglected youngsters (Larcen, Spivack, & Shure, 1972), and of emotionally disturbed ones (Higgens & Thies, 1981), as well as when the disturbed in special schools were compared to normals in regular school classes (Shure & Spivack, 1972).

To illustrate, a normal youngster created this story about a child who wanted to make friends in a new neighborhood.

> First Al got talking to the leader (*mean*). He found out the kids liked basketball but Al didn't know how to play (*obstacle*). When Al got to know the leader better (*time*) he asked him to get the kids down to the skating rink (*mean*). The kids went and saw him practicing shooting goals. So the kids asked him, "Would you teach us how to do that?" (*mean*). So he did and they organized two teams (*mean*) and the kids liked that and Al had lots of friends. (Spivack *et al.*, 1976, p. 66)

At the other extreme, a more disturbed child would more typically think of the end goal rather than the means to obtain it. An 11-year-old disturbed girl told her story this way.

> She (Joyce) will go out and meet some kids and then she'll have lots of friends. Then she won't be lonely anymore and her mother will be happy because she went out and made lots of friends. She was happy too because she wasn't lonely anymore. She and her friends had lots of fun together because they played a lot during recess and after school. (Spivack *et al.*, 1976, pp. 66–67)

Not only did this girl's story move to immediate goal consummation (no statement was given about how she met the kids), but most of it described feelings and events which occurred *after* the goal was reached. (Similar stories are not uncommon in ICPS-deficient public school children as well [Shure, 1980].)

While Higgens and Thies (1981) found emotionally disturbed youngsters as a group to be poorer problem solvers than normals, their findings suggest the sensitivity with which means–ends thinking can distinguish relative differences in social competence within that special population.

Alternative solution thinking, when measured by asking the child to name all the different ways to solve an interpersonal problem (called the "what else" procedure), plays an important role in adjustment of second- to fifth-grade children before training (McKim, Weissberg, Cowen, Gesten, & Rapkin, in press; Richard & Dodge, 1981; Shure & Spivack, 1970a), and as tested to date in fourth and fifth graders after training (Elardo & Caldwell, 1979; Shure, 1980). When this kind of thinking was measured by number of different, spontaneously offered solutions embedded within MEPS-type stories, McClure, Chinsky, and Larcen (1978) found that after training fourth graders, it significantly predicted the judged effectiveness of problem-solving strategies (strategies that maximize positive, and minimize negative social and personal consequences). In simulated (but to the child, seemingly real) problem situations (e.g., a confederate "mother" concerned about her "child" making friends), youngsters who generated more alternatives not only proposed more effective solutions but offered them with less adult prodding (interpreted as problem sensitivity) and continued to volunteer them in the face of prearranged adult-initiated obstacles (interpreted as persistence). That this effectiveness was predicted by number of solutions conceptualized (in hypothetical situations) and applied (in simulated ones) supports the efficacy of our process versus a content approach to training.

The spontaneous tendency to weigh the pros and cons of an act before deciding whether to transgress has not differentiated adjustment groups in dependent–neglected 9- to 12-year-olds (Larcen, Spivack, & Shure, 1972), and to date, it has not been studied in other populations of this age. In Black urban public school fifth graders, the "what else" technique to elicit alternative consequences best highlights the deficiencies of (peer-rated) inhibited children (Shure, 1980), a finding notably similar to that of our preschoolers.

On the matter of training, most studies of elementary school-aged children show ICPS improvement following intervention and indicate that these gains are not merely a function of initial IQ or IQ change (e.g., Elias, 1980; Enright, 1980a; Larcen, 1980; Weissberg, Gesten, Carnrike, Toro, Rapkin, Davidson, & Cowen, 1981). In one study which did not show immediate change, Bensky (1978) did find significant improvement in fourth and fifth graders on most subtests of the SPSAM 7 weeks later. However, it is becoming increasingly clear that ICPS programs lasting from 6 weeks to 3 or 4 months may have less dramatic impact on immediate behavior change, at least in the lower class, than has been demonstrated with younger children (see also Weissberg, Gesten, Rapkin, Cowen, Davidson, Flores de Apodaca, & McKim, 1981). Encouragingly, Gesten, Rains, Rapkin, Weissberg, Flores de Apodaca, Cowen, and Bowen (in press) found that 1 year later, trained second and third graders (who showed immediate ICPS gains) began to show prosocial and acting-out behavior gains as rated by new teachers who were unaware of the child's previous training experience. That such behavior gains were not due to natural development or to time alone was evidenced by control children, whose ICPS skills never improved. Any immediate control group behavior gains (in the first year) returned to baseline when reevaluated at the 1-year follow-up.

There are two posssible explanations for Gesten's delayed results. It may be that it simply takes longer for ICPS to affect behavior in older children. Elardo and Caldwell (1979) showed immediate behavior change, but only when their program was implemented over an entire school year. Weissberg and his associates (in press) obtained adjustment gains and, for the lower-socioeconomic-status sample especially, attribute this in part to closely monitored training, supervision, and consultation efforts. However, school curricula do not generally allow time for daily ICPS sessions, as is possible for the younger groups. And because most homeroom teachers do not supervise recess (on the playground), "dialogues" cannot be exercised in the very place interpersonal problems so typically occur.

If length or intensity of training is one issue, another is the possibility of teacher bias (but in the direction opposite to that discussed earlier). Allen, Chinsky, Larcen, Lochman, and Selinger (1976) did not find immediate behavior gain in third graders, and he suspects that teachers of older children may be *less* flexible or sensitive to change and, therefore, less likely and/or willing to indicate such on the behavior ratings. If this was the case, it is conceivable that the natural behavior of Gesten *et al.*'s (in press) second and third graders really did improve and first surfaced in the ratings of the new teachers who were unaware of the children's behavior or teacher-judged behavior a year earlier. This conjecture becomes still more likely when we discover that in simulated, but seemingly real, problems (in this study, a confederate child refusing another a magic marker), the trained youngsters of Gesten *et al.* not only verbalized but acted out more solutions and with greater persistence than controls. These observations, and those of McClure *et al.* (1978) are consistent with the Krasnor–Rubin (1981) model of social competence, a model which embraces flexibility, effectiveness, and persistence. Until now, potential benefits of ICPS training for elementary school-aged children have been, perhaps, outweighed by the challenges of conducting that training. These investigators inspire optimism that this trend may soon be reversed.

In adolescents, means–ends and solution skills continue to distinguish adjustment groups (Platt *et al.*, 1974). In samples of sexually active teenagers, those less able to plan means toward an interpersonal goal (e.g., making friends) were likely to experience more unplanned pregnancies (Steinlauf, 1979), and regardless of pregnancy they were less likely to use contraceptive devices at all (Marecek, Flaherty, Olsen, & Wilcove, 1980). Flaherty (1981) noted that further analyses are showing that noncontraceptive users were also less likely, when asked, to consider the consequences of nonuse (e.g., pregnancy), nor did they consider any facets of the longer-range responsibilities of bearing or raising a child. Perhaps the behavior of the nonuser is a reflection of a specific form of impulsivity, behavior often characteristic of poor problem solvers. In addition, Spivack and Levine's (1963) *spontaneous* consequential thinking appears to distinguish normals from severely impulsive teenagers, though not from hospitalized psychiatric patients (Platt *et al.*, 1974).

In adulthood, the relationship between alternative solution skills and adjustment is not completely independent of IQ, a finding not observed before this period. Perhaps in adults, the more demanding task of means–ends thinking is a clearer predictor (Gotlib & Asarnow, 1979; Platt & Spivack, 1973). Also, for the first time, spontaneous causal thinking independently distinguishes adjustment groups. These, together with other measured social thinking skills suggest a possible paradigm for maximally developed thought–behavior linkages. Perhaps sophisticated problem solvers first define the problem (such awareness relates to other ICPS skills, though not directly to behavior), have a tendency to look back and consider its causes, carefully plan step-by-step means to solve it (taking the perspective of others into account), anticipate what might happen next, and then, if necessary, construct a different plan.

Intervention has not yet tested this paradigm in full. However, emerging studies show that modified ICPS training has helped hospitalized adult psychiatric inpatients decrease depression and increase self-esteem, introspectiveness, a sense of mastery, and feelings of social competence (Coché, 1976). Intagliata (1978) adapted the ICPS program of Platt and Spivack (1976), and 1 month after treatment, young adult alcoholics had actually employed such skills in their daily lives. Acknowledging that every process has not been measured in all age groups, leaving a notable gap in information, the flexibility of the ICPS approach appears to be adaptable from at least age 4, and to individuals experiencing a wide variety of behavioral difficulties.

Social Perspective Taking as a Problem-Solving Skill

During our intervention years with 4- and 5-year-olds, social perspective taking, sometimes called "role taking," was not systematically measured. However, included in our training program were exercises and games to help children recognize that the same person can feel the same way at different times, that different people can feel the same way at the same time, and that different people can feel different ways at different times. Teaching that the same person can feel different ways at the same time would have been, as Cooney and Selman (1978) and Harter (this volume, Chapter 1) have noted, developmentally too advanced for this age group. Ability to recognize that a person who is angry now may not be angry later was considered important for problem solving, because *timing* can be crucial. Knowing that feelings can change and be influenced can help a child see that he/she need not feel helpless in the face of anger. Appreciation that different people can feel different ways about different things—that is, that preferences can differ—is also important in deciding what to do: "I feel happy about this, but he feels sad." "I like to paint but he does not."

Our conception was that for optimal adjustment, such perspective taking alone might not be enough. Knowing how someone feels cannot resolve a problem and thus relieve the tension unless one also knows what to do about it. We have now systematically tested this skill in 4-year-olds, using the measure adapted and created for this age by Urberg and Docherty (1976). Evaluated were ability to recognize: (1) how another feels in a variety of situations (e.g., receiving a present, being alone in the dark); (2) how two children may feel differently about the same thing (e.g., a broken bike); and (3) that an event may benefit one person at the expense of the other (e.g., one child receives a toy from the teacher; the other does not). These perceptions significantly distinguished adjustment groups (Shure & Standen, in preparation). Discriminant analyses revealed solution thinking to be the most powerful predictor of overall behavior group classification; consequential thinking, the least powerful; and measured role taking, intermediate. The addition of such role taking to solution skills best identified deficiencies of impulsive children and helps to fill the gap between solution and consequential skills highlighted in earlier studies as significant processes associated with adjustment in young children.

That deficient role taking as measured supersedes consequential thought as a predictor of impulsivity could be expected because, as noted earlier, impulsive children who have a limited repertoire of solutions may not restrain their actions to obtain their wish. However cognizant of the consequences, any recognition or concern that what they do may lead to their own happiness at another's expense is disregarded. For inhibited children, is it possible that any knowledge or sensitivity to feelings without the wherewithal to deal with them may be frightening enough to cause social withdrawal?

Whether preschoolers are really able to take the role of the "other" —as advanced by Kessler (1977), by Marvin, Greenberg, and Mossler (1976), and by Urberg and Docherty (1976)—or whether they are simply ascribing their own emotions to another person in a familiar situation—as Chandler and Greenspan (1972) submit—our data suggest that such emotional sensitivity is an immensely important skill for healthy social adjustment at this age. Whether or not such skills are actually prerequisite to those of solution thinking, it is reasonable to believe that emotional sensitivity, however it is called, should enrich problem-solving ability; the child who appreciates the viewpoint of others should evolve a broader range of solutions from which to choose. Perhaps such a child would also better evaluate possible solutions because of his/her greater sensitivity of how his/her actions might affect others. Some supportive evidence for this conjecture is provided by a study of second graders (Hudson, Peyton, & Brion-Meisels, 1976).

Would a higher level of perspective taking further enhance problem-solving ability, as one might surmise from the work of Selman and Jaquette (1978)? Though a sequential pattern has not yet been established, there is substantial evidence that appreciation of another's perspective and problem-solving skills are intimately related: (1) in 4-year-olds, the previously described perceptions, with PIPS (Shure & Standen, in preparation), and Flavell, Botkin, Fry, Wright, and Jarvis's (1975) measure of recognition of appropriate gifts for others, with PIPS (Schiller, 1978); (2) in third to sixth graders, Selman, Jaquette, and Lavin's (1977) measure of interpersonal awareness, assessing growth of maturity from focus on the self (e.g., what friends can do for "me") to understanding of reciprocal relationships between self and others (e.g., friends are to learn from, share with, feel good with),

with MEPS (Pelligrini, 1980); and (3) in fifth and eighth graders, and in adults (relationships of adolescents not analyzed), Feffer's (1970) analysis contrasting focus on the self versus awareness and coordination of multiple viewpoints (as told from the perspective of two or more characters in an interpersonal situation), with MEPS (Marsh, 1981; Platt & Spivack, 1973; Shure, 1980). Even though these studies measured different qualities of perspective taking, these relationships existed in a variety of age and social class groups regardless of specific solution content, or of the given goal to be reached (e.g., getting even for a nasty remark, making friends). Importantly, however, the correlations in all these studies generally ranged from the .30s to the .50s. Thus, with an average overlap of 10% to 30%, it is evident that processes of perspective taking and problem solving are associated, but not interchangeable or assumed to be measuring the same thing.

To test the possibility that perspective taking may be prerequisite to problem solving, Marsh, Serafica, and Barenboim (1980) provided training for middle-class eighth graders in the former only. The idea was to determine if increasing ability to coordinate perspectives of others (à la Feffer) would naturally improve a child's ability to solve problems involving people. They found that compared to controls, trained youngsters improved significantly on a measure of interpersonal problem solving (including alternative solutions and consequences), based on the D'Zurilla and Goldfried (1971) framework. However, the children did not improve significantly on the MEPS nor on social perspective taking. It turned out that many of these youngsters had relatively high levels of perspective taking from the start, and that role playing during training did, in fact, include open-ended discussions of problem situations, discussions which were more consistent with processes of solution and consequential skills than with those of means–ends thinking per se (the latter of which would have had to include sequenced steps, potential obstacles, and appreciation that goal attainment may take time). When Enright (1980a) trained only perspective-taking skills (in sixth graders), he, too, found that MEPS scores did not increase. When skills *were* specifically trained, Enright found in first graders that increased level of perspective taking was associated with increased PIPS; and in 10-year-olds, with solutions as well as MEPS (Shure, 1980).

These studies do not, we believe, suggest that outcome might be due to mere training to task (see Enright, 1980a, for support of this position), but rather, suggest (as we have argued) that perhaps perspective-taking skills are necessary, but not sufficient, antecedents to optimal problem solving. Without specific training, the process of problem solving will not automatically improve, whether that process involves sequenced planning or multiple options, even though the children may become more sensitive to the feelings and viewpoints of others. If a prerequisite pattern is still unknown, we can ask whether high problem solvers are at least not low perspective takers. As can be implied from the developmental studies of McGillicuddy-DeLisi (1980), Marsh et al. (1980), and Feldgaier and Serafica (1980), we can also ask whether, within a given age group, better problem solvers more typically consider reciprocity, including viewpoints of others, in the problem-solving strategies they verbalize and/or apply. A beginning in that direction is a current study by D. W. Shantz and C. U. Shantz (in progress). As part of a study of natural conflicts between children (ages 6 and 7), they are examining how still another dimension of perspective taking (Flavell et al.'s [1975] "privileged information" task—in this case, the extent to which children attribute information to others, information which only they really have) relates to the number and type of solutions given to a modified version of the PIPS. In addition, the relation between problem solving and children's behavior during conflicts will be explored. For example, will high perspective takers offer more reciprocal solutions, and will they show different ways of handling peer conflict than children deficient in one or both of these skills? Also, will children who have more competent cognitive capacities be moved to try another way if the first attempt should fail?

Though not specifically studying conflict, Pelligrini (1980) found in third to sixth graders that it was the combination of level of interpersonal awareness (Selman & Jaquette, 1978) and means–ends thinking that best predicted behavior, especially prosocial ones. While conflict is not the same as general patterns of behavior, it will be interesting to learn, in light of S. Feshbach's position (in Shure & Selman, 1977), how much cognitive capacity is typically applied during actual conflict as observed by Shantz and Shantz.

Whether the mothers we trained could encourage problem-solving thinking in their children, at least in part because they learned to recognize and accept their children's point of view, is still open to question. Bearison and Cassel (1975) have found that youngsters of "person-oriented" mothers who appealed to human needs, thoughts, and feelings, were more sensitive to the perspective of a listener while communicating than were children of "position-oriented" mothers who appealed to rules or who merely demanded conformity. Herman (1979) has learned that in retarded 9- to 11-year-olds, supportive mothers who allow their children to make their own decisions have children with better developed problem-solving skills than those of restrictive mothers. Regarding content, Jones, Rickel, and Smith (1980) discovered that regardless of social class, 4-year-olds of restrictive mothers (concerned with rules and authority) offered evasion strategies to the PIPS mother-type problem, strategies that Jones *et al.* interpret to require no attempt to deal with the thoughts, feelings, and needs of the other (e.g., hide, hide the [broken flower pot]; "Say 'I didn't do it.'"). In light of Bearison and Cassel's (1975) findings, it is interesting that children of nurturant mothers offered more solutions of personal appeal and negotiation (e.g., "Mom, don't be mad"; or, in the peer-type story, "I'll give the [truck] right back."), reciprocal solutions that recognize others' thoughts, feelings, and wishes. Earlier described chronological cognitive maturity notwithstanding, it is particularly noteworthy that within the youngest age group studied, some children can conceptualize more cognitively advanced solutions than others, suggesting that the *capacity* to think this way is well within the realm of possibility for children as early as age 4.

How childrearing style, parent and child perspective-taking skills, and the ability of each to problem solve interdigitate—and how each affects the child's subsequent behavior—could open an inviting channel to swim. So, too, could the synthesis of other forms of social cognition, such as referential communication (e.g., Chandler, Greenspan, & Barenboim, 1974) and moral reasoning (e.g., Damon, 1977).

We recognize that links connecting thought and behavior can also be strengthened by other means, such as those of more direct self-instructional techniques of Meichenbaum (1977) or the combination of ICPS and self-instruction by Camp and Bash (1981). We also know that emotional blockage can inhibit thought any time. Behavior can be modified in a multitude of ways, including a direct reinforcement of it. Recognizing the variety of ways there may be, our research and that of the SRCD study group (1978) has shown that social cognition, including interpersonal problem solving, stands high on a list of mediators that determine the quality of social adjustment and interpersonal competence. How to decipher the role each plays in the total interpersonal world of the young child, and at what age, is perhaps our next problem to be solved.

ACKNOWLEDGMENTS

The author's problem-solving research with 4- and 5-year-olds was supported in part by grant number MH-20372, National Institute of Mental Health; with 10-year-olds, by grant number MH-27741, National Institute of Mental Health; and by Biomedical Research Support grant number 5-S07-RRO-5413.

162 SHURE

REFERENCES

Allen, G., Chinsky, J., Larcen, S., Lochman, J., & Selinger, H. *Community psychology and the schools: A behaviorally oriented multilevel preventive approach.* Hillsdale, N.J.: Erlbaum, 1976.

Arend, G., Gove, F. L., & Sroufe, L. A. Continuity of individual adaptation from infancy to kindergarten: A predictive study of ego-resiliency and curiosity in preschoolers. *Child Development,* 1979, *50,* 950–959.

Bazar, J. W. *An exploration of the relationship of affect awareness, empathy, and interpersonal strategies to nursery school children's competence in peer interactions.* Unpublished doctoral dissertation, University of California, Berkeley, 1976.

Bearison, D. J., & Cassel, T. Z. Cognitive decentration and social codes: Communicative effectiveness in young children from differing family contexts. *Developmental Psychology,* 1975, *11,* 29–36.

Bensky, J. M. *Differential effectiveness of a social problem solving curriculum with regular and special education children.* Unpublished doctoral dissertation, University of Connecticut, Storrs, 1978.

Block, J. H., & Block, J. *The California Child Q Set: A procedure for describing personological characteristics of children.* Berkeley: Department of Psychology, University of California, Berkeley, 1971. (Mimeo)

Camp, B. W., & Bash, M. A. *Think Aloud: Increasing social and cognitive skills—A problem solving program for children.* Champaign, Ill.: Research Press, 1981.

Chandler, M. J., & Greenspan, S. Ersaltz egocentrism: A reply to H. Borke. *Developmental Psychology,* 1972, *7,* 104–106.

Chandler, M. J., Greenspan, S., & Barenboim, C. Assessment and training of role-taking and referential communication skills in institutionalized emotionally disturbed children. *Developmental Psychology,* 1974, *10,* 546–553.

Chilman, C. S. *Growing up poor* (Welfare Administration Pub. No. 13). Washington, D.C.: U.S. Department of Health, Education and Welfare, 1966.

Clark, A. H., Wyon, S. M., & Richards, M. Free play in nursery school children. *Journal of Child Psychology and Psychiatry,* 1969, *10,* 205–216.

Coché E. *Therapeutic benefits of a problem-solving training program for hospitalized psychiatric patients.* Paper presented at the meeting of the Society for Psychotherapy Research, San Diego, 1976.

Cooney, E. W., & Selman, R. L. Children's use of social conceptions: Towards a dynamic model of social cognition. In W. Damon (Ed.), *New directions for child development* (Vol. 1: *Social cognition*). San Francisco: Jossey-Bass, 1978.

Damon, W. *The social world of the child.* San Francisco: Jossey-Bass, 1977.

D'Zurilla, T. J., & Goldfried, M. R. Problem-solving and behavior modification. *Journal of Abnormal Psychology,* 1971, *78,* 107–126.

Elardo, P. T., & Caldwell, B. M. The effects of an experimental social development program on children in the middle childhood period. *Psychology in the Schools,* 1979, *16,* 93–100.

Elias, M. J. *The development of a theory-based measure of how children understand and attempt to resolve problematic social situations.* Unpublished master's thesis, University of Connecticut, Storrs, 1978.

Elias, M. J. *Developing instructional strategies for television-based preventive mental health curricula in elementary school settings.* Unpublished doctoral dissertation, University of Connecticut, Storrs, 1980.

Emmerich, W. *Structure and development of personal–social behaviors in preschool settings: Head Start longitudinal study.* Princeton, N.J.: Educational Testing Service, November 1971.

Enright, R. D. An integration of social cognitive development and cognitive processing:

Educational applications. *American Educational Research Journal*, 1980, *17*, 21–41. (a)

Enright, R. D. Personal communication, June 9, 1980. (b)

Enright, R. D., & Sutterfield, S. J. An ecological validation of social cognitive development. *Child Development*, 1980, *51*, 156–161.

Feffer, M. Developmental analysis of interpersonal behavior, *Psychological Review*, 1970, *77*, 197–214.

Feldgaier, S., & Serafica, F. C. *Interpersonal problem solving: A developmental analysis.* Paper presented at the meeting of the Eastern Psychological Association, Hartford, April 1980.

Flaherty, E. Parental influence on children's social cognition (Final Summary Report, No. 29033). Washington, D.C.: National Institute of Mental Health, 1978.

Flaherty, E. Personal communication, July 28, 1981.

Flavell, J. H., Botkin, P. T., Fry, C. L., Wright, J. W., & Jarvis, P. E. *The development of role-taking and communication skills in children.* New York: Krieger, 1975.

Gesten, E. L., Rains, M., Rapkin, B., Weissberg, R. G., Flores de Apodaca, R., Cowen, E. L., & Bowen, G. Training children in social problem-solving competencies: A first and second look. *American Journal of Community Psychology*, in press.

Gotlib, I., & Asarnow, R. F. Interpersonal and impersonal problem solving skills in mildly and clinically depressed university students. *Journal of Consulting and Clinical Psychology*, 1979, *47*, 86–95.

Granville, A. C., McNeil, J. T., Meece, J., Wacker, S., Morris, M., Shelly, M., & Love, J. M. *A process evaluation of project developmental continuity interim report IV* (Vol. 1: *Pilot year impact study—Instrument characteristics and attrition trends*, No. 105-75-1114). Washington, D.C.: Office of Child Development, August 1976.

Hartup, W. W. Peer relations and the growth of social competence. In M. W. Kent & J. E. Rolf (Eds.), *The primary prevention of psychopathology* (Vol. 3: *Promoting social competence and coping in children*). Hanover, N.H.: University Press of New England, 1979.

Herman, M. S. *The interpersonal competence of educable mentally retarded and normal children and its relation to the mother–child interaction.* Paper presented at the meeting of the Society for Research in Child Development, San Francisco, March 1979.

Higgens, J. P., & Thies, A. P. Problem solving and social position among emotionally disturbed boys. *American Journal of Orthopsychiatry*, 1981, *51*, 356–358.

Hoffman, M. L. Father-absence and conscience development. *Developmental Psychology*, 1971, *4*, 400–406.

Hudson, L. M., Peyton, E. F., & Brion-Meisels, S. Social reasoning and relating: An analysis of videotaped social interactions. In H. Furth (Chair), *Integrations of development in social cognition and social behavior.* Symposium presented at the meeting of the American Psychological Association, Washington, D.C., September 1976.

Intagliata, J. Increasing the interpersonal problem-solving skills of an alcoholic population. *Journal of Consulting and Clinical Psychology*, 1978, *46*, 489–498.

Johnson, J. E., Yu, S., & Roopnarine, J. *Social cognitive ability, interpersonal behaviors, and peer status within a mixed age group.* Paper presented at the meeting of the Southwestern Society for Research in Human Development, Lawrence, Kansas, March 1980.

Jones, D. C., Rickel, A. U., & Smith, R. L. Maternal childrearing practices and social problem-solving strategies among preschoolers. *Developmental Psychology*, 1980, *16*, 241–242.

Kessler, E. S. *Cognitive aspects of imaginative role-playing in young children.* Unpublished master's thesis, University of Chicago, 1977.

Krasnor, L. R., & Rubin, K. H. The assessment of social problem-solving skills in young children. In T. V. Merluzzi, C. R. Glass, & M. Genest (Eds.), *Cognitive assessment.* New York: Guilford Press, 1981.

Larcen, S. W. *Enhancement of social problem-solving skills through teacher and parent collaboration.* Unpublished doctoral dissertation, University of Connecticut, Storrs, 1980.

Larcen, S. W., Spivack, G., & Shure, M. *Problem-solving thinking and adjustment among dependent-neglected preadolescents.* Paper presented at the meeting of the Eastern Psychological Association, Boston, April 1972.

Marecek, J., Flaherty, E. W., Olsen, K., & Wilcove, G. Correlates of teenagers' contraceptive use. In S. H. Newman (Chair), *Adolescent sexual behavior and contraceptive use.* Symposium presented at the meeting of the American Psychological Association, Montreal, September 1980.

Marsh, D. T. Interrelationships among perspective taking, interpersonal problem solving, and interpersonal functioning. *Journal of Genetic Psychology,* 1981, *138,* 37-48.

Marsh, D. T. The development of interpersonal problem solving among elementary school children. *Journal of Genetic Psychology,* 1982, *140,* 107-118.

Marsh, D. T., Serafica, F. C., & Barenboim, C. Effect of perspective-taking training on interpersonal problem solving. *Child Development,* 1980, *51,* 140-145.

Marvin, R. S., Greenberg, M. T., & Mossler, D. The early development of conceptual perspective taking: Distinguishing among multiple perspectives. *Child Development,* 1976, *47,* 511-514.

McClure, L. F., Chinsky, J. M., & Larcen, S. W. Enhancing social problem solving performance in an elementary school setting. *Journal of Educational Psychology,* 1978, *70,* 504-513.

McGillicuddy-DeLisi, A. V. Predicted strategies and success in children's resolution of interpersonal problems. *Journal of Applied Developmental Psychology,* 1980, *1,* 175-187.

McKim, B. J., Weissberg, R. P., Cowen, E. L., Gesten, E. L., & Rapkin, B. D. A comparison of the problem solving ability and adjustment of suburban and urban third grade children. *American Journal of Community Psychology,* in press.

Meichenbaum, D. *Cognitive-behavior modification: An integrative approach.* New York: Plenum Press, 1977.

Mussen, P., & Rutherford, E. Parent-child relations and parental personality in relation to young children's sex-role preference. *Child Development,* 1963, *34,* 589-607.

Muuss, R. E. Mental health implications of a preventive psychiatry program in the light of research findings. *Marriage and Family Living,* 1960, *22,* 150-156. (a)

Muuss, R. E. The relationship between 'causal' orientation, anxiety, and insecurity in elementary school children. *Journal of Educational Psychology,* 1960, *51,* 122-129. (b)

Ojemann, R. H. Incorporating psychological concepts in the school curriculum. *Journal of School Psychology,* 1967, *5,* 195-204.

Pellegrini, D. *The social-cognitive qualities of stress-resistant children.* Unpublished doctoral dissertation, University of Minnesota, Minneapolis, 1980.

Platt, J. J., & Spivack, G. Studies in problem-solving thinking of psychiatric patients: Patient-control differences and factorial structure of problem-solving thinking. *Proceedings of the 81st Annual Convention of the American Psychological Association,* 1973, *8,* 461-462. (Summary)

Platt, J. J., & Spivack, G. *Workbook for training in interpersonal problem solving thinking.* Philadelphia: Department of Mental Health Sciences, Hahnemann Medical College and Hospital, 1976.

Platt, J. J., Spivack, G., Altman, N., Altman, D., & Peizer, S. B. Adolescent problem-solving thinking. *Journal of Consulting and Clinical Psychology,* 1974, *42,* 787-793.

Radin, N. Observed paternal behaviors as antecedents of intellectual functioning in young boys. *Developmental Psychology*, 1973, *8*, 369–376.

Richard, B. A., & Dodge, K. A. *Social maladjustment and problem solving in school-aged children.* Manuscript submitted for publication, 1981.

Schiller, J. D. *Child care arrangements and ego functioning: The effects of stability and entry age on young children.* Unpublished doctoral dissertation, University of California, Berkeley, 1978.

Selman, R. L., & Jaquette, D. Stability and oscillation in interpersonal awareness: A clinical–developmental analysis. In C. B. Keasey (Ed.), *Nebraska Symposium on Motivation* (Vol. 25). Lincoln: University of Nebraska Press, 1978.

Selman, R. L., Jaquette, D., & Lavin, D. R. Interpersonal awareness in children: Toward an integration of developmental and clinical child psychology. *American Journal of Orthopsychiatry*, 1977, *47*, 264–274.

Shantz, C. U. The development of social cognition. In E. M. Hetherington (Ed.), *Review of child development research* (Vol. 5). Chicago: University of Chicago Press, 1975.

Shantz, D. W., & Shantz, C. U. *Children's behavior during interpersonal conflicts: Situational and social-cognitive correlates.* Project of the Department of Psychology, Oakland University, Rochester, Minn., and Department of Psychology, Wayne State University, Detroit. (In progress)

Shure, M. B. Training children to solve interpersonal problems: A preventive mental health program. In R. E. Muñoz, L. R. Snowden, & J. G. Kelley (Eds.), *Social and psychological research in community settings.* San Francisco: Jossey-Bass, 1979.

Shure, M. B. *Interpersonal problem solving in ten-year-olds* (Final Report No. MH-27741). Washington, D.C.: National Institute of Mental Health, 1980.

Shure, M. B. Social competence as a problem-solving skill. In J. D. Wine & M. D. Smye (Eds.), *Social competence.* New York: Guilford Press, 1981.

Shure, M. B., Newman, S., & Silver, S. *Problem solving thinking among adjusted, impulsive and inhibited Head Start Children.* Paper presented at the meeting of the Eastern Psychological Association, Washington, D.C., May 1973.

Shure, M. B., & Selman, R. L. (Co-Chairs). *Issues in social cognition.* Conversation Hour at the meetings of the Society for Research in Child Development, New Orleans, March 1977.

Shure, M. B., & Spivack, G. *Cognitive problem-solving skills, adjustment and social class* (Research and Evaluation Report No. 26). Philadelphia: Department of Mental Health Sciences, Hahnemann Medical College and Hospital, 1970. (a)

Shure, M. B., & Spivack, G. *Problem-solving capacity, social class and adjustment among nursery school children.* Paper presented at the meeting of the Eastern Psychological Association, Atlantic City, April 1970. (b)

Shure, M. B., & Spivack, G. *Solving interpersonal problems: A program for four-year-old nursery school children: Training script.* Philadelphia: Department of Mental Health Sciences, Hahnemann Medical College and Hospital, 1971.

Shure, M. B., & Spivack, G. Means–ends thinking, adjustment and social class among elementary school-aged children. *Journal of Consulting and Clinical Psychology*, 1972, *38*, 348–353.

Shure, M. B., & Spivack, G. *A preventive mental health program for four-year-old Head Start children.* Paper presented at the meeting of the Society for Research in Child Development Philadelphia, March 1973.

Shure, M. B., & Spivack, G. *A mental health program for kindergarten children: Training script.* Philadelphia: Department of Mental Health Sciences, Hahnemann Medical College and Hospital, 1974. (a)

Shure, M. B., & Spivack, G. *Preschool interpersonal problem-solving (PIPS) test: Manual.* Philadelphia: Department of Mental Health Sciences, Hahnemann Medical College and Hospital, 1974. (b)

Shure, M. B., & Spivack, G. *A mental health program for preschool and kindergarten children, and a mental health program for mothers of young children: An interpersonal problem solving approach toward social adjustment* (A comprehensive report of research and training, No. MH-20372). Washington, D.C.: National Institute of Mental Health, 1975.

Shure, M. B., & Spivack, G. *Problem solving techniques in childrearing.* San Francisco: Jossey-Bass, 1978.

Shure, M. B., & Spivack, G. Interpersonal cognitive problem solving and primary prevention: Programming for preschool and kindergarten children. *Journal of Clinical Child Psychology,* 1979, *2,* 89–94.

Shure, M. B., & Spivack, G. Interpersonal problem solving as a mediator of behavioral adjustment in preschool and kindergarten children. *Journal of Applied Developmental Psychology,* 1980, *1,* 29–43.

Shure, M. B., & Spivack, G. Interpersonal problem solving in young children: A cognitive approach to prevention. *American Journal of Community Psychology,* in press.

Shure, M. B., Spivack, G., & Gordon, R. Problem-solving thinking: A preventive mental health program for preschool children. *Reading World,* 1972, *11,* 259–273.

Shure, M. B., Spivack, G., & Jaeger, M. A. Problem-solving thinking and adjustment among disadvantaged preschool children. *Child Development,* 1971, *42,* 1791–1803.

Shure, M. B., Spivack, G., & Powell, L. *A problem solving intervention program for disadvantaged preschool children.* Paper presented at the meeting of the Eastern Psychological Association, Boston, April 1972.

Shure, M. B., & Standen, C. *The relationship between social role-taking, interpersonal problem solving and adjustment in preschool children.* Philadelphia: Department of Mental Health Sciences, Hahnemann Medical College and Hospital. (In preparation)

Society for Research in Child Development. Study Group on Social Cognition and Social Relations, Columbus, Ohio, June–July 1978.

Spivack, G., & Levine, M. *Self-regulation in acting-out and normal adolescents* (Report M-4531). Washington, D.C.: National Institute of Health, 1963.

Spivack, G., Platt, J. J., & Shure, M. B. *The problem solving approach to adjustment.* San Francisco: Jossey-Bass, 1976.

Spivack, G., & Shure, M. B. *Social adjustment of young children.* San Francisco: Jossey-Bass, 1974.

Steinlauf, B. Problem-solving skills, locus of control, and the contraceptive effectiveness of young women. *Child Development,* 1979, *50,* 268–271.

Urberg, K. A., & Docherty, E. M. Development of role-taking skills in young children. *Developmental Psychology,* 1976, *12,* 198–203.

Weissberg, R. P., Gesten, E. L., Carnrike, C. L., Toro, P. A., Rapkin, B. D., Davidson, E., & Cowen, E. Social problem-solving skills training: A competence-building intervention with 2nd–4th grade children. *American Journal of Community Psychology,* 1981, *9,* 411–423.

Weissberg, R. P., Gesten, E. L., Rapkin, B. D., Cowen, E. L., Davidson, E., Flores de Apodaca, R., & McKim, B. J. The evaluation of a social problem solving training program for suburban and inner-city third grade children. *Journal of Consulting and Clinical Psychology,* 1981, *49,* 251–261.

Wowkanech, N. Personal communication, August 26, 1978.

5

Children's Understanding of Social Rules and the Social Context

CAROLYN UHLINGER SHANTZ

Introduction

Children's interest in regularities they encounter in their day-to-day lives is known to most parents by what children choose to comment upon, the direct questions they ask, and the content of their play. The types of assumptions and questions of children about various kinds of regularities are illustrated in the following anecdote which occurred when a child came home from her first day in the second grade (Mrs. McIntyre is the teacher):

CHILD: Mom, guess what? Two and three is five in Mrs. McIntyre's room, too!

MOTHER: What do you mean?

CHILD: It's the *same* as first grade—two and three is five. Is it the same in every room? . . . Everywhere? . . . In China, too?

MOTHER: Yes, it is.

CHILD (*musing*): It's a rule everywhere. . . . Can't anybody make it be something else?

OLDER SISTER: No, it's a rule. It's always five. And you better not say anything else or Mrs. McIntyre will say you're wrong. You can't fool around with rules about numbers.

Sometimes baffled, sometimes amused, and sometimes in earnest seriousness, parents respond to questions about the generality and mutability of rules.

CAROLYN UHLINGER SHANTZ. Department of Psychology, Wayne State University, Detroit, Michigan.

It is relatively recently that developmental researchers have explored systematically children's understanding of rules. The questions guiding this corpus of research are: What domains do children conceptualize as being rule-governed? What is their understanding of the origins, generality, and changeability of rules, and the consequences for violating particular rules? In this chapter, children's reasoning about social rules, both conventional and moral, is examined. I also discuss some of the possible relations between social rule understanding and the social context within which the child operates.

Background: Theory and Research

The larger conceptual framework out of which this research and discussion come is based on the view that there is adaptive significance for both the child and those around her/him to share an understanding of specific rules and the function of rules. For the child, the social world becomes a more predictable place, one in which more mutually satisfying interpersonal relations are possible as one shares an understanding of the rules. That is, one can more easily act or "operate in concert" (co-operate) with others. For the adult generation, there is adaptive significance in transmitting rules to maintain the social system.

How children acquire an understanding of rules and their function has been the subject of a good deal of theorizing and speculating. Two primary positions are evident, one which emphasizes the role of the social environment and one which emphasizes the role of the child's own conceptual resources. The first stems from the view of the child as acquiring social concepts, rules, and expectations from models and direct tutoring, and the contingent rewards and punishments for rule following and rule violating. In short, the child's social knowledge is basically a "copy" of the external social reality. The second view appears to be a particular version of Piagetian research in which social knowledge per se is focused on with, unfortunately, little appreciation for the social context in which it is embedded. That is, the child is sometimes portrayed as mentally constructing social reality in virtual social isolation. Such a "bootstrapping" portrayal is, of course, a distortion of Piaget's constructivist position, but an understandable distortion. Piaget's own research focused to such an extent on the processes and structures of the mind as they change in ontogenesis that little attention was given to the "aliments" upon which the mind works. His theoretical views, on the other hand, assume an interactionist position of organism and environment, of a constant assimilation and accommodation of each to one another. The environmental side of the interaction, despite its theoretical centrality, has been neglected in research. It has been left for others to specify how logic and social knowledge develop in the social context, and how they serve as tools for adaptation to that context.

Neither of these extreme positions is adopted here. Rather, the child is viewed as constructing a workable social theory (or belief system) that is constantly manifested in content and structure by the social environment. How does the child build such a belief system? Presumably she/he gathers and creates social information by a variety of methods, such actions as observing social behavior of others and self, imitating, communicating to others, being communicated to, abstracting regularities across time and situations, taking the role of the other, and experiencing affective relations with others. In short, the child both represents social realities and transforms them. And what are the social "aliments" that the child confronts and creates? I would propose that there are at least four major domains of social experience: (1) *the self and other persons* as organisms that have psychological events such as thoughts, feelings, intentions, preferences, reasoning, attitudes, and the like; (2) *social dyadic relations* such as relations of authority, friendship, conflict, etc.; (3) *social group relations* such as linear or configurational systems that relate several individuals to one another, encompassed by concepts of dominance, affiliation, leadership, and rules that are shared by members within the group; and (4) *larger social systems* (family, school, social institutions, nations, etc.). It is not assumed that these are exclusive categories, but rather that they are embedded categories such that individuals operate within dyadic relations which are at any one point in time part of group and larger relations. Whether these are psychologically different domains for the child is moot; but there is heuristic value for purposes of inquiry in demarcating domains of the social environment.

While the child constructs and reconstructs social beliefs, at the same time the social environment acts and reacts in ways that provide essential social information and structure as well. For example, in the diversity of people and behaviors to which the child is exposed, adults in all societies provide distinctions or classifications that are important to the society as a whole, such as "children," "adults," "male," "female," etc., each with their associated attributes, behaviors, expectations, and functions. Such messages may be communicated directly. Bearison and Cassel (1975), for example, found that when some parents deal with conflicts with their children, they appeal for compliance to their rule by focusing on the status of being a child ("All *children* should go to bed by nine o'clock."). Or such messages may be communicated less directly by adults' behavior. Fry and Willis (1971) reported, for example, that when children (who were confederates of the experimenter) stood unusually close to adults in a theater ticket line (i.e., they violated a culturally defined appropriate distance rule), the adults responded differently depending on the apparent age of the child: accepting and friendly toward a 5-year-old; ignoring or being tolerant of the 8-year-old; and reacting to a 10-year-old as they would to adults, moving away, leaning away or fidgeting. That is, the "passive" characteristic of the child, the apparent age, elicited different behavior from adults, which in turn gave different messages of expected behavior, however subtle, to the child.

The peer group also provides social structure. From preschool groups to older groups, children themselves generate an organization that is shared among its members: who likes who (affiliative networks); who can make who do what they want them to do (dominance or power hierarchies); who is good at doing things the group does (competence hierarchy) (Glidewell, Kantor, Smith, & Stringer, 1966). And the available evidence suggests that these social dimensions are, in most groups, quickly formed and quite stable over time. The child, then, both participates in the creation and maintenance of this social structure, and is the recipient of its advantages and disadvantages. Likewise, children provide discrimination of rules in social settings for one another. For example, Nucci and Turiel (1978) found that children seldom make an issue of violations of social conventions ("Sand is to stay in the sandbox.") but do make an issue over moral rule violations ("One should not hit other people."), particularly the victim of the violation.

In summary, then, the view held here is that the child gathers and creates social information and interrelates it to form an understanding of the social structure in which she/he operates. But at the same time, the social environment provides information about expected behavior, rules, and social relations in different situations. There is bidirectional influence in this process: the child on others and others on the child.

Rules shared by members of a group are one way the group manifests its structure. That is, it ceases to be a mere collection of individuals when the members agree, however tacitly, upon certain expectations for one another's relations and coordinated actions within a setting. The rules may not be apparent until there is a perturbation in the system of relations. The "perturbation" often used in research is a violation of a rule. Thus, the major research on children's understanding of rules (e.g., Damon, 1977; Kohlberg, 1969; Selman, 1976; Turiel, 1978a, 1978b) has used a conflict paradigm in which either a rule is broken (behavior is in conflict with expectation) or two rules are in conflict with one another (as in stories of social or moral dilemmas). For example, children are interviewed about their reasoning on a rule violation such as addressing teachers by their first name or stealing something of value to another. The focus of such research is not how serious the violation is ranked by children or the action they select to solve a dilemma, but the reasons underlying their rankings and solutions.

Several researchers have outlined the ontogenesis of social rule conceptions from late preschool ages through adolescence, the more recent of which are briefly summarized here. Turiel (1978a) has proposed that social-conventional rules form a conceptual domain that is distinct from moral principle rules, in contrast to the views held by Piaget (1932) and Kohlberg (1969). Social conventions are defined as rather arbitrary uniformities that function to coordinate the actions of individuals within a social system, such as mode of dress or greeting, the "content" of which can be changed to serve a particular function. Moral rules, on the other hand, are not arbitrary since they are derived from factors intrinsic to the actions (such as harming others or their rights). Thus, evaluation of conventional rules would be based on their social context, while moral acts would be evaluated in relation to their consequences for others. The distinction between social-conventional rules and moral rules has had some empirical support (e.g., Much & Shweder, 1978; Nucci & Turiel, 1978; Turiel, 1978b).

Turiel (1978b) has identified in clinical interviews with people 6 to 25 years of age seven sequential levels of social-conventional concepts, the levels alternating between affirmation and negation of particular concepts. The first identified level, occurring usually in 6- and 7-year-olds, is the concept of convention as a social uniformity, followed during the next 2 years by negation of that view; a new conception follows of conventions as part of a rule system around 10 to 11 years of age, followed by negation of that view, with four levels following through young adulthood (see Turiel, 1978b).

Damon (1977) has elucidated a somewhat different view of the ontogenesis of social rule reasoning. The levels Damon found were based on interviews with children, ages 4 to 9, in which they were probed for their views about violations of sex roles, table manners, and stealing. Rather than finding evidence of an affirmation–negation cycle such as proposed by Turiel, Damon proposed four qualitatively different levels, the ages cited as those from illustrative interview protocols:

- *Level 0* (4–4, 8): Personal desire is paramount in deciding whether to follow rules and justify noncompliance; reasoning is very specific to the act and situation. Others' possible reactions to violation are construed to match self's desires. No differentiation is made between conventional and moral principle-based rules.
- *Level 1* (4½–7, 4): Consequences are the critical basis for obeying rules, especially authority reactions but also peer group reactions. Some concrete forms of intrinsic rationales emerge. There is no differentiation between convention and principle rules.
- *Level 2* (6, 2–8, 10): Consequences are still the basis for obeying rules (both authorities' and peers' reactions). The major change is the view that convention violations are less serious than principle violations, although not consistently so.
- *Level 3* (8, 8–9½): The organizational function of rules is recognized. Violations of conventions are seen as clearly less serious than principle violations, but the "social impact" of convention violation is recognized.

Two aspects of this ontogenetic picture deserve attention. First, Damon suggests that Levels 0 and 1 are characterized by the child not making any clear distinction between social-conventional and moral rules (in contrast to Turiel's view [1978b] that such a distinction is made by 6 years of age). Such a distinction defines the difference between Levels 1 and 2. Second, rule following is based on different criteria at different levels: at Level 0 it is personal desire which justifies compliance or noncompliance, whereas beginning at Level 1 the determining factor is the consequences for obeying or disobeying rules. Social consequences, that is, the reactions of authorities and peers, are particularly emphasized.

The Study of Rules

These qualitatively different types of reasoning about social convention and moral principles afforded by Turiel's and Damon's work conclude with two somewhat different outlines of social-conceptual ontogenesis. The present investigation was undertaken to "sketch in" in greater detail the rule reasoning of one particular age group to determine: (1) whether children distinguish between conventions and moral principles, (2) the types of rule reasoning that occur, and (3) the extent to which reasoning varies as a function of the type of violation and age.

Forty-eight children were interviewed about rule reasoning and four other domains of social knowledge and reasoning[1] as part of a larger study on peer conflict behavior in natural settings and social-cognitive correlates (Shantz & Shantz, 1977). The children were drawn from eight first- and second-grade classrooms, and equally divided between the sexes. They attended a large regional elementary school near Rochester, Michigan. The school serves a broad socioeconomic range of families from poverty level to upper middle class. The children were randomly selected from over 140 whose parents gave permission for their being interviewed about their social understanding.

Each child was interviewed individually for approximately 40 minutes, and her/his responses were tape-recorded for later verbatim transcription. The child was told five stories of violations, of which two were social-conventional rule violations and three were moral-principle violations. Each violation was ranked by the child as to its seriousness, and then the child told why she/he gave that rank.

The rule violation interview was introduced by acquainting children first with the ranking material: Five faces were presented, ranging from a broad-smiling face on the left ("very good") to a neutral face in the middle ("O.K."), to a severe, frowning face on the right ("very bad"). The children were asked to nominate some food they loved to eat and show how they felt when they ate it, and to name some food they disliked a lot and point to the face that showed how they felt when they ate it. Children quickly understood the continuum, essentially from "rah rah ice cream" to "icky pooh stew"!

---

1. Besides the interview about rules reported here, children were interviewed about their understanding of individuals (role-taking ability and free descriptions of known peers) and their understanding of interpersonal relations (concepts of friendship and strategies for resolving peer conflicts). Random orders of administration of domains were used.

Then the five rule-violation stories and questions were presented in random order:

1. Social-conventional violations
   a. Dave doesn't like to comb his hair. He gets up in the morning, washes his face, gets all dressed, but he doesn't comb his hair. He goes around like that all day—to school, to play, everywhere.

      QUESTION: What do you think of that—of Dave not combing his hair? Point to the face that shows what you think of that.

      QUESTION: Why do you think it is (*child's rank*—very good, good, O.K., bad, very bad)? [Probed further for clarity and encouraged to give as many reasons as possible.]
   b. This boy named George likes to play with dolls, especially a Barbie doll. He has other toys—a ball, puzzles, trucks, model airplane—but *he* plays with *dolls* mostly.

      QUESTION: What do you think of that—of the boy playing mostly with dolls? [Questions continue as in 1. a.]
2. Moral-principle violations
   a. One day Mike and another boy were playing at recess time. Mike didn't like the other boy and Mike went over and hit him real hard—on purpose—to hurt him.

      QUESTION: What do you think of that—of Mike hitting the other boy to hurt him? Why?
   b. Mary eats lunch at school, and one day when she looked in her lunch box, she saw that she didn't have any candy in her box. But at lunch time she saw that the girl next to her had candy. So, when that girl wasn't looking, Mary took her candy and ate it quick. [Questions as in 1. a.]
   c. Betty was making a picture book for her school project one day. She was pasting in the pictures to finish the book up. Another girl wanted to use the paste too, to finish *her* book. She asked Betty if she could use the paste some too. Betty said, "No, you can't use it too." [Questions as in 1. a.]

After each story, then, the child indicated what she/he thought of the event by pointing to a face on the scale (from 1, very good, to 5, very bad), and each child justified her/his rankings. In the following section, the rankings, the rationales, and the relation between rankings and rationales are presented.

Ranked Evaluations of Violations

Two types of data are presented here: mean ranks and consistency of ranks. The mean ranks for different rule violations (Table 5-1, bottom row) indicate that sex role violation was ranked, on the average, just below "O.K.," the midpoint; this was followed by the more serious violation of not combing one's hair, which in turn was followed in increasing "badness" by not sharing, stealing, and unprovoked aggression. A three-way analysis of variance (Age $\times$ Sex $\times$ Stories) revealed a significant main effect for Stories, F (4, 176) = 21.25, $p < .01$, and no significant interactions. Rankings did not differ significantly for 6- and 7-year-olds, nor by sex of child. Newman–Keuls tests of the significant main effect of Stories revealed the following: All moral-principle violation stories were ranked significantly worse ($p < .01$) than both convention violations; moral-principle violations were not ranked significantly differently ($p > .05$) from one another; and, within social-conventional rules, not combing one's hair was ranked significantly worse ($p < .01$) than sex role violation.

TABLE 5-1. *Frequencies of Different Rule Rationales by Story*

Category number	Category name	Convention stories		Moral-principle stories			Total
		Sex role	Hair	Hit	Steal	Not share	
1	Nominal–evaluative	0	7	2	10	8	27
3	Legalistic	0	0	6	7	4	17
5	Authority reactions	0	4	17	13	4	38
2	Individual's preference	29	8	3	6	9	55
4	Peer reactions	5	15	0	1	9	30
8	Victim's emotional reaction	0	0	7	13	3	23
6	Negative physical consequences to "self"	2	17	0	6	2	27
9	Social standards	27	3	6	0	1	37
7	Negative physical consequences to victim	0	0	21	8	16	45
10	Intrinsic social principle	1	0	0	2	5	8
	Total frequencies	64	54	62	66	61	307
	Mean rank evaluation	3.33	4.04	4.85	4.63	4.42	

These findings on *mean ranks* seem to support the view that children make a distinction between social conventions and moral principles, as proposed by Turiel (1978a). In addition, despite the differences in mean ranks for moral violations (Table 5-1), these differences were not significant. This indicates that there are factors which, in the minds of children, make not sharing, hitting, and stealing "equally" reprehensible. Turiel (1978b) has suggested that these factors are intrinsic consequences of the acts themselves (violating property rights, safety of others, etc.). In summary, the rankings indicate a significant difference *between* domains (social conventional vs. moral) but not *within* the moral domain.

There was a significant difference, however, within the social-conventional domain: Not combing one's hair is worse than sex role violation. It may well be that the conventional domain is less homogeneous than the moral domain in that some convention violations have less serious consequences than others, such as disturbing others' sensibilities (looking messy, eating noisily) or disturbing the social order.

The emphasis during the last decade within the culture of the arbitrary nature of sex roles may well have had an influence on that particular convention violation. Children were not, however, *very* liberated in this regard: Twenty-one ranked George's preference for doll play as bad or very bad, six as very good or good, and the rest at the midpoint, "O.K." This tolerance-to-approval rating by a little over half the sample is in some contrast to Damon's findings (1977) on sex role violation. Children from 4 to 9 years of age were questioned by Damon about occupational restrictions ("Can a boy become a nurse?" "Can a girl become a truck driver?"), and the most sex-stereotyped responses occurred in the age group of 6 to 7. More "liberated" views were held both by younger children (ages 4 to 6) and by older children (ages 8 to 9). Damon interpreted these similar degrees of approval by the youngest and oldest children as based on the Level 0 tendency to ignore social convention ("one does as one pleases") and Level 3 children's respect for the law of equal treatment of the sexes. Level 1, typical of reasoning at ages 5 to 7, is based on blind allegiance to social uniformities and, as such, would be consistent with high sex role stereotyping. The data here would indicate less "blindness" for this age group, a majority indicating tolerance to high approval. It may be that the *kind* of behavioral uniformity related to gender is important: When it comes to children's own behavior being restricted to a type of play material, they show a more liberated attitude than toward a future adult behavior of occupations!

It is noteworthy that the rank ordering of the seriousness of violations that children gave matches the rank ordering of a group of 15 undergraduates, although the latter viewed convention violations as less serious than did the children. To the extent that this small sample of young adults represents the cultural views as a whole, it is clear that young children already hold views similar to the larger cultural view on the relative seriousness of rule violations, and on the cultural distinction between conventions and moral principles.

There is a final and important finding related to the ranking of violations. Each child's rankings were examined to determine whether both conventional violations were ranked relatively less serious (one rank or greater) than the three moral violations. The majority ($n = 30$) did not consistently rank convention violations lower than moral violations; only 18 did so. Apparently the difference in *mean* ranks between conventions and principles described earlier is due largely to the more extreme positive rankings by 6 of the 18 children. Such data draw attention to the hazard of characterizing individual children of a particular age group from the *means* of the group. Thus, the consistency data of individual children clearly support the view that conventional–moral distinction is not typical for children in the age span of 6 to 7.[2]

Rule Rationales

What are the reasons children offer for justifying their evaluations? These reasons are partial representations of children's understanding of the rationales underlying social rules. The open-ended interview elicited a variety of rationales, and the classification of them required some theoretical assumptions, as does any coding scheme. One option was to adopt a developmental-structuralist position and code responses

2. In response to a preprint of this chapter, Turiel (1979) reexamined the ratings of importance of rules reported in the study by Turiel (1978b) and found that there was consistency in individual ratings, with the majority of children making the distinction between conventions and moral rules. Thus, the issue remains unclear. The differences between the data reported here and those reported by Damon (1977) and by Turiel (1978b) may be due in part to what, specifically, children were asked to do (rank the seriousness of rule violations vs. rank the importance of rules) and what kinds of conventions and moral rules were sampled in each of the studies.

according to the levels described in previous studies. However, it seemed advisable to use a more molecular coding system to determine the extent to which particular responses co-occurred, forming the patterns (levels) found in previous research.

The categories of rationales developed for this study were, essentially, based on an "event structure" scheme that minimized inferences about the child's global understanding of rules. "Event structure" refers to the analysis of aspects of the stories upon which the child focuses or about which inferences are made. Such an approach is exemplified by the use of story grammars (e.g., Stein & Glenn, 1979) in which stories are divided into settings, initiating events, internal responses of the protagonist, goal-directed actions, and consequences and reactions (of the protagonist and others). Whereas such story-grammar-based research has provided systematic variations of stories to describe memory, comprehension, and causal reasoning of children, the taxonomy was used here to loosely structure the initial coding scheme. It conforms, in some respects, to the content categories used by Damon (1977), Sigel (1977), and others. The major dimensions of the rationales were: (1) *emotional factors* (as preexisting states or as consequences) of the protagonist (self), the victim, peers, or authorities; (2) *physical consequences* to the self, victim, or others; (3) the *rule* and/ or *standard* involved, whether these were more concrete references to rules and procedures or more abstract principles; and (4) *no rationale*.

The exact ways in which these various dimensions were combined into the categories used by children are given in Table 5-2. The first category, nominal–evaluative, is made up of statements that give no rationale for the ranking; each is merely a statement that a rule has been violated and/or a restatement of the evaluation the child just gave. Category 2 is based on the notion that the protagonist is justified or not justified in her/his behavior by whether it satisfied the wishes or preferences of the protagonist (individual preference) or was justified by saying "I do that" (idiosyncratic). According to Damon (1977), this is typical reasoning for a child at Level 0. Category 3 includes statements referring to the legality or illegality of the behavior, or in a few cases, an implied contractual procedure being broken. The following three categories concerned rationales that focused on the consequences to the rule violator: social approval or disapproval of peers (Category 4) or of authorities (Category 5), and physical consequences to the rule violator (Category 6). The next two categories were statements focusing on the other person (the "victim"), her/his physical well-being (Category 7) and emotional well-being (Category 8). Statements which were

TABLE 5-2. *Definitions of Rule Rationale Categories*

Category number	Category name	Definition
1	Nominal–evaluative	Statement of rule being violated ("He should/shouldn't do that"; "She's supposed to share"; etc.) or evaluation of behavior ("That's not good/bad/nice/ugly"; etc.).
2	Individual's preferences	The actor("self")-satisfying wish; preference, likes, or dislikes of self; or idiosyncratic, as in "I do that."
3	Legalistic	Reference to the legality or illegality of behavior or breaking rule; procedural violations ("If she asks, you got to share.").
4	Peer reactions	Approval or disapproval of peers; to avoid ridicule, rejection by peers.
5	Authority reactions	Approval or disapproval of authority figures (parents, teachers, principal), either explicit or implied ("Get into trouble"; "Go to jail.").
6	Negative physical effects to self	Negative physical consequences such as uncombed hair getting ratty, dirty; getting germs from stolen candy; etc.
7	Negative physical consequences to victim	Physical or material "well-being" of victim in story such as being physically hurt, being deprived of needed objects (food, goods), or detrimental outcome (can't finish school project).
8	Victim's emotional reaction	Victim in story will have negative or positive emotional reaction (feelings hurt; won't like it; will feel bad, mean, happy, glad; etc.).
9	Social standards	Normative statement of group consensus or standard such as personal appearance standard; sex role stereotype or androgynous standard; insufficient justification for aggression; etc.
10	Intrinsic social principle	Statement of violation of property rights, personal safety, fairness principle.

more abstract than Category 1 and referred, implicitly or explicitly, to group consensus or standards were classified in Category 9. Finally, statements of abstract principles of fairness, personal safety, and the like were classified in Category 10. The interrater reliabilities on a third of the interviews for each category, assessed by total agreements divided by total statements scored, ranged between 77% and 100%, with a mean of 92%. Interrater reliabilities for each story ranged between 92% and 98%, with an average of 94%.

After all statements were categorized, three criteria were adopted for subsequent analyses: (1) Nominal–evaluative statements were not counted if they were the first statement followed by other codable statements. It appeared that some children in assimilating the story contented themselves first with merely stating the rule violated or affirming their evaluation (both Category 1), and then went on to give rationales. To count such initial statements seemed to distort the frequency data. Nominal–evaluative (Category 1) statements were counted, then, only if they were the *only* response the child gave. (2) Only one response within each category was counted since our interest was in the diversity of rationales the child could generate, and repetitions within categories would inflate the data. (3) The first three *different* rationales only were counted to standardize scoring, but since children seldom had more than three rationales for any one story, this criterion did not seem to distort their responses.

The frequency of different rule categories for the total sample across different stories is given in Table 5-1. The most frequent justification for rankings is based on the wishes and preferences of the protagonist (Category 2); and next, on the effects of the violation on the physical state of the other child in the story (Category 7). Somewhat less frequent rationales concerned the reactions of authorities (Category 5) and statements of group standards (Category 9). This indicates that children in this age range frequently use a wide variety of factors, ranging from the focus on the protagonist and victim in the stories to factors beyond the stories—authorities' reactions and group standards. Those categories which most closely match those cited by Damon in his analysis of levels of reasoning (Categories 2, 4, 5, and 10) are evident in this age group, including the low frequency of intrinsic rationales (Category 10). However, the fact that ten different categories were required to code responses indicates a wider diversity of reasoning than has been demonstrated previously. Part of this diversity is related to the diversity of stories used, as indicated in Table 5-1, and that point is discussed more fully later.

One of the major interests of this study was to clarify possible co-occurrences of different types of rationales. For example, is a child who justifies the badness of an act by the negative reactions of authorities likely to also use the negative reactions of peers? To determine this, the data were scored for co-occurrences for each child across the five stories, and a cluster analysis was performed to determine co-occurrences beyond a chance level of co-occurrence. Johnson's hierarchical method (1967) was used to describe the "natural clustering" of those nominal data. Category 1 was excluded from the cluster analysis since these rationales occurred so frequently with all other rationales as to be nondiscriminating.

The results of the cluster analysis are presented in Table 5-3. Beginning at the top of the table, the first cluster is made up of Categories 7 and 10. That is, there is a high probability, well beyond chance level, that if Category 10 is used in reasoning about any of the stories, Category 7 is also. These rationales focus on the *intrinsic effects* of violation—the concrete physical effects on the victim and the more abstract violation of a principle. In Category 7, for example, the statements are that one should not steal or refuse to share because the other person in the story (the victim) has need for food (candy) and goods (paste), and one doesn't hit because one might actually hurt the other person, such as break her/his bones, etc. These appear to be concrete statements underlying abstract rationales of personal safety, fairness, and property rights. It is the "intrinsic factor" Damon observed also in which concrete forms in the early levels (1 and 2) are found later, in Level 3, as abstract statements or principles recognized in the larger society.

It is worth noting at this point that focusing on the other person's physical well-being (Category 7) does not co-occur with reasons about the other person's emotional well-being (Category 8). Instead, the latter co-occurs with Categories 2 and 4: These are rationales in which the focus is on the protagonist's wishes, likes, and dislikes for justifying the breaking of rules (Category 2), the peer group's affective reaction to rule breaking (Category 4), and the victim's affective state (Category 8). In short, this cluster of Categories 2, 4, and 8 suggests that some children are particularly attuned to the *emotional factors* as rationales, be they the emotions of the protagonist, victim, or peer group.

This is an interesting cluster in that Category 2 rationales have been cited previously (Damon, 1977) as the most immature reasoning, and yet they co-occur with rationales used at more mature levels (Categories 4 and 8). Are we dealing, then, with developmental differences or individual differences, that is, conventional versus moral reasoning? As

TABLE 5-3. *Cluster Analysis of Responses to All Stories*

Level	Category clusters	γ
1	7, 10	1.00
2	(2, 8) (7, 10)	1.00
3	(2, 8, 4) (7, 10)	1.00
4	(6, 9) (7, 10) (2, 4, 8)	.95
5	(3, 5) (6, 9) (7, 10) (2, 4, 8)	.88
6	(3, 5) (6, 9, 10, 7) (2, 4, 8)	.70

indicated in Table 5-1 where children are summed across, the most frequent use of Category 2 is to justify rankings of George's playing with dolls, and the most frequent use of Category 4 is to justify rankings of messy hair, both conventions; and Category 8 consists of statements about the sadness or madness of the victim in having her candy taken (moral violation). Further, of the 31 children who used self's wishes to justify their ranking on one or both of the conventions, only 9 also used self's wishes to justify rankings on any of the three moral-violation stories. The frequent use of self's wishes for conventional violations may be the way in which children of this age indicate their understanding of the arbitrary nature of conventions; that is, "one does as one pleases" when confronted with arbitrary rules, either following or not following. At the same time, what George plays with has consequences mainly for George and not the social order or others' basic sensibilities. Thus, the particular type of convention violation may also "pull" for Category 2 reasoning. Clearly, it was very infrequent for children to use self's wishes to justify rankings on moral violations (e.g., "people like to share so it's bad not to share the paste").

Since age varied so little in this group, it is impossible to determine the extent to which reasoning based on self's wishes is a *developmentally immature* form of reasoning. Clearly it is related to *story differences*, and it may well represent individual differences among children as well—to focus on emotional factors rather than other factors in stories. It will be necessary to interview other age groups to assess the relative impact of age, types of stories, and factors within stories to answer the question posed.

Finally, this *emotional factors* cluster might be interpreted by some as representing children who are vigilant to or likely to infer others' emotional reactions (victim's and peers'), that is, who are empathetic. The problem is that "empathy" means different things to different people (Shantz, 1975). For some, vigilance to others' emotions is an expression of concern or compassion for others' negative emotions and of pleasure in others' positive emotions. Although this may be the case sometimes (one cannot tell in this type of category system), it may be that some children are expressing an understanding of the emotional state as a predictor of future behavior. This was most clearly illustrated by one child who said about the hitting story: "He'll [the victim] feel bad. He'll feel mean. He'll *get* mean!" Thus, the recognition of the likely emotional state of the victim may be an expression of concern, or it may be merely a statement of fact used in the "what happens next?" sense as a predictor of retaliation by the victim.

Another major cluster that occurred, Categories 6 and 9, is not immediately interpretable. Category 9 is essentially a rather abstract statement of group standards, norms, or expectations, while Category 6 captures negative physical consequences to the protagonist. This co-occurrence may reflect the high frequency of using these rationales when reasoning about conventions, the common pattern being to cite for the sex role violation the stereotype standard ("Boys aren't supposed to play with dolls.") or the androgynous standard ("Dolls are for everybody."), and to invoke physical effects for not combing one's hair ("It will get lumpy . . . knots . . . lice . . . bugs, etc."; and "It will hurt when you *do* comb it.").

Finally, the cluster of Categories 3 and 5 appears to reflect that some children are particularly attuned to authorities' reactions to rule violations, and tend to conceive of rules in legal and illegal terms.

In summary, the within-child co-occurrence of rationales suggests some basic general categories (clusters) of intrinsic effects, emotional effects, authority reactions, and group standards–physical effects. These four clusters were retained for the remaining analyses, and the nominal–evaluative category (1) was added.

Rationale Use for Different Stories

Given these clusterings, the next question is whether they occurred about equally for each type of rule violation. Cochran Q tests were run on each type of cluster. For example, of the 32 children in the sample who used the authority–legalistic rationales (either Category 3 or 5 or both) for any of the five stories, did the frequency of use vary with the violation? Yes, the type of reasoning varied significantly ($p < .01$) with the type of story. In addition, it appears that the major difference is that the type of reasoning about conventions differs from reasoning about principle violations, as alluded to in the prior discussion. Rationales about convention violations involved almost entirely emotional reactions (Categories 2, 4, and 8) and standards–physical effects (Categories 6 and 9), and there was no significant difference ($p < .05$) between the two convention stories for these two clusters. This indicates some homogeneity of reasoning about convention breaking. On the other hand, reasoning about principle violations was not quite so uniform.

Emotional reactions and intrinsic rationales differed significantly ($p < .05$), depending on the story being about sharing, stealing, or hitting; but authority reactions reasoning did not differ in frequency among the stories. The pattern of these data supports Turiel's thesis (1978b) that children's reasoning about violations differs depending on the type of violation involved.

Relation between Ranks and Rationales

The remaining analyses used only children's reasoning about moral-principle violations: hitting, stealing, and not sharing. Each child was given a modal designation of the most frequently occurring rationale on these three stories. Table 5-4 indicates how the sample of 48 children was distributed among the major rationale clusters and how those related to the rankings of badness of breaking conventions versus principles.

Three clusters of reasoning account for the majority of children: emotional reactions ($n = 14$), intrinsic rationales ($n = 13$), and authority reactions ($n = 11$). Their use occurred about as frequently in 6-year-olds as 7-year-olds. Children who could only offer nominal-evaluative statements were quite rare—only 5 children of the 48, but all were first graders.

The rankings of the seriousness of the violations indicate that 30 of the 48 children did not consistently judge both convention violations as less serious than principle violations, as noted previously. Those children seem to view a rule as a rule, and not combing your hair, for example, is as bad as hitting someone with no provocation. Children who modally reasoned on the basis of authority reactions or emotional reactions showed a disproportionate tendency to view all rule breaking as equally bad (binomial tests, $p = .11$ and .09, respectively), and particularly so children who gave nominal–evaluative statements ($p = .03$). They knew rule breaking was bad, but they didn't know (say) why. The only opposing pattern was children who invoked the intrinsic rationales on most stories: There was a tendency (though not statistically significant, $p = .13$) to view convention violations as less serious than moral-principle violations.

In my view, these data suggest only three levels of rule reasoning in this age group. At the lowest level are those children ($n = 5$) who modally fail to have any rationale at all for their rankings but merely reaffirm the badness of breaking rules (nominal–evaluative, Category 1),

TABLE 5-4. *Distribution of Subjects by Modal Rationale and Rankings of Violations*

Modal category on moral stories	n	Number of children		Rankings on conventions and principle stories		Binomial test on ranks
		6-year-olds	7-year-olds	No difference	Conventions less	
Authority/legalistic (Cluster 3, 5)	11	6	5	8	3	$p = .11$
Emotional reactions (Cluster 2, 4, 8)	14	6	8	10	4	$p = .09$
Intrinsic rationales (Cluster 7, 10)	13	5	8	4	9	$p = .13$
Standards/physical effects to "self" (Cluster 6, 9)	5	2	3	3	2	$p = .50$
Nominal-evaluative (Category 1)	5	5	0	5	0	$p = .03$
Totals	48			30	18	

and who, in addition, make no consistent distinction between convention and principle violations. At the other extreme are children
who often invoke the intrinsic physical effects and principle violations,
and consistently distinguish between the two types of violations ($n = 9$).
The majority of the age group fall in between, tending not to distinguish between conventions and principles but using a wide variety
of rationales for their rankings.

This picture bears some similarity to Damon's levels of rule reasoning, but the clustering of categories makes a direct comparison
difficult. To compare more precisely, the data were reanalyzed according to the major criteria cited by Damon (1977). Level 0 children
make no distinction in their rankings as to the seriousness of convention versus principle violations, and use the self's own wishes
(Category 2) as the primary rationale for explaining their rankings on
one or more moral stories. A total of 12 children in this sample met
these two criteria for Level 0 assignment; half were 6-year-olds, and
half were 7-year-olds. Level 1 was defined as children who also failed to
make the convention–principle distinction and, in addition, used any
other rationales than self's wishes (Category 2) or intrinsic principles
(Category 10). A total of 17 children in this sample met these two
criteria, 11 being first graders and six second graders. The next pattern,
Level 2, was defined as children who consistently ranked conventions
less serious and used any rationales other than Categories 2 or 10.
There were 14 children who had such a pattern, six being first graders,
and eight second graders. Finally, two children met the criteria for
Level 3 in that they used intrinsic rationales (Category 10) on two of the
three moral stories and consistently viewed convention violations as
less serious; they represented each grade.

Thus, 45 of the 48 children met the specific combinations or
criteria Damon suggests to define the levels. Three children showed an
aberrant pattern: consistent ranking of convention violations as less
serious combined with rationales based on self's desires.

On the one hand, the ability of Damon's system to account for 45
of the 48 children's rankings and rationales is quite remarkable given
the differences in stories and methods of scoring. On the other hand,
there are several differences that should be noted: the types of rationales,
the age distribution, and the story effects. First, Levels 1 and 2 could
not be distinguished by the types of rationales used, as is also true in
Damon's descriptions. He posits that both levels emphasize peer and
authority reactions to violations. Children here demonstrated a much
wider variety of rationales and particularly tended to focus on the

emotional and physical effects of the victim more than the reactions of peers and authorities.

Second, and perhaps more important, is the fact that in this narrow age range from 6 to 7, children were distributed among all developmental levels (Levels 0 to 3, $n = 12, 17, 14$, and 2, respectively), and a sizable proportion of them were at the lowest level, which is supposed to be characteristic of reasoning of 4- to 4½-year-olds. In addition, each level was almost equally represented by the two age groups; that is, there was no apparent age trend from lower to higher levels. Thus, the question arises: Do the different patterns represent developmental differences or individual differences in social reasoning? It would be expected that developmental differences would show one of three criteria: some relationship (however modest) to differences in chronological age, some developmental characteristics in the pattern of behavior (such as different degrees of differentiation or concreteness to abstractness), and/or characteristics in which, logically, one pattern would have to precede another. Clearly, this modest cross-sectional study of a narrow age range cannot provide definitive answers. The kinds of studies that are needed would be to follow these children longitudinally to determine whether they continue to reason basically in the same fashion or change systematically, or, alternatively and less preferably, to sample cross-sectionally other age groups to determine whether the same differences occur at each age.

Restricted to these data, however, it could be that despite the narrow age range, these children do evidence developmental social reasoning typical of children ages 4 to 9. That is, it could be argued that there are developmental differences here masquerading as individual differences, such that what is captured here is a cross-sectional "still picture" of different *rates* of development. My earlier proposal that the data suggest three basic levels of reasoning is based, in part, on this argument, as well as on increasing differentiation (between convention and moral principles) and an increasing focus on underlying abstract principles rather than immediate, concrete behavioral consequences of violations. The small variability in age, then, may mask whatever slight relationship there is between different patterns of ranking and reasoning.

Finally, the different patterns of ranked "badness" of violations and reasoning are associated most consistently with the different content of the stories, that is, whether they dealt with violations of social conventions or moral principles. Turiel (1978b) claims that this basic distinction is not age-related since the majority of preschoolers and kindergartners, behaviorally or in interviews, make the distinction (Turiel, 1979). On the other hand, Damon (1977), in comparing stealing to eating with one's fingers, found that only 37% of 4- and 5-year-olds thought stealing was worse. At age 6, however, there was a significant increase to 60% citing stealing as worse. Such relative data suggest that the distinction *is* age-related. The issue becomes more complicated by the data of this study: Mean ranks suggested that these 6- and 7-year-olds as a group were making the distinction between conventions and moral rules. But the mean ranks were not descriptive of the majority of children since a few children's extreme ratings weighted the means. In fact, the analysis of each individual's rankings indicated that only 38% were consistently ranking convention violations as less serious than moral ones. Perhaps the low figure, compared to Damon's, reflects the number of different rule violations sampled.

At this juncture, it is not possible to reconcile the various data on the issues: Is the distinction between conventions and moral principles an age-related phenomenon? If so, when in ontogenesis do the majority of children make such a distinction? This formulation of the issues may be too broad, however, since it is possible that some types of conventions are differentiated from moral principles earlier in ontogenesis than are others. Suffice it to say that future research could profitably be directed at a broad sampling of rules as well as age groups. Likewise, there are two hazards that bear mention regarding the use of group means or modal group reasoning to characterize particular age groups: The group performance may not describe even a majority of the children, and the attribution of modal reasoning patterns runs the risk of masking important individual differences. And it is the individual and the individual's ontogenetic changes, after all, that we are trying to understand.

The Social Context

This study has been an examination of only one side, the child's, of what is fundamentally a two-sided interchange. What of the environmental side? How does it provide social rule information?—not just what rules apply in particular settings at particular times but the larger society's ways of providing rule information and the rationales behind rules.

As suggested in the introduction to this chapter, very little research or theory has been devoted to the way in which social organization is manifested to the child. Although the child lives from birth in a world of social rules, these probably are seldom evident until the child or another person violates them. For the child, then, the "perturbation" in the social system makes the rules more apparent, as it does for the scientist as well. For the purposes of the remaining discussion, then, the events of rule violations are the focus of my speculations concerning the "social embeddedness" of rule understanding of children.

It seems likely that there is a complex of factors that draw the child's attention, provide discriminations of rules, and give meaning to the rule: *who* responds to a rule violation, *what* an adult or peer might say or do in response to a rule violation; and *how severe* the consequences are. In the first case, "who responds," there is some very recent evidence that violations of social conventions are responded to by adults much more frequently than children, while violations of moral principles are responded to equally by children and adults. Nucci and Turiel (1978) observed in ten preschools the transgressions responded to by either children or adults, and interviewed children who observed (as bystander or participant) about 30% of such transgressions. Social-conventional violations included such events as doing things different from the group while in group activities, standing while snacking rather than sitting, and violations of other such "school rules." Moral violations included taking another's belongings, failing to share, intentional hitting, and the like. Of 246 transgressions, 54% were social convention and 46% were moral. Of the convention violations, 92% were responded to solely by adults, 5% by adults and children, and the remaining by children only. For moral violations, 46% of the time only children responded, for 38% only adults responded, and for 16% both reacted.

However, a somewhat different picture is afforded by Much and Shweder's study (1978) of "breaches of rules" which were accompanied by an accusation or an account. A total of 628 such breaches occurred in 60 hours of observation over several weeks in a nursery school and a kindergarten class. The types of breaches which adults and/or children responded to differed, but not in the exact way Nucci and Turiel (1978) found. First, Turiel's (1978a) social-conventional rule category was subdivided into two types: regulations (which derive from authorities and are specific to a setting, such as "school rules") and conventions (derived from group consensus and not setting-specific, such as returning a greeting, shaking with the right hand, etc.). Such regulations, conventions, and the third category (moral violations) accounted for 90–95% of all breaches in both nursery school and kindergarten. It was found that adults respond more often to regulation violations than do children, but adults and children respond equally often to convention violations (cultural expectations). Thus, it is "school rule" violations that seem to largely account for adults' more frequent responsiveness in Nucci and Turiel's findings on "social conventions," rather than violations of conventions of a general cultural type. Of all moral breaches, Much and Shweder (1978) found that 75% were responded to by children, and 25% on the average were responded to by adults in both nursery school and kindergarten. Much and Shweder noted that since children, rather than adults, are the much more likely victims of moral transgressions, and it is the victim who often responds, it is more likely that children than adults respond to moral violations. In addition, they added, children are apt to judge more events to be moral breaches than do teachers. In short, it is not likely that teachers are less concerned about moral breaches than children, it is merely less likely that teachers are the victims and/or less likely that they view as many events as moral transgressions. What is particularly important to note, by way of summary, is that both of these studies indicate that domains of rule violations are differentiated by different patterns of who responds to the violations. The types of domains behaviorally differentiated match quite well the types of domains differentiated in children's representations and rankings at least by middle childhood.

There is also evidence that "what is said" in response to different types of rule violations also varies. Nucci and Turiel (1978) found that in response to moral violations, the primary responses of adults were to provide a rationale and comment on the feelings of others involved. In contrast, children responded to moral violations with commands, and they cited the consequences of the acts, specifically, the emotional reactions and physical consequences (injury or loss). In the latter case, it is often the victim talking! In this regard, Piaget (1967) speculated on the origin of the concept of justice:

> Where does this feeling of justice come from? Awareness of what is just and unjust ordinarily appears as a *reaction* [emphasis added] to the adult rather than an acquisition from him. Through some unintentional or imaginary injustice of which the child is a victim, he starts to dissociate justice and submission. (p. 57)

The speculation, it appears, can be expanded upon: It is also a reaction to intentional injustice at the hands of peers as well as adults. Finally, Nucci and Turiel (1978) found that social-convention violations elicited a different pattern of responses in which adults gave commands, statements of the rule, and (to a lesser extent) statements about sanctions and disorder.

Much and Shweder (1978) found differences in the accounts kindergarten children themselves gave to different types of violations (or breaches of rules) as they occurred in the classroom. Although no statistical data are given, it was found that violations of regulations and conventions seemed to elicit "a legalistic orientation rich in references to conditions, consequences, and rule formulations," whereas moral violations were responded to by descriptions of what was done so as to turn the act into a nonmoral issue. For example, one child accused another of stealing her chair, to which the accused responded that it was empty, she didn't steal it, she "sat in it." The authors suggest that the force of moral rules makes violations of them nonnegotiable, so one attempts to reinterpret the act.

Finally, a third set of data suggest that what is said differs depending on whether the violation is a conventional or moral one. Steinlauf (1975) interviewed the mothers of kindergarteners about their likely response to common conflicts with their children, known in the larger literature on moral development as "disciplinary strategies" (Hoffman, 1970; Hoffman & Saltzstein, 1967). Ten stories were given in which the mother was to imagine her own child violating the expectation or rule (e.g., failure day after day to put toys away after playing, striking another child, stealing, teasing a child, etc.). The open-ended responses were classified according to Hoffman's "parental discipline strategy" system (1970): (1) power assertion, in which the parent punishes physically or threatens to, and capitalizes on her/his power and authority over the child; (2) love withdrawal, a type of psychological punishment by expressing anger, disapproval, and rejection of the child; and (3) induction, a discipline appealing to reason by giving the child information about the reactions and consequences of the violation for the child and others. Steinlauf found, first, that the use of each of the three types of strategies varied significantly with the type of parent–child conflict involved. Since the interest was in rational versus punishment strategies of mothers, the following analyses were made comparing induction to the other two combined (power assertion and/or love withdrawal). Violations of adults' rules in the home elicited in a high percentage of mothers' power assertion and love withdrawal responses; and very seldom, inductive responses. Typical violations were refusal to go to bed at bedtime, failure to put toys away, being silly and impolite in front of a guest in the home: These fit Turiel's definition of social conventions in that they deal with the social order in a particular setting and do not involve aspects of justice intrinsic to the violation act itself. On the other hand, peer conflicts and violations outside the home elicited from a high percentage of mothers inductive responses and very few power assertive or love withdrawal statements. Conflicts of these kinds involved teasing a child, stealing, and causing a disturbance in school. The first two cases are moral-principle violations, but the latter is not clearly so. Some mothers, however, treated the "social order of the school" as a moral issue of being "fair" to the rest of the children in the class so they could hear the teacher and learn. Interestingly, two items elicited in a high percentage of mothers all three types of strategies: hitting another child and destroying another child's property. A recent study by Grusec and Kuczynski (1980) on mothers' reported discipline strategies in response to rule violations of their children, ages 4 to 8, largely confirm the results of the study by Steinlauf (1975). In summary, Steinlauf's findings indicate, in general, that the convention violations tend to elicit punishment-oriented responses, and that moral violations tend to elicit inductive responses. This is consistent with Nucci and Turiel's (1978) findings that adults tended to respond in nursery schools to convention violations with commands, statements about rules and disorder, and sanctions. Likewise, when teachers responded to moral violations, they tended to provide a rationale for the moral rule and to comment on the feelings of others involved (inductive responses). At the same time, Steinlauf's data give hints that both the type of rule and the setting (home vs. outside the home) may be important in the way mothers respond. Turiel (1978b) has found significant differences in ratings of importance of conventional versus moral rules *within* settings (home or school settings), but no analysis was made of differences *between* settings. It would be expected that settings as a factor would have less impact on moral violation responses and ratings than on convention violation responses and ratings.

Finally, the distinction between conventional and moral acts, Damon (1977) suggests, may be exemplified in the social world of the child by the fact that violations of conventional acts are more often ignored than moral violations, or, if responded to, the consequences are less severe. The prior observational studies in nursery schools and a kindergarten (Much & Shweder, 1978; Nucci & Turiel, 1978) do not give any information concerning the "ignoring" measure since only those violations responded to were analyzed. Likewise, the severity of consequences has not been examined in any study to date.

In sum, these recent studies indicate that the social environment does show differential responses to convention violations (specifically, regulation) and moral violations, both in terms of *who* tends to respond (adults or children) and *what* is said. In the latter case, there are three different category systems used, so it is difficult to draw definite conclusions. The single most evident finding is for adults (teachers or parents) to respond to moral violations with rationales and statements about the consequences for the other, particularly the emotional consequences. Children, too, tended to respond by pointing out the consequences of the acts (injury, loss, emotional reactions), often as victims of the moral violation; but, in contrast to adults, they more often gave commands and responded physically, not surprisingly. These studies provide, then, some indication of a "match" between the child's representation and reasoning about rule violations and the kind of discriminations and rationales provided in the social environment—in this case, by who responds to violations predominantly and what they say. This is not an argument for viewing the child as passively "mapping on" to the distinctions made in the social environment. Rather the child's understanding is determined, it is presumed, by both the cognitive level at which she/he is operating and the nature of the social events themselves.

It is apparent from this survey of recent studies that there has been only a bare beginning to "contextualizing" children's representation of rules, and, indeed, I suspect only a bare beginning to "contextualizing" social-cognitive development in general. If we are to understand how social-cognitive competencies serve adaptation to the social world of the child, we need to have a much more thorough account of the dynamics and structure of that social world, which, in turn, facilitate development.

Research Directions

In concluding this chapter, it is worth noting that, circa 1980, the term "contextualizing" social-cognitive development seems to have several different meanings to those endeavoring to chart and clarify social-cognitive ontogenesis. Perhaps the most frequent meaning is embedded in the elucidation of the relation between certain social-cognitive concepts or skills and how children actually behave in social situations, experimental or naturally occurring. Typically, the social-cognitive abilities (e.g., perspective taking) are assessed in one situation using standardized tasks, and then in another situation, children's social behavior is assessed (e.g., cooperation, aggression) to determine whether, for example, children advanced in perspective taking tend to be more cooperative, less aggressive, etc.

A different approach to the contextual analysis of children's social knowledge is the examination of social behavior as it occurs in specific social contexts. What children do and say in relation to each other as they interact form the basis for inferring their social-cognitive concepts, rules, etc. The focus most often, then, is not on the individual child but on the *dyadic* relations and interchanges. The partial bases of this approach are most succinctly described by Glick (1978):

> The social world is not only "known about," it is acted within. . . . The main problem of social life is . . . to maintain and sustain coherent courses of action which are related coherently to an interactive context. . . . Knowledge for an actor is governed as much by its conditions of application . . . as it is by its structure as a known field of information. (p. 5)

Chapter 6 in this volume, by Bearison, details such an approach.

Yet a third approach to contextualization is apparent in the study of the social environment to elucidate its informational properties: the structuring of social life, the kinds of information given and modeled for the child (concepts, rules, etc.). A good deal of the research on rule concepts falls under this rubric. In some cases the focus is limited to an analysis of the social environment (e.g., the ways in which mothers respond to rule violations of a hypothetical sort, as previously described in the work of Steinlauf [1975] and of Grusec & Kuczynski [1980]). And other approaches more directly assess the match between social-environmental information and the child's information (e.g., the analysis of rule structuring by adults and children in preschools and interviewing participants in those settings, as illustrated by the Nucci & Turiel study [1978]).

This latter approach has had a long history in American developmental psychology for the study of social development but not social-cognitive development. That is, the influence of various social events were examined, such as the rules given to children, the social contingencies in the environment, the models provided children, etc. This research, often from a social learning perspective, examined the influence of social events on children's social *behavior* and very rarely examined how children understood or represented these events (models, contingencies, etc.). But the mind of the child is not easily ignored! The events to which children attend, their abstraction of rules, their representations of the meanings of social events were not, in many important respects, like those of adults; and these factors had to be taken into acount if the goal, ultimately, was to systematically relate the social environment to the social behavior of the child. It was this influence of the child's cognitive development that led in large measure to some of the major revisions in modern social learning theory. For example, Bandura (1971) speaks of modeling as operating primarily in terms of its *informational* function—that is, operating at the level of "symbolic representations of modeled events rather than specific stimulus–response associations" (p. 16). Mischel (1973), too, suggests a variety of cognitive factors influencing social learning, such as expectations, encoding strategies, self-guiding rules, etc.

With the rise of the definable area of study called social-cognitive development, many theoretical positions besides the social learning tradition are evident in attempts to understand the match between the social environment and social cognition–social behavior. Earlier in this chapter I abstracted what appears to be a rather good "match" between the distinctions made in the environment between conventional and moral rules, and the same distinctions made at a behavioral and/or representational level by children as they develop. But what is one to make of such a relation? Are children directly acquiring from others the distinctions others are making between rules, as children are exposed to rules and rule violations? This is a very likely interpretation of the meaning of the "match," particularly if one assumes a rather "passive" child who "maps on" to the environmental structure, acquires information wholesale (more or less), and is highly influenced in a unilateral manner by others (particularly by adults, and more particularly, by parents). Since such matches between the child's social concepts and the social environment are likely to be searched for in future research, it seems useful to briefly discuss some of the hazards of such searches, and particularly, hazards of interpretátions where substantial matches are found.

The gist of this speculative "cautionary tale" is that matches between children's social-cognitive concepts and the social environment will often be found to be weaker, less direct, and less adult-derived than is often presumed. To clarify, let us briefly consider just two aspects of the child's functioning vis-à-vis her/his social world. First, to understand what aspects of the social environment are related to the child's social-cognitive concepts, and how they are related, two large classes of environmental events are likely to be searched: the *direct experiences* the child has in the social world as observer and participant, and the *representations* of social events and information given by parents, the media, teachers, etc. The impact on the child historically has been presumed to be a quite direct one, but that presumption has been based on little appreciation of the child's own contribution to the process—selective attention, current level of cognitive functioning, and meanings attributed to behavior of others and of the self. A study by Campbell (1975) provides an illustration of the importance of cognitive functioning in understanding the impact of the social environment. He studied children's conception of illness, as both a biological and social-role-related phenomenon. He interviewed 264 children, ages 6 to 13, who were short-term patients in a pediatric hospital, concerning their understanding of illness, and he also interviewed their mothers. He wished to determine whether the child's conceptions were largely based on her/his mother's representation of illness. They were not: A mother's conception was found not to be a prototype of her child's conception at any age. And a second possibility was examined: Perhaps the level of sophistication in the child's concept of illness was related instead to the child's direct experiences in being ill. Health history was related to the level of sophistication, but not in a simple and direct way. Rather, it interacted with age: Children younger than 9 with poor health histories had the least sophisticated concepts, whereas those older than 9 with poor health histories had the most mature illness concepts. In short, younger children's own frequent illnesses were not related to more sophisticated understanding of illness. Here, then, is one example where the representation and the direct experience bore a much less direct relation to the child's conceptions than might be expected.

The second point in this "cautionary tale" is that some social concepts are probably not *acquired from* adults but rather are formed at least in part in *reaction to* adults' behavior, as noted earlier in this chapter. In relation to rules, the presumption is often made that concepts such as justice are modeled and directly taught by adults and serve as a root-source for moral judgment. While adults clearly influence children's justice concepts, it seems likely that at least the primitive concept of justice is based on a direct reaction of the child to being treated unjustly by others. Likewise, social-relational concepts such as dominance hierarchies and affiliative networks in peer groups and in interaction with adults are probably based on reactions to others' behaviors over resources and the like in dyadic interchanges. That is, children's structuring of their own groups along dimensions of power and liking appears to occur spontaneously, without adult tuition, and to be maintained over time (Shantz, in press).

It remains for the future to determine whether this cautionary tale, as "tale" is defined in the dictionary, deals with real or imagined hazards for research in the next decade on the social-cognitive–social-contextual relations. The multiplicity of theoretical positions and research strategies promises, at the least, significant and broadening appreciation of the ways in which children adapt to their social world and society adapts to its new members.

ACKNOWLEDGMENTS

Preparation of this chapter was made possible in part by a grant from the National Science Foundation (BNS77-07901) to the coprincipal investigators, Dr. David Shantz and the author. Special thanks are extended to Ms. Diane Jones for her skillful interviewing and coding of the data, and to the principal, Mrs. Esther Bowen, and the teachers and children of Brooklands Elementary School, Rochester, Michigan.

REFERENCES

Bandura, A. (Ed.). *Psychological modeling: Conflicting theories.* Chicago: Aldine-Atherton, 1971.

Bearison, D. J., & Cassel, T. Z. Cognitive decentration and social codes: Communicative effectiveness in young children from differing family contexts. *Developmental Psychology,* 1975, *11,* 29–36.

Campbell, J. D. Illness is a point of view: The development of children's concepts of illness. *Child Development,* 1975, *46,* 92–100.

Damon, W. *The social world of the child.* San Francisco: Jossey-Bass, 1977.

Fry, A. M., & Willis, F. N. Invasion of personal space as a function of the age of the invader. *Psychological Record,* 1971, *21,* 385–389.

Glick, J. Cognition and social cognition: An introduction. In J. Glick & A. Clarke-Stewart (Eds.), *The development of social understanding.* New York: Gardner Press, 1978.

Glidewell, J. C., Kantor, M. B., Smith, L. M., & Stringer, L. A. Socialization and social structure in the classroom. In L. W. Hoffman & M. L. Hoffman (Eds.), *Review of child development research* (Vol. 2). New York: Russell Sage Foundation, 1966.

Grusec, J. E., & Kuczynski, L. Direction of effect in socialization: A comparison of the parent's versus the child's behavior as determinants of disciplinary techniques. *Developmental Psychology,* 1980, *16,* 1–9.

Hoffman, M. L. Moral development. In P. H. Mussen (Ed.), *Carmichael's manual of child psychology* (Vol. 2). New York: Wiley, 1970.

Hoffman, M. L., & Saltzstein, H. D. Parent discipline and the child's moral development. *Journal of Personality and Social Psychology,* 1967, *5,* 45–57.

Johnson, S. C. Hierarchical clustering schemes. *Psychometrika,* 1967, *32,* 241–254.

Kohlberg, L. Stage and sequence: The cognitive-developmental approach to socialization. In D. A. Goslin (Ed.), *Handbook of socialization theory and research.* Chicago: Rand McNally, 1969.

Mischel, W. Toward a cognitive social learning reconceptualization of personality. *Psychological Review*, 1973, *80*, 252–283.

Much, N. C., & Shweder, R. A. Speaking of rules: The analysis of culture in breach. In W. Damon (Ed.), *New directions for child development: Moral development.* San Francisco: Jossey-Bass, 1978.

Nucci, L. P., & Turiel, E. Social interactions and the development of social concepts in preschool children. *Child Development*, 1978, *49*, 400–407.

Piaget, J. *The moral judgment of the child.* New York: Harcourt Brace, 1932.

Piaget, J. *Six psychological studies.* New York: Random House, 1967.

Selman, R. Social-cognitive understanding. In T. Lickona (Ed.), *Moral development and behavior.* New York: Holt, Rinehart & Winston, 1976.

Shantz, C. U. The development of social cognition. In E. M. Hetherington (Ed.), *Review of child development research* (Vol. 5). Chicago: University of Chicago Press, 1975.

Shantz, C. U. Social-cognition. In P. H. Mussen (Ed.), *Carmichael's manual of child psychology* (Vol. 3: *Cognitive development*, J. H. Flavell & E. Markman, Eds.). New York: Wiley, in press.

Shantz, D. W., & Shantz, C. U. *Children's behavior during interpersonal conflicts: Situational and social-cognitive correlates* (BNS 77-07901). Research grant proposal to the National Science Foundation, 1977.

Sigel, I. E. Personal communication, 1977.

Stein, N. L., & Glenn, C. G. An analysis of story comprehension in elementary school children. In R. O. Freedle (Ed.), *Advances in discourse processing* (Vol. 2: *New directions in discourse processing*). Norwood, N.J.: Ablex, 1979.

Steinlauf, B. *Role-taking abilities of young children and maternal discipline strategies.* Unpublished master's thesis, Wayne State University, 1975.

Turiel, E. The development of concepts of social structure: Social convention. In J. Glick & A. Clarke-Stewart (Eds.), *The development of social understanding.* New York: Gardner Press, 1978. (a)

Turiel, E. Social regulations and domains of social concepts. In W. Damon (Ed.), *New directions for child development: Social cognition.* San Francisco: Jossey-Bass, 1978. (b)

Turiel, E. Personal communication, May 1979.

6

New Directions in Studies of Social Interaction and Cognitive Growth

DAVID J. BEARISON

> There are many unnecessary problems arising from the fact that some have committed themselves from the outset to a dichotomy "individual or society" while forgetting that there is a relational perspective according to which there exist only interactions, which can be globally studied either sociologically or ontogenetically during the course of individual development.
>
> *Piaget (1966, p. 249; translated from the French)*

Introduction

Social cognition, as a field of inquiry in developmental psychology, has traditionally been defined as the study of how children conceptualize other people and social relations (Shantz, 1975). Interest in social cognition grew out of earlier concerns among developmentalists with more general problems regarding how children conceptualize object relations. Influenced by the cognitive-stage developmental model of Piaget, early studies of object relations focused on children's knowledge of such object properties as space, time, number, weight, volume, etc. When interest shifted in the late 1960s to children's knowledge of such person properties as feelings, thoughts, needs, and intentions, it seemed reasonable at the time to adapt experimental paradigms from the already empirically established domain of physical or object cognition. According to this general paradigm, subjects are interviewed alone by an adult experimenter who administers a series of problems

DAVID J. BEARISON. Doctoral Programs in Educational and Developmental Psychology, The Graduate Center of the City University of New York, New York, New York, and Department of Psychiatry, Harvard Medical School and The Children's Hospital Medical Center, Boston, Massachusetts.

that can be solved according to different levels of cognitive analysis. These levels of analysis reflect theoretically determined stages of cognitive growth and development. In social-cognitive research, subjects typically are asked to solve problems about people and the kinds of social relationships that people construct and maintain for themselves. The levels of analysis in social-cognitive research usually reflect children's ability to logically infer various kinds of inner psychological experiences in others and to organize such inferences in a coordinated manner. However, the presentation of others as social agents in the vast majority of studies of social cognition has been in the form of hypothetical people engaging in hypothetical social acts apart from a social context that has any subjective meaning for the knower (Chandler, 1977).

Some of the more popular kinds of social-cognitive problems that have been studied within this experimental paradigm have included: (1) age-related changes in social-cognitive development (Barenboim, 1977; Berndt & Berndt, 1975; Miller, Kessel, & Flavell, 1970; Peterson, Danner, & Flavell, 1972; Selman, 1971), (2) correspondences between Piagetian stages of logical operations and social-cognitive development (Chandler, Paget, & Koch, 1978; Damon, 1975; Feffer & Gourevitch, 1960), (3) correspondences between different domains of social cognition (Hudson, 1978; Piche, Michlin, & Rubin, 1975; Rubin, 1973; Urberg & Docherty, 1976), (4) relationships between social cognition and social behavior (Barrett & Yarrow, 1977; Blotner & Bearison, 1980; Chandler, 1973; Levine & Hoffman, 1975; Rardin & Moan, 1971; Rothman, 1976), and (5) socioenvironmental conditions that affect the rate of social-cognitive development (Bearison & Cassel, 1975; Hollos, 1975; Hollos & Cowan, 1973).

The general findings that have emerged from these types of studies have been often contradictory and equivocal. As children get older they become more adept at making inferences about other people's psychological experiences and use this knowledge to mediate their judgments about others. However, these age-related changes are not generally uniform across contextual domains of social-cognitive reasoning, nor are changes in social reasoning clearly reflected in social behavior. Very little is presently known about how children's reflective knowledge in socially isolated contexts is related to their social reasoning and behavior in naturally occurring interactive settings.

The logical transformations that explain the structure of physical knowledge do not strongly correspond with the emergence of increasingly sophisticated concepts of social relations, and it is questionable whether these logical transformations even constitute necessary, if not sufficient, conditions for social-cognitive development. For example, Lempers, Flavell, and Flavell (1977) have shown that children as young as 2 years seem surprisingly precocious in their accommodations to another's perspective. If all knowledge is logically organized in a stage-sequential pattern of ontogenesis, we are much less aware how logical transformations are embedded in children's reasoning about the social compared to the physical domain. The idea of a logical basis of social cognition was strongly questioned by Gelman (1979) when she stated that "there is little, if any reason to continue to entertain the notion of a stage theory for the development of perspective taking abilities. Instead, it looks as if the development of perspective taking starts very early and is something children keep getting better and better at" (p. 2).

While studies have shown that there are some socioenvironmental conditions that facilitate social-cognitive growth more than others, these conditions have not been delineated in ways that could lead to positive intervention or the formulation of effective social and pedagogical policies that would promote child development.

These kinds of problems have led some to reevaluate the methods being used to study social-cognitive development. Research in this area has been increasingly criticized for using experimental paradigms that fail to capture the dialectics of subject-to-subject interaction (Chandler, 1977; Damon, 1979). Many have argued that there are formal and contextual factors that substantially differentiate social from object cognition, and that these differences are not being considered in social-cognition paradigms that are extensions of earlier experimental paradigms used to study children's development of object knowledge. For example, Hoffman (1981) has maintained that "social knowledge is based less on logic and more on probability, shared cultural belief systems, cultural stereotypes and scripts" (p. 67). According to Damon (1981), "social knowledge is structured according to different categories and principles than physical knowledge because social interactions have unique features not pertaining to physical interactions" (p. 6). These "unique features" have to do with the mutual intentionality that people interacting with each other maintain for themselves and that is totally lacking in actions on objects. Knowledge of objects is not necessarily more or less complex than knowledge of people, but—because objects lack psychological experiences (e.g., intentions, feelings, thoughts)—there are different classes of categories by which we structure object interactions compared to social interactions.

For Glick (1978), social knowledge is "more uncertain and more sensitive to current informational conditions than physical knowledge" (p. 3). Glick goes on to note that this sensitivity might only be reflected in interactive situations and not in our isolated cognitive reflections about such interactions. "The main problem of social life is not necessarily to emerge with a 'theory' of social actions. It is rather to maintain and sustain coherent courses of action which are related coherently to an interactive context" (Glick, 1978, p. 5).

Social Development of Knowledge

These considerations of differences between social and physical cognition have led to new ways of defining social cognition as a domain of psychological inquiry and new methods of investigation. The earlier emphasis on social cognition in terms of a particular class of objects of knowledge (people v. things) is being broadened to encompass the general process by which all classes of knowledge are constructed. Thus, social cognition not only reflects the development of *social knowledge* but also the *social development* of knowledge. All knowledge is inherently social in that the ontogenesis of mental development is motivated and maintained by social discourse. Social cognition, understood within this broader framework, is entirely consistent with Piaget's theorizing about mental development, while limiting social cognition to the study of particular classes of knowledge is not. According to Piaget, all knowledge is social because the categories of knowledge derive their meaning from social discourse, and because "it is precisely by a constant interchange of thought with others that we are able to decentralize ourselves . . . to coordinate internal relations deriving from different viewpoints" (1963, p. 64). As Chandler (1977) has noted, Piaget's theory disavows conventional distinctions between social and nonsocial classes of knowledge and assumes that all classes of knowledge are subsumed by the same cognitive structures. "The reaction of intelligence . . . to the social environment is exactly parallel to its reaction to the physical environment" (Piaget, 1963, p. 160). Cognitive development, then, rests on intraindividual as well as interindividual coordinations, and these coordinations are similarly structured.

As Damon (in press) has previously noted, a popular illustration from Piaget is misleading: how a child in social isolation might construct logicomathematical knowledge by arranging and rearranging a group of pebbles in different perceptual configurations—first arranging them in a straight line, then in a circle, a triangle, etc.—and hence discover the logic of associativity (Piaget, 1964). Such an illustration fails to acknowledge that even logicomathematical knowledge would have no meaning to the child unless it could be assimilated into a social context in which others confirm, share, and use this knowledge to mediate their social discourse. If one would imagine children developing in relative social isolation without the press to coordinate their knowledge with others, it is likely that they would never cognitively emerge from their own egocentrism, and their egocentrism would bias all categories of knowledge, not just social knowledge.

The logical necessity that characterizes higher forms of cognitive reasoning are not embedded in earlier forms of sensorimotor and preoperational reasoning. The ontogenesis of higher forms of reasoning requires social interactions within a given cultural context whereby individuals face others who contradict their own intuitively derived concepts and points of view, and thereby create cognitive conflicts whose resolutions result in the construction of higher forms of reasoning. Thus, social interaction and the coordination of perspectives are essential components of cognitive growth. The relationship between social–contextual and cognitive–organismic structures is reciprocal, presupposing as well as determining both individual and interindividual actions.

Thus, cognitive development cannot be accounted for solely in terms of children's solitary reflections upon a hypothetical reality. Children's social knowledge is not acquired independently of their social actions. Efforts to experimentally disentangle social concepts from the interactive concepts in which they are acquired forces investigators to propose various systems of conceptual bridges, feedback mechanisms, or mediating links to account for how social reasoning influences social activities. Instead of proposing such kinds of mediating links between cognitive reasoning and social interaction, Piaget has proposed that there is a structure to the social context that is isomorphic with the structure of children's knowledge derived within that context, and therefore, coordination of actions of individuals obeys the same laws as intraindividual coordination (Piaget, 1970). This isomorphism should not be surprising since the social contextual structures are a product of a knowing system that is itself structured. Thus, the relationship between social cognition and social interaction can be studied without recourse to externally derived, environmentally determined mediators or cognitive feedback systems (Damon, in press).

Seen in this light, Piaget's theory is not as inconsistent as might have been previously thought with such social-dialogical theories of mental development as those proposed by Mead and Vygotsky. Mead emphasizes the social-interactive context as the primary process by which knowledge is acquired. He states that there is a "temporal and logical preexistence of the social process of the self-conscious individual that arises in it" (1934, p. 29). Similarly for Vygotsky, "the true direction of the development of thinking is not from the individual to the socialized but from the social to the individual" (1962, p. 29). An essential difference that remains, however, between a dialogical model such as Mead's or Vygotsky's and a constructivist model like Piaget's is that, whereas for dialogical theories it is language, as a shared social symbol system, that embodies the social origins of thought; for Piaget, it is from the coordination of actions that thought arises.

Certain dialectical theories of cognitive development also account for growth in terms of mutual social exchanges between individuals. These theorists have criticized Piaget for unduly emphasizing the role of the individual thinker apart from the social context in which concepts derive their relevance and meaning. According to Riegel (1976), dialectical exchanges occur at all levels of development throughout the life span and account for the potential of continued cognitive growth during adulthood and aging.

We have maintained that early conceptions of social cognition as referring to a particular class of knowledge have promoted dubious distinctions between the organization of physical and social knowledge. Such conceptions have also promoted theoretical confusion regarding the social origins of all knowledge. They have also led to many empirical problems, including the relationship between social knowledge and social behavior. Therefore, we have tried to present a more expanded view of social cognition that recognizes social interaction as a cognitive process that develops in tandem with the cognitive structural status of the individual. In the next section we present a particular experimental paradigm that captures this view of cognitive development and social interaction.

Social Interaction and Cognitive Change

As was previously noted, most studies of social cognition are based on experimental paradigms derived from Piaget's studies of children's knowledge of space, time, number, weight, and volume. Piaget's own studies of social reasoning in children have been limited to studies of the development of autonomous moral concepts (Piaget, 1965) and the coordination of listener–speaker perspectives in verbal communication

(Piaget, 1967). In the communication studies, Piaget used a dyadic context in which children were asked to repeat stories to other children. In the moral-reasoning studies, Piaget interviewed children individually and asked them to consider hypothetical justice problems. However, in discussing his studies of moral reasoning, Piaget acknowledged the differences between "verbal or theoretical judgment and the concrete evaluations that operate in action" (1965, p. 117), and he cautioned readers that the "verbal evaluations made by our children are not of actions of which they have been authors or witnesses, but of stories which are told to them" (p. 119). Despite Piaget's caution about confusing reflective knowledge with practical action, "the predominant Genevan experimental paradigm over the last 40 years has been the testing of the young child-as-scientist, in solitary reflection, wrestling with problems of math or science" (Damon, 1979, p. 209). However, Piaget's theory is considerably broader in scope than the research it has thus far generated. The theory is not limited to studies of the type Chandler (1977) described as "the private contemplations of individuals working in social isolation" (p. 36). Thus, there appears to be a strong foundation for studies of the social aspects of cognitive development within an organismic–developmental perspective.

Perhaps because of growing interest in social learning theories (Bandura, 1977; Rosenthal & Zimmerman, 1978), renewed interest in the work of Vygotsky and his colleagues (Luria, 1976; Vygotsky, 1962, 1978), and greater recognition of dialectical methodologies (Lerner, Skinner, & Sorell, 1980; Riegel, 1978), increasing numbers of investigators have begun examining the role of social interaction in cognitive development. Damon (1977), for example, has made a substantial contribution to this area of research. He studied the development of children's concepts of distributive justice, but, instead of relying on children's verbal responses to hypothetical justice problems, he created social settings in which children actually had to collectively reach a consensus regarding how "rewards" were to be distributed among themselves. Among other things, he found that children resorted to higher levels of justice reasoning when considering hypothetical situations than when engaging in practical judgments. On the other hand, Bearison and Gass (1979) found that children used higher levels of interpersonal persuasion in a practical, as opposed to a hypothetical, situation.

According to Damon (in press), children's social interaction for the purpose of collectively resolving a problem reveals cognitive conflicts and resistances that are missing in children's solitary attempts to solve problems. In the collective situation, children are pressed not only to satisfy themselves regarding the best solution but to satisfy other members of the group as well. This need to verify one's own actions in coordination with another's structures the process of social interaction in ways which promote cognitive growth. Thus, systematic observations of how children socially interact in attempting to solve cognitive problems have the potential to reveal more about the process of cognitive change than the verbal products of children's solitary reflections.

The efficacy of social interaction on cognitive change has been, to date, most clearly demonstrated in a series of studies by Willem Doise and his colleagues in Geneva. They have shown that children working in dyads solve cognitive problems at a significantly more advanced level than children working individually on the same problems. According to Doise, "conflicts of cognitive centrations embedded in a social situation are a more powerful factor in cognitive development than a conflict of individual centrations alone" (Doise & Mugny, 1979, p. 105).

In some of the Doise studies, children's collective performance was simply compared to that of control subjects working alone. In other studies, however, children were initially pretested to determine basal levels of performance on a target problem. They were then randomly assigned within pretest levels to individual or collective conditions, and several days later were individually posttested in order to determine which particular pairings of pretest performance levels maximized the cognitive effects of social interaction. Different studies used different cognitive problems as the focus of social interaction, including conservations of length, number, and liquid, and the coordination of spatial perspectives. In these studies it was found that it was not necessary to pair a subject with a more advanced partner for the subject to show individual improvement on a posttest, and that a subject paired with a less advanced partner did not regress (Perret-Clermont, 1980). The most successful dyadic combinations were those in which subjects functioning at intermediate levels of mastery worked collectively (Mugny & Doise, 1978). In such pairings, both the less and the more advanced subjects showed progress. A substantial number of subjects in collective conditions who progressed on conservation tasks used logical arguments to justify their conservation responses in an individually administered posttest which were not produced during the course of social interaction (Perret-Clermont, 1980).

The general superiority found in the collective performance of peers compared to subjects working individually has been explained in the following manner:

> The cause of the cognitive development observed is to be found in the conflict of centrations which the subject experiences during the inter-action. The interaction obliges the subject to coordinate their [sic] actions with those of others, and this brings about a centration in the encounter with other points of view which can only be assimilated if cognitive restructuring takes place. (Perret-Clermont, 1980, p. 148)

According to this explanation it should not be necessary for subjects in the course of social interaction to be exposed to the "correct" solution but only a "conflict of centrations." This was demonstrated in a study by Doise, Mugny, and Perret-Clermont (1976) in which social conflict (and, hence, cognitive growth) was produced by preoperatory centrations that were contrary to the subject's own preoperatory centrations in a conservation-of-length problem.

A conflict-equilibration explanation of cognitive change such as the one just proposed is in marked contrast to explanations of social-interaction effects proposed by social learning theorists. They have shown that children experience significant cognitive gains by observing a model demonstrate the correct solution (Rosenthal & Zimmerman, 1972; Zimmerman & Lanaro, 1974; Zimmerman & Rosenthal, 1972, 1974). However, it has been shown that even preoperatory subjects who interact with less advanced partners who do not provide them with "correct" solutions benefit from the social experience. The modeling effect, thus, might be better understood as a particular instance of the general effects of social conflict. Where modeling does appear to work it is not in response to the model but in the conflict that is generated between the subjects' expectations and the model's behavior.

Studies of peer interaction and cognitive change have also been reported in this country by Botvin and Murray (1975), Kuhn (1972), Miller and Brownell (1975), Murray (1972), Murray, Ames, and Botvin (1977), Silverman and Geiringer (1973), and Silverman and Stone (1972). All but Kuhn's study focused on conservation attainment, and they generally found that social interaction facilitated concept attainment. Although Botvin and Murray (1975) found social conflict to be as effective a change agent as simple modeling, a more recent study by Ames (1980) found that having two nonconservers (length and mass) work together, each with a subject whose preoperational centration was contradictory to their own, produced greater cognitive gains than having nonconservers observe a "model" who asserted nonconservation based on the centration opposite the subject's. For example, in the social-interaction condition, if a subject thought the transformed rod in a conservation-of-length task was longer, he/she was paired with a subject who thought the transformed rod was shorter, and the two children were asked to resolve their differences on their own. In the "modeling" condition, a subject who thought that the transformed rod was longer simply watched another child judge that it was shorter and heard a nonconservation reason for the judgment.

Coordination of Spatial Perspectives

Almost all of the social interaction–cognitive change paradigm studies reported in the literature have had to do with conservation attainment. However, there have been few studies in which the coordination of spatial perspectives was the object of social interaction (Doise, Mugny, & Perret-Clermont, 1975; Mugny & Doise, 1978). The spatial perspective problem, as originally designed by Piaget in 1948 (Piaget & Inhelder, 1956), consisted of a papier-mâché model of a landscape of three different-size mountains. Children were asked to identify the visual perspective of another (a doll) in various locations around the landscape. Three different types of responses were measured: (1) reconstruction of the scene, (2) selection of a photograph from a set which matched the doll's location, and (3) placement of the doll to match a particular perspective. Piaget found variations in scores from children between 4 and 9 years. This measure has subsequently been criticized for being too susceptible to task-specific variations such as substituting a live person for a doll (Cox, 1975), varying the number and type of stimuli in the spatial array (Eiser, 1974; Shlecter, 1977), and varying the number of degrees the "other" is oriented in relation to the subject's position (Cox, 1977; Eiser, 1974; Nigel & Fishbein, 1974). These studies have found that such task variations significantly affect the mean age when children show mastery of spatial coordination concepts (see Fehr, 1978, for a critical review of these findings).

However, in Doise's studies, these variations are held constant across experimental conditions (individual vs. collective), and mean scores are compared across conditions, not ages. Of the three types of response measures, Doise used the reconstruction measure. Children were shown a model and were given materials to construct a copy of it with the base of the copy at different spatial orientations relative to the base of the model. Compared to most measures of concrete operations, and conservation in particular, the spatial perspective task is particularly appropriate for social-interaction studies. Whereas a conservation task is a verbal-reasoning problem, the spatial perspective task, using the construction response, relies more on task-directed activities and less on verbal reasoning. In a social-interaction condition, the task can be solved by two children directly acting on the task materials without the need to completely talk the problem out with one another. As will be seen later, this aspect of the task became an important consideration in our own studies of social interaction and cognitive change.

Based on the findings from Geneva, as well as those from this country, there is little doubt that peer conflict generated in the course of social interaction promotes cognitive development. On a theoretical level, the causative factor appears to be cognitive conflict generated by subjects' attempts to coordinate their partners' viewpoints when they differ from their own. However, to date, investigators have not specified what particular aspects of the interactive experience reflect the coordination of interindividual actions and what aspects facilitate cognitive growth.

In the remainder of this chapter we describe a preliminary study of this problem and interpret some very tentative findings in terms of the directions they suggest for future research on the cognitive effects of social interaction. The study reported here is adapted from Doise *et al.* (1975), and adheres rather closely to their procedures and measures. Our study thus tests the replicability of their findings.

The subjects were predominantly middle-class children enrolled in kindergarten and first grade in a large urban school system. The children ranged in age from 5.50 years to 7.67 years (mean age = 6.47 years). All subjects were administered a pretest of spatial coordination, and then, within grade and pretest levels, they were randomly assigned to either a collective or individual condition. Seventy-six children took part in the collective condition (38 pairs) and 22 in the individual condition. There were approximately equal numbers of males and females. However, in the collective condition, children were always paired with someone of their own sex and in their own grade.

The apparatus, as adapted from Doise *et al.* (1975), consisted of two cardboard bases, onto each of which was affixed a sheet of graph paper marked out in millimeter squares and measuring about 50 by 40 cm. In the same place on each sheet an irregular piece of blue transparent paper ("mark") was affixed to serve as a reference point.

The "mark" was set off to one corner of the base. Along with each base there was a set of three clearly distinguishable solid pine blocks which served as houses. They were painted red, blue, and yellow, with windows and a door painted on one side in order to identify the front of each house. The largest house (A) measured 17.14 × 8.89 × 7.62 cm and had a flat roof. The other two houses had peaked roofs and measured 12.06 × 6.35 × 16.51 cm (B) and 5.08 × 3.18 × 7.62 cm (C), respectively. One set of houses was used to construct the model by placing each house at a precisely defined position on the base. The other set of houses was for the subjects to use to make a copy of the model on the second, identical base.

The model was set on a table that was placed at an angle of 90 degrees to the left of a second table on which was placed the base of the copy (see Figure 6-1). The subjects were permitted to move around the model but were told that they must remain in front of the base of the copy while constructing their copy. The "mark" on the model was identified to the subjects as a lake, and they were told to build their copy so that a man who was coming out of the lake would find his houses the same way on the subjects' copy as on the model.

There were four items on the task, consisting of a construction of four models differing from each other in terms of their rotation and orientation of the bases to the copies. The relative positions of the houses on the base of the models remained constant, however. The composition of the four models is shown in Figure 6-2. Following Doise *et al.* (1975), "the items were classified as 'simple' or 'complex,' depending on the structure of the transformations they required. The subjects had to make the copy from position B [Figure 6-1] and could do this for the simple items by making a simple rotation through 90° of the copy of the model. For the complex items, this rotation had

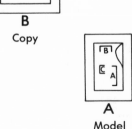

FIG 6-1. *Placing of subjects relative to the tables for the model and for the copy. (From "Social Interaction and Cognitive Development: Further Evidence" by W. Doise, G. Mugny, and A. Perret-Clermont,* European Journal of Social Psychology, *1975, 5, 371. Reprinted by permission.)*

B
Copy

A
Model

FIG. 6-2. *The four models as seen from position A (cf. Fig. 6-1). (From "Social Interaction and Cognitive Development: Further Evidence" by W. Doise, G. Mugny, and A. Perret-Clermont, European* Journal of Social Psychology, *1975, 5, 372. Reprinted by permission.)*

to be combined with an imaginary inversion of the copy or with a copy obtained by going around to the other side of the model to observe it" (p. 372). Subjects in the collective condition were told to work together on the task and to tell the experimenter when they were satisfied that their copy matched the model.

Measures

Doise *et al.* (1975) used two related measures to reflect the accuracy of the construction of the copies in relation to the models: a deviation score (DS) and a structural index (SI). For each copy, the DS was computed by noting the exact position of each of the three houses taken from numbered vertical and horizontal coordinates on the graph paper mounted to the base. The coordinates were read from the two ends of the front side of each house. The sum of the differences between the three sets of coordinates from the copy and those from the model, divided by two, determined the DS. The SI consisted of the number of houses correctly placed with respect to the position and orientation of the fronts. A score of 1 was assigned for each house placed in the correct relative position and orientation. Thus, for each item, scores ranged from 0 to 3, and from 0 to 12 for the four items together. The DS and the SI were expected to negatively correlate with each other. High SI and low DS scores reflected good performances. In addition to the DS and SI scores, a third score consisted of the number of seconds (recorded from a stop watch) subjects spent working on each item.

Several weeks before testing in the individual or collective condition, each subject was individually administered a pretest for the coordination of spatial perspectives. The pretest was adapted from Brodzinsky (1980). Subjects were presented with a model made from a toy farm scene consisting of a brightly colored plastic barn, truck, doll, fence, and cow. Instead of constructing a copy of the model, as in the interaction condition, subjects selected one of eight 12.70 × 17.78 cm colored photographs representing 45-degree increments around the model. There were four items on the pretest, each one representing a different orientation of the model in relation to the subject—90, 135, 180, and 270 degrees. The order of the items was counterbalanced among all subjects. Subjects received a score of 1 each time they made a correct choice. Thus, scores ranged from 0 to 4.

The pretest scores were used to arrange particular dyadic combinations and to ensure that mean scores for the collective and individual conditions were matched within grade and sex. Among 94 subjects pretested, 31 received a score of 0, 33 a score of 1, 20 a score of 2, 9 a score of 3, and 1 received a score of 4. The mean pretest score for subjects in the individual condition was 1.45, and it was 1.12 for subjects in the collective condition. Individual posttest measures of spatial coordination were not obtained.

Results

The mean performance scores on the simple and complex items for subjects in the individual and collective conditions are reported in Table 6-1. As expected, subjects did significantly better on the simple compared to the complex items on the analyses of the SI scores, F (1, 58) = 14.09, $p < .001$; and the DS scores, F (1, 58) = 20.32, $p < .001$. The

TABLE 6-1. *Mean* (SD) *Performance Scores of Subjects in Collective and Individual Conditions*

| Condition (n) | Mean (SD) performance scores | | | | | |
| | Simple | | | Complex | | |
	SI	DS	Time	SI	DS	Time
Individual (22)	2.14	114.41	68.04	1.36	137.70	74.04
	(2.32)	(46.15)	(30.88)	(1.79)	(43.55)	(42.13)
Collective (38)	3.55	78.38	221.16	2.47	108.73	190.45
	(2.33)	(51.04)	(166.39)	(2.32)	(61.83)	(142.85)

length of time subjects spent on the simple and complex items did not differ significantly. Of greater interest, however, is the comparison between subjects who worked on the problems individually with those subjects who worked in dyads. As expected, subjects working collectively received significantly higher SI scores, F (1, 58) = 5.35, $p < .05$, and significantly lower DS scores, $F(1,58) = 6.19, p < .05$, than subjects working individually. Subjects in the collective condition also spent significantly more time working on the task than subjects in the individual condition, F (1, 58) = 18.58, $p < .001$.

In addition to the gross comparisons between subjects in the individual and collective conditions, SI and DS scores were analyzed for selected groups of subjects based on their pretest scores. The following comparisons were made: dyads each having pretest scores of 0 against individuals with pretest scores of 0, dyads consisting of subjects with pretest scores of 0 matched with subjects with scores of 1 against individuals with scores of 1, and dyads each having pretest scores of 2 against individuals with pretest scores of 2. The mean scores of these selected groups of subjects are presented in Table 6-2. Among these comparisons, the only significant main effect for condition (collective vs. individual) was on the analyses of the SI and DS scores for dyads each with pretest scores of 0 against individual subjects with pretest

TABLE 6-2. *Mean (SD) Performance Scores of Selected Subjects in Particular Collective and Individual Conditions*

		Mean (SD) performance scores			
		Simple		Complex	
Condition by pretest scores[a]	(n)	SI	DS	SI	DS
I-0	(9)	1.22 (2.05)	124.33 (37.60)	.89 (1.62)	153.50 (37.60)
C-0 × 0	(8)	3.62 (2.33)	63.56 (38.61)	2.00 (1.69)	123.69 (65.61)
C-0 × 1	(6)	2.50 (2.50)	111.92 (40.03)	1.33 (2.33)	131.97 (55.49)
I-1	(7)	2.71 (2.21)	111.00 (54.72)	1.29 (1.60)	141.29 (27.13)
C-1 × 1	(7)	2.43 (2.57)	98.64 (59.40)	1.71 (2.63)	129.36 (78.41)
I-2	(3)	2.00 (3.46)	99.50 (51.36)	.67 (1.15)	134.50 (35.39)
C-2 × 2	(4)	3.50 (1.73)	87.62 (50.41)	2.00 (1.83)	108.50 (32.16)

[a]I = individual condition; C = collective condition.

scores of 0, F (1, 15) = 4.84, $p < .05$, and F (1, 15) = 4.74, $p < .05$, respectively. Subject pairs with pretest scores of 1 did not perform significantly better than subjects with pretest scores of 1 working alone. Also, subjects with pretest scores of 1 paired with other subjects with pretest scores of 1 did not perform significantly better than subjects with pretest scores of 1 working alone, and dyads of subjects both having pretest scores of 2 did not perform significantly better than subjects with scores of 2 working individually.

These findings are presented primarily to illustrate the application of the social-interaction paradigm in studying cognitive change. They are preliminary and do not represent all the different kinds of analyses that could be performed on the data. The findings are also limited because individual posttest measures of cognitive change were not obtained, and the correlation between pretest scores and the total SI scores in the experimental condition was only .47 (based only on scores from subjects working individually in the experimental condition, $n = 22$).

The significant overall difference between subjects in the collective compared to the individual condition supports Doise's previous findings. However, Mugny and Doise (1978) found that more progress took place when children with different initial levels of task ability worked together on the spatial perspective problems than when children with the same initial levels worked together, particularly when the initial levels were low. This finding was interpreted to imply that children with different abilities were more likely to experience cognitive conflict when working together than children with similar abilities. However, we did not find this to be the case. The particular dyadic combination that showed the greatest progress was the one in which both children had pretest scores of 0. The mean SI scores for this combination exceeded the mean SI scores for all other combinations reported in Table 6-2. While this finding is not consistent with that of Mugny and Doise (1978), it is also inconsistent with any social learning type of explanation of social interaction effects.

Our findings compared with Doise's findings, however, point to the need to consider other methods of establishing the presumption of cognitive conflict in the course of social interaction and problem solving. The use of pretest scores to compare the effectiveness of particular dyadic combinations places too much emphasis on organismic states of "readiness" and fails to recognize the dynamic aspects of mutual exchanges of influence that can occur in the interactive context. Consistent with our earlier discussion of the social origins of knowledge, cognitive conflict is as much a function of the context in which ideas are constructed as it is of the cognitive state of the thinker. Cognitive conflict does not occur as a singular perturbation that suddenly disrupts the cognitive equilibrium of the thinker in solitary reflection. Instead, it is a process which unfolds in tandem with a coordinated system of actions and representations that arise from different approaches (centrations) to a problem. We believe that it is simply more likely that the coordination of contrary centrations will occur in an interactive context than in a context of solitary reflection. While one child working alone can remain embedded within his/her own egocentric intuitions, it is considerably more difficult for two or more children working together on a problem to each adhere to his/her own egocentric point of view. This is not to imply that all social interactions will facilitate cognitive growth in all children. The cognitive state of the individual remains an important determinant of what kinds of social contexts are likely to induce conflicts and how the ensuing coordinations will be operationally structured. However, the social context in which ideas are represented, exchanged, confirmed, and contradicted should be regarded as an equally important factor in establishing conflict and promoting cognitive growth.

Our own observations of children working together on the spatial perspective problems have led us to consider the ways in which the activity of one subject either confirms or contradicts the immediately previous activity of the other subject. When a subject acts in a way to contradict the other subject's activity, the first subject will then reconsider his/her previous activity as if to validate the activity both for him/herself and his/her partner. To illustrate, suppose Subject B places a house at point x on the copy. Subject A then takes the house from point x and places it at point y. The immediate effect on Subject B of this replacement is to consider both points x and y as possible solutions, and to compare the placement of the house at point y in relation to the model and the placement at point x in relation to the model. These comparisons are not induced by Subject B him/herself but by Subject A's action on Subject B's previous act. Thus, Subject B is faced with a dilemma that he/she would not have had if he/she were working alone. The dilemma can be resolved by either leaving the replaced house at point y, putting it back at point x, or selecting a third point on the model for placing the house. The resolution by Subject B, when different from Subject A's resolution, will set the stage for Subject A to then engage in further validation of his/her own activity in relation to Subject B. This mutual and sequential validation of one's own activity in light of one's partner's activity continues back and forth until both partners reach agreement.

This description of the coordination of task-related actions adheres to the principles of a dialectical perspective as described by Riegel (1978). When true coordination occurs it is a synthesis of each subject's responses which had previously stood in a contradictory relationship as thesis and antithesis. As long as the acts of both subjects yield a synthesis of both the opponent's acts and the subject's own preceding acts, coordination will continue and the interactive context will facilitate cognitive growth. When this condition is not met, when one subject acts independently of the previous acts of the other subject, the interaction collapses into parallel and uncoordinated activities.

We are currently engaged in a series of pilot studies to attempt to empirically verify our informal observations of the process by which task-directed social activity becomes mutually coordinated. Our purpose is to be able to reliably distinguish between dyads who show significant progress on tasks, such as the spatial perspective problem, from those who do not in terms of the kinds of specific social exchanges in which they engage. The problem, however, is knowing what to observe in interactions. We have found that not only do children in dyadic conditions spend more time on the task than children working individually, but that within the dyadic condition, at least among pairs of children with low performance abilities, the amount of time spent on the task is positively related to levels of progress. Thus, we might speculate that whatever it is that children do together in attempting to solve the problems, the more successful groups of children do more of it than the less successful groups.

Our observations of children's task-related activities in the spatial perspective problem have also led us to realize that the coordination of actions can be carried out on a purely motoric plane without the aid of verbal dialogue. Indeed, some of the most successful dyads spoke very little to each other but spent a lot of time placing and replacing houses on the bases in response to their partner's placements and replacements.

In one of our current studies, an observer notes the occurrence of each of the following events separately for each member of the dyad as they work together on the spatial perspective problem.

- subject touches the other subject (1)
- subject moves the other subject's hand (2)
- subject gives a house to the other subject (3)

- subject touches a house (4)
- both subjects touch a house simultaneously (5)
- subject places a house on the base (6)
- subject replaces a house already on the base (7)
- subject removes a house already placed on the base (8)
- subject points to a house (9)
- subject points to the base (10)

These observations are recorded as a string of connected events that begins when a subject initiates a task-related act in regard to the placement of a house and continues until either subject initiates an act in regard to the placement of another house. If a subject returns to a previously placed house, the string is again picked up by the observer. For example, a particular string of observations of the interactions between subjects X and Y in regard to a given house on a given item might look like the following: X3-X6-X9-X7-XY5-Y8-Y6-X7.

As we continue with this line of research, new events will be added or will replace other ones in our observations. The test of this observational method will be how well different kinds of statistical analyses can account for variations in the progress shown by pairs of children working together. Analyses will be made of patterns of interaction (strategies) rather than the simple aggregation of elemental events. Once we are able to identify the characteristics of successful interaction strategies, further research will test the generalizability of these strategies across different task contents. We will be interested in how strategies change in relation to different task characteristics. We will also be interested in how strategies carried out in the motoric plane in the spatial perspective task are translated into forms of verbal discourse in other types of tasks.

Conclusions

The theme of this chapter is that cognitive development cannot be adequately explained solely in terms of children's solitary reflections upon hypothetical problems. Knowledge is not constructed independently of the social contexts in which it is shared, confirmed, and used to mediate social discourse. While the thrust of previous studies of children's cognitive development has been on the structuration of intra-individual coordinations, there are increasing signs of a major shift in research paradigms from intraindividual coordinations to the study of interindividual coordinations in the context of social interaction. Paradigms, such as Doise's, in which two or more subjects collaborate on solving cognitive problems appear to be a useful strategy to examine the role of social interaction in cognitive development. However, in order to arrive at an adequate explanation regarding why social interaction facilitates cognitive growth, investigators will have to move beyond the simple documentation of the effect and identify specific aspects of the interaction experience that will reliably predict cognitive growth. These aspects will have to capture the dialectical exchanges inherent in the coordination of interindividual activities. Ideally, they will reflect levels of cognitive conflicts that co-occur within the individual and within the interactive context, as well as the ensuing attempts to collectively resolve such conflicts at increasingly higher levels of cognitive organization.

The collaborative problem-solving situation has an advantage over the more traditional individual problem-solving situation in providing objective data about the cognitive processes used to solve problems. Cognitive reasoning that would be covert in an individual context becomes externalized in the collaborative context because of the need to represent and communicate one's ideas to another.

One approach to identifying those aspects of social interaction that facilitate cognitive growth would be to use functional criteria that simply pose the question of what kinds of interactive activities within a given context do groups of subjects working together who demonstrate significant positive change engage in that are lacking among groups who do not show change. However, even a functional–contextual approach as simple as this one will have to consider structural–universal issues regarding the cognitive developmental status of individual subjects as they enter the social-interactive experiences. Thus, the "new directions" in social-cognitive research alluded to in the title of this chapter appear as attempts toward an integration of classically independent models of development: structural versus functional and universal versus contextual.

REFERENCES

Ames, G. *When two wrongs make a right: Promoting cognitive change through social conflict.* Paper presented at the Southeastern Conference on Human Development, Alexandria, Va., 1980.

Bandura, A. *Social learning theory.* Englewood Cliffs, N.J.: Prentice-Hall, 1977.

Barenboim, C. Developmental changes in the interpersonal cognitive system from middle childhood to adolescence. *Child Development,* 1977, *48,* 1467–1474.

Barrett, D., & Yarrow, M. R. Prosocial behavior, social inferential ability, and assertiveness in children. *Child Development*, 1977, *48*, 475–481.

Bearison, D., & Cassel, T. Cognitive decentration and social codes: Communicative effectiveness and the coordination of perspectives in young children. *Developmental Psychology*, 1975, *11*, 29–36.

Bearison, D., & Gass, S. Hypothetical and practical reasoning: Children's persuasive appeals in different social contexts. *Child Development*, 1979, *50*, 901–903.

Berndt, T., & Berndt, E. Children's use of motives and intentionality in person perception and moral judgment. *Child Development*, 1975, *46*, 904–912.

Blotner, R., & Bearison, D. *Developmental consistencies in socio-moral knowledge: Relationships between justice reasoning and altruistic behavior.* Paper presented at the meetings of the American Psychological Association, Montreal, September 1980.

Botvin, G., & Murray, F. The efficacy of peer modeling and social conflict in the acquisition of conservation. *Child Development*, 1975, *46*, 796–799.

Brodzinsky, D. Cognitive style differences in children's spatial perspective taking. *Developmental Psychology*, 1980, *16*, 151–152.

Chandler, M. Egocentrism and anti-social behavior: The assessment and training of social perspective taking skills. *Developmental Psychology*, 1973, *9*, 326–332.

Chandler, M. Social cognition: A selective review of current research. In W. Overton & J. Gallagher (Eds.), *Knowledge and development*. New York: Plenum Press, 1977.

Chandler, M., Paget, K., & Koch, D. The child's demystification of psychological defense mechanisms: A structural and developmental analysis. *Developmental Psychology*, 1978, *14*, 197–205.

Cox, M. V. The other observer in a perspective task. *British Journal of Educational Psychology*, 1975, *45*, 83–85.

Cox, M. V. Perspective ability: The relative difficulty of the other observer's viewpoints. *Journal of Experimental Child Psychology*, 1977, *24*, 254–259.

Damon, W. Early conceptions of positive justice as related to the development of logical operations. *Child Development*, 1975, *46*, 301–312.

Damon, W. *The social world of the child.* San Francisco: Jossey-Bass, 1977.

Damon, W. Why study social-cognitive development? *Human Development*, 1979, *22*, 206–211.

Damon, W. The developmental study of children's social cognition. In J. Flavell & L. Ross (Eds.), *New directions in the study of social-cognitive development*. New York: Cambridge University Press, 1981.

Damon, W. The nature of social cognitive change in the developing child. In W. Overton & H. Reese (Eds.), *Knowledge and development* (Vol. 4). Hillsdale, N.J.: Erlbaum, in press.

Doise, W., & Mugny, G. Individual and collective conflicts of centrations in cognitive development. *European Journal of Social Psychology*, 1979, *9*, 105–108.

Doise, W., Mugny, G., & Perret-Clermont, A. Social interaction and the development of cognitive operations. *European Journal of Social Psychology*, 1975, *5*, 367–383.

Doise, W., Mugny, G., & Perret-Clermont, A. Social interaction and cognitive development: Further evidence. *European Journal of Social Psychology*, 1976, *6*, 245–247.

Eiser, C. Recognition and inference in the coordination of perspectives. *British Journal of Educational Psychology*, 1974, *44*, 309–312.

Feffer, M., & Gourevitch, V. Cognitive aspects of role taking in children. *Journal of Personality*, 1960, *28*, 383–396.

Fehr, L. A. Methodological inconsistencies in the measurement of spatial perspective taking ability: A cause for concern. *Human Development*, 1978, *21*, 302–315.

Gelman, R. Why we will continue to read Piaget. *The Genetic Epistemologist*, 1979, *8*, 1–3.

Glick, J. Cognition and social cognition: An introduction. In J. Glick & A. Clarke-Stewart (Eds.), *The development of social understanding*. New York: Gardner Press, 1978.

Hoffman, M. L. Perspectives on the difference between understanding people and understanding things. In J. Flavell & L. Ross (Eds.), *New directions in the study of social-cognitive development*. New York: Cambridge University Press, 1981.

Hollos, M. Logical operations and role-taking abilities in two cultures: Norway and Hungary. *Child Development*, 1975, *46*, 638–649.

Hollos, M., & Cowan, P. Social isolation and cognitive development: Logical operations and role-taking abilities in three Norwegian social settings. *Child Development*, 1973, *44*, 630–641.

Hudson, L. M. On the coherence of role-taking abilities: An alternative to correlational analyses. *Child Development*, 1978, *49*, 223–227.

Kuhn, D. Mechanisms of change in the development of cognitive structure. *Child Development*, 1972, *43*, 833–844.

Lempers, J. D., Flavell, E., & Flavell, J. The development in very young children of tacit knowledge concerning visual perception. *Genetic Psychology Monographs*, 1977, *95*, 3–53.

Lerner, R., Skinner, E., & Sorell, G. Methodological implications of contextual/dialectic theories of development. *Human Development*, 1980, *23*, 225–235.

Levine, L., & Hoffman, M. Empathy and cooperation in 4-year-olds. *Developmental Psychology*, 1975, *11*, 533–534.

Luria, A. R. *Cognitive development: Its cultural and social foundations*. Cambridge, Mass.: Harvard University Press, 1976.

Mead, G. H. *Mind, self and society*. Chicago: University of Chicago Press, 1934.

Miller, P., Kessel, F., & Flavell, J. Thinking about people thinking about people thinking about . . . : A study of social cognitive development. *Child Development*, 1970, *41*, 613–623.

Miller, S., & Brownell, C. Peers, persuasion and Piaget: Dyadic interaction between conservers and nonconservers. *Child Development*, 1975, *46*, 992–997.

Mugny, G., & Doise, W. Socio-cognitive conflict and structure of individual and collective performances. *European Journal of Social Psychology*, 1978, *8*, 181–192.

Murray, F. Acquisition of conservation through social interaction. *Developmental Psychology*, 1972, *6*, 1–6.

Murray, F., Ames, G., & Botvin, G. Acquisition of conservation through cognitive dissonance. *Journal of Educational Psychology*, 1977, *69*, 519–527.

Nigel, A., & Fishbein, H. Perception and conception in coordination of perspectives. *Developmental Psychology*, 1974, *10*, 858–866.

Perret-Clermont, A. Social interaction and cognitive development in children. *European monographs in social psychology* (Vol. 19). London: Academic Press, 1980.

Peterson, C., Danner, F., & Flavell, J. Developmental changes in children's responses to three indications of communication failure. *Child Development*, 1972, *43*, 1463–1468.

Piaget, J. *The psychology of intelligence*. Patterson, N.J.: Littlefield, Adams, 1963.

Piaget, J. Cognitive development in children: The Piaget papers. In R. Ripple & V. Rockcastle (Eds.), *Piaget rediscovered: A report of the conference on cognitive studies and curriculum development*. Ithaca, N.Y.: School of Education, Cornell University, 1964.

Piaget, J. *The moral judgment of the child*. Glencoe, Ill.: Free Press, 1965.

Piaget, J. La psychologie, les relations interdisciplinaires et le système des sciences. *Bulletin de Psychologie*, 1966, *254*, 242–254.

Piaget, J. *The language and thought of the child.* London: Routledge & Kegan Paul, 1967.

Piaget, J. Piaget's theory. In P. Mussen (Ed.), *Carmichael's manual of child psychology.* New York: Wiley, 1970.

Piaget, J., & Inhelder, B. *The child's conception of space.* London: Routledge & Kegan Paul, 1956.

Piche, G., Michlin, M., & Rubin, K. Relationships between fourth graders' performance on selected role taking tasks and referential communication accuracy tasks. *Child Development,* 1975, *46,* 965–969.

Rardin, D. R., & Moan, C. Peer interaction and cognitive development. *Child Development,* 1971, *42,* 1685–1699.

Riegel, K. The dialectics of human development. *American Psychologist,* 1976, *31,* 689–700.

Riegel, K. *Psychology mon amour: A countertext.* Boston: Houghton-Mifflin, 1978.

Rosenthal, T., & Zimmerman, B. Modeling by exemplification and instruction in training conversation. *Developmental Psychology,* 1972, *6,* 393–401.

Rosenthal, T., & Zimmerman, B. *Social learning and cognition.* New York: Academic Press, 1978.

Rothman, G. The influence of moral reasoning on behavioral choices. *Child Development,* 1976, *47,* 397–406.

Rubin, K. Egocentrism in childhood: A unitary construct. *Child Development,* 1973, *44,* 102–110.

Selman, R. Taking another's perspective: Role taking development in early childhood. *Child Development,* 1971, *42,* 1721–1734.

Shantz, C. U. The development of social cognition. In E. M. Hetherington (Ed.), *Review of child development research* (Vol. 5). Chicago: University of Chicago Press, 1975.

Shlecter, T. M. *Children's spatial coordination and the influences of environmental differentiation.* Paper presented at the meetings of the Society for Research in Child Development, New Orleans, 1977.

Silverman, I., & Geiringer, E. Dyadic interaction and conservation induction: A test of Piaget's equilibration model. *Child Development,* 1973, *44,* 815–820.

Silverman, I., & Stone, J. Modifying cognitive functioning through participation in a problem-solving group. *Journal of Educational Psychology,* 1972, *63,* 603–608.

Urberg, K., & Docherty, E. Development of role-taking skills in young children. *Developmental Psychology,* 1976, *12,* 198–203.

Vygotsky, L. S. *Thought and language.* Cambridge, Mass.: MIT Press, 1962.

Vygotsky, L. S. *Mind in society.* Cambridge, Mass.: Harvard University Press, 1978.

Zimmerman, B., & Lanaro, P. Acquiring and retaining conservation of length through modeling and reversibility cues. *Merrill–Palmer Quarterly,* 1974, *20,* 145–161.

Zimmerman, B., & Rosenthal, T. Concept attainment, transfer, and retention through observation and rule provision. *Journal of Experimental Child Psychology,* 1972, *14,* 139–150.

Zimmerman, B., & Rosenthal, T. Conceptual generalization and retention by young children: Age, modeling and feedback effects. *Journal of Genetic Psychology,* 1974, *125,* 233–245.

7

Social Cognition and Social Structure

MICHAEL J. CHANDLER

Introduction

This chapter is intended as a navigational aid to those interested in exploring the contemporary social cognition literature, and it attempts to plot certain currents and directional trends operating within this research area. While a fuller agenda would have included a more systematic mapping and cataloging of recent studies, reviews of this sort have recently become something of a glut upon the academic marketplace (Chandler, 1977; Chandler & Boyes, 1982; Hill & Palmquist, 1978; Shantz, 1975), and in this bearish atmosphere there seems little margin in issuing still another such stock report. Instead, what will hopefully prove to be more helpful to persons unfamiliar with this territory is to attempt to locate certain pressure patterns or gathering fronts within this shifting research atmosphere, and to chart areas of apparent turbulence which may signal something about the way the wind is blowing.

Any attempt such as this to identify present or future direction in the growth of social cognition research is dependent as its starting point upon an analysis of a brief history of this field. While in many research areas any such retrospective undertaking would necessarily carry the reader back to the earliest beginnings of psychology, the developmental history of social cognition research is relatively brutish and short, and requires no such farsightedness. As recently as a decade ago the term had almost no currency in the literature and appears to have been minted in the late 1960s by essentially the same group of investigators who currently employ it as regular coinage in their ongoing work. Related interests in how children go about cognizing their

MICHAEL J. CHANDLER. Department of Psychology, University of British Columbia, Vancouver, British Columbia, Canada.

social worlds has, of course, always existed, and pioneers such as Piaget (1926, 1932) were already contributing to our understanding of such matters as early as half a century ago. During this earlier period, however, there appears to have been no need felt to distinguish knowledge of social events from knowing more generally, and whether the object of one's knowledge was to be an impersonal event or another subject was generally regarded as a simple content consideration requiring no special theoretical adjustments—and certainly not the christening of a distinct research domain.

What Is Social about Social Cognition?

Over the last decade or so, however, a sentiment arose among rank-and-file workers in this area that more was at stake than the trivial substitution of one set of content considerations for another. According to advocates of this view, interpersonal events were seen to demand for their proper understanding, modes of thought which are different from those required for understanding the world of impersonal objects. While there has been less than universal agreement among representatives of this view as to precisely what is required to qualify a cognition as social, even a partial listing of such separationist claims would need to include the following assertions: (1) that social laws or norms are qualitatively different from physical laws (Habermas, 1971; Kohlberg, 1958; Toulmin, 1974; Turiel, 1966; Wright, 1971); (2) that psychological causality is distinct from physical causality (DeCharms & Shea, 1976); (3) that social, but not impersonal, knowledge can be gained reflexively (Youniss, 1975); and (4) that social events and social cognitions are both recursive in ways that physical events and impersonal cognitions are not (Barenboim, 1978; Miller, Kessel, & Flavell, 1970; Oppenheimer, 1977; Selman & Byrne, 1974). By all of these accounts, it is either stated or implied that social knowledge is qualitatively different from, and nonreducible to, nonsocial knowledge, and, as such, involves procedures and structures of knowing which have no counterpart in the world of impersonal cognition.

Such secessionist arguments in favor of the separate-but-equal status of social cognition have not, however, gone unchallenged. From the vantage of more traditional cognitive-developmental theory, the struggle on the part of some to establish the conceptual independence of social cognition as an autonomous realm of intellectual functioning has seemed an unnecessarily divisive and parochial assault upon the hoped for unity of science. From this perspective, such separatist arguments have seemed subversive, if not dangerously European. Where such immigrant notions have gained a foothold on the soil of mainstream North American psychology, they have commonly been discouraged from retaining their pluralistic ways and have been quickly sanitized and homogenized and added to the common melting pot of less alien quantitative, as opposed to qualitative, distinctions. According to this standard view, what is especially interesting about cognition tends to be both formal and content-free, and quick or exaggerated uniqueness claims concerning social or any other kind of cognition seem awkwardly particularistic and out of keeping with psychology's universalistic mission. The process by which one comes to know social events is best regarded, from this perspective, as essentially the same as the process of knowing anything else. Social cognition, by this measure, is little more than an unnecessarily muddled case of cognition more generally, best left to those practical-minded investigators willing to exchange an embarrassing loss of rigor for the dim prospect of social relevance.

While the independence of social cognition research from the parent domain of impersonal cognition is far from established, interest in such identity issues is not nearly so keen at present as it was in the past. Having seemingly argued their case to a draw, investigators interested in the development of children's understanding of the social world have proceeded to consolidate their identity by the familiar path of simply assuming an independence that could not be accomplished by negotiation, and by affirming their separate existence by their own substantive efforts. Having moved off the defensive, the social cognition literature has grown in recent years until it occupies more journal space than almost any area of developmental study. Here, then, as with most such bids for independence, the authenticity and separate identity of social cognition research appears to rest more upon its accomplishments than upon any persuasive argument for its uniqueness.

The Role of the Social Stimulus Environment

Despite its recent successes, not all of the expansion which has taken place in the social cognition literature appears to be at or near its own growth edge, and much that is written seems to involve methodologic debates on in-house controversies over fine-grained measurement issues. Without wishing to dismiss as unimportant the necessary management of such housekeeping details, much that seemed fresh and promising about this field at the beginning of the current growth spurt appears to have been misplaced in favor of increasingly shopworn concerns over matters of procedural elegance.

Despite such grounds for concern, there does, however, continue to be reason to be hopeful that this line of inquiry may still offer solutions to some of cognitive developmental psychology's oldest problems. Now that the dust has settled somewhat, what seems to be peculiarly unique about the study of social cognition is not that it focuses upon thoughts about people rather than things, but that social events as objects of such thought stubbornly refuse to surrender their separate identities simply because they are thought about. Historically, the principal shortfall of research and theory regarding the processes of impersonal cognition appears to be that it has sacrificed the stimulus environment to the constructivistic appetites of its subjects, and left them suspended in an objectless world of pure assimilation. Responsibility for this lack of evenhandedness is largely traceable to the relativistic posture into which most cognitive theorists feel they have been forced. In an earlier and simpler era, psychology sought a solution to its organizational problems by neatly subdividing its subject matter into nonoverlapping classes of objective stimuli and subjectively organized responses. After decades of cognitive research, however, psychologists have been forced to abandon their simple packaging principle, as repeated evidence has shown that persons choose and subjectively deform their own stimulus environments. Persons, according to this now standard view, actively impose different sorts of human order upon events capable of supporting an infinity of such alternative constructions. Whatever commonalities found to exist across such various constructive efforts are consequently presumed to reflect something of the nature of the human mind but nothing about the stimulus world. The environment, in this view, becomes an infinitely malleable grist for the mills of thought—fickle to the point of total untrustworthiness and, consequently, unsuitable as a variable for scientific study. This one-sided constructivism has had the effect of reducing knowable order to an exclusively human byproduct; and the study of cognition, to a monocular science of pure assimilation (Chandler, Siegal, & Boyes, 1980).

Thus, deserted by the object side of the subject–object interactions, cognitive developmentalists have been forced into a lopsided, subject-centered psychology where organization, when it is observed, must be assumed to be the consequence of persons rather than the object or task variables with which they interact. In the typical moral judgment study (e.g., Kohlberg, 1969; Kohlberg & Turiel, 1971), to take only a single example, a common set of moral dilemmas is typically administered to a range of subjects, who represent all potential levels of moral maturity. Different subjects are then shown to utilize these same story details as raw materials out of which they fashion diverse moral judgments, reflective of their own current levels of cognitive maturity. Because any and all levels of moral reasoning maturity can be indexed from responses to the same stimulus events, it is assumed that all of the variability worthy of comment is traceable to the subjects and not to the objects or events upon which they operate. Within such active organism–passive environment orientations (Payne, 1968), persons are viewed as radical constructivists (Von Glasersfeld, 1974) who are seen to so thoroughly assimilate external reality into existing cognitive structures that only the most limited attention to the stimulus environment, in its premasticated form, is required. Any value-laden episode, such as the now standard story of Heinz and his cancer-stricken wife, is thought to be equally legitimate grist for any moral-reasoning mill, and the only remaining matter thought to be of real psychological significance is the style or character of the reconstructive process to which such events are submitted.

The common effect of this and similarly conceived research strategies has been to enforce upon psychology a kind of inequitable double standard which excludes from systematic study the organized character of the targeted objects of knowledge and, in a less than evenhanded fashion, restricts research attention to the subject side of such subject–object interactions. By this lopsided standard, people are seen to be lost in a subjective world of their own making, cognitive psychology is transformed into a science of pure assimilation, and theoretical access to the study of compelling adaptational issues is cut off.

Social Cognition as a Subject by Subject-as-Object Transaction

While investigators concerned with social-cognitive development have commonly assumed the burden of the same relativistic dilemma which has plagued more traditional theories of impersonal cognition, there would appear to be no compelling justification for their doing so. On the contrary, the inherently recursive character of social cognition would appear to offer a readily made solution to this problem. The key to this solution lies in the fact that, at least within the interpersonal context which social-cognitive theories are intended to elucidate, the objects of knowledge are also simultaneously subjects. If persons in their role as research subjects can be legitimately held to think in organized ways which express the presence of underlying cognitive structures, then there would seem to be no easily defensible justification for forbidding them these same structures simply because they change hats or places and become the social objects of the cognition of others. In other words, as objects of other people's knowledge, it seems only fitting that persons should be understood to retain the same structured organization which they were said to have had when they were thinking rather than being thought about. At least, then, in this special "quarry is the hunter" case, both subjects and the intended objects of their knowledge, who happen to be subjects in their own right, need to be seen as varying along a common dimension or organized complexity, and any adequate description of the means by which such people know must also count as a fair description of that which they are attempting to be knowledgeable about. This fact does not, of course, excuse subjects from the necessity of construing their own experience, but it does require that social objects be understood to have a separate, premasticated existence which is independent of the ways in which they are understood. The consequence of this obligatory and more evenhanded "what is good for the goose is good for the gander" orientation is that it restores to social cognition research an independent means of indexing the object half of subject–object interactions, and rescues the study of social thought from the relativistic sink of unchecked assimilation. If, for example, an investigator were to ask subjects to observe and characterize some person or group of persons, it is almost certain that individuals at different stages in their own cognitive development would construe these same social situations differently. In the case where the proposed target of understanding is an organized social group or institution, some would see only a conglomerate of juxtaposed people, others would detect seriated sequences of power and status relations, and still others would recognize hierarchical, lattice-like structures more expressive of the group's own functional table of organization. Similarly, as objects of other people's knowledge, each of us presumably retains those same structures which we are said to have when we are thinking rather than being thought about. Reasonable and accurate knowledge about us as persons would, therefore, seem to necessarily require that the intellectual machinery brought to bear on the problem of us in some way be equal to the complexity of ourselves as targets. We would anticipate that persons less intricately structured than ourselves—young children, for example

—would fail to follow our more complexly reasoned thoughts and could be fairly said to have failed in their efforts to properly understand us. By this standard, we do not simply pose unspecifiable comprehension problems to one another but, at specific times and in quantifiable ways, represent preoperational or concrete operational, or formal operational puzzles to those who seek to understand us. The point is that any and all of these alternative constructions are possible and even predictable, depending upon the developmental age of the subjects involved. There is, in the case of any particular targeted social stimulus person or group, some specifiable structure which does, in fact, characterize its operation, and some attempted constructions of it are accurate and others are mistakes. Social objects, in other words, bear the structural stamp of their own developmental station, and they function in accordance with specifiable human rules which must be comprehended and mirrored in thought if one is to navigate them smoothly.

What all of this suggests is that, because of its inherently reflexive character, the study of social cognition requires a binocular splitting of research attention, with equal emphasis being given to both the structural characteristics of one's subjects and the structural features of the social events with which they are expected to come to terms. By proceeding simultaneously on both of these fronts, cognitive-developmental theory would be in a position to consider the full transactional consequences of studying organized individuals in interaction with an equally structured or organized social stimulus environment.

What is required to accomplish such a transactional analysis of subject–object interactions is some form of double-entry bookkeeping by means of which the changing complexities of children's cognitive abilities can be coordinated and cross-referenced with counterpart complexities in the objects of their understanding which are also subjects. While studies which have self-consciously adopted this kind of binocular focusing are in short supply, much of the existing social cognition literature can be conveniently reinterpreted within this framework. The highly fragmented research literature on social role taking, for example, can be seen to contribute and sum to a larger mosaic which, in the aggregate, follows the format of subject-by-object interactions being proposed (Chandler et al., 1980). Some of this literature (i.e., Lempers, Flavell, & Flavell, 1977; Masankay, McCluskey, McIntyre, Sims-Knight, Vaughn, & Flavell, 1974; Shantz & Gelman, 1973), primarily concerned with exploring the earliest reaches of role-taking competence, has tested the ability of children to appreciate that other individuals possess presymbolic knowledge of concrete events to which they have been exposed. Three- and 4-year-old children, with presumably no more than preoperational competencies, have regularly been shown to possess such figurative knowledge about the figurative knowledge of others. Other studies (see Chandler, 1977, for a review of this literature), concerned with documenting the abilities of somewhat older children to appreciate that others subjectively construe their own experiences, have amassed considerable evidence which suggests that symbolic representational skills are necessary cognitive prerequisites to the accurate recognition of such symbolic representational abilities in others. Still other investigators (Feffer, 1959; Feffer & Gourevitch, 1960; Selman, 1971; Selman & Byrne, 1974), intent upon identifying the cognitive prerequisites to reciprocal role-taking abilities (which involve knowing that others know that one knows), have demonstrated that only adolescents with formal operational competencies are able to successfully disembed such nested recursions. Considered as a group, these various studies accomplish what none of them has achieved singly; they establish that the developmental course of social role-taking competencies is a joint function of both the cognitive-developmental abilities of one's subjects and the structural complexities of the objects of their attempts at understanding, which are also subjects.

In the remainder of this chapter, an attempt is made to further illustrate this kind of joint focus upon both the subject and object poles of social cognition by referencing some recently published and unpublished research carried out by the writer and his colleagues which was undertaken from this proposed binocular perspective. The first two of these studies investigated the relationship between children's levels of cognitive-developmental competencies and their ability to decode and interpret various psychological defenses in others, chosen to represent conceptual transformations of different orders of structural complexity. The third study references a recently completed research effort in which the moral deliberation process was interpreted as a transaction between the structural characteristic of various moral dilemmas and the structural features of the cognitive machinery leveled against them.

Children's Understanding of Mechanisms of Psychological Defense

The purpose of the first of the two research efforts in this area (Chandler, Paget, & Koch, 1978) was to explore possible relationships between children's developing cognitive abilities and their successes and failures in interpreting various psychological defenses in others. In this study, several familiar mechanisms of defense were identified as representing instances of transformations upon more candid and straightforward expression of affect-laden subject–subject interactions. Denial and repression, in this formal descriptive model, were taken as representative of simple logical negations in which present affects were flatly obliterated out of psychological existence. Through transformations of this relatively primitive sort, unacceptable affects such as "I am angry at you" converted into more acceptable alternatives such as "I am *not* angry at you" or "*Not I* am angry at you." Other more formally intricate defenses, such as reaction formation and displacement, were interpreted as instances of somewhat more complex logical transformations in which unacceptable events are replaced by their logical opposites, or *reciprocals.* Through logical transformations of this sort, circumstances such as "I am angry at you" can be made to read "I am the opposite of angry at you" (reaction formation) or "I am angry at the opposite of you" (displacement). Finally, it was argued that unacceptable events of the "I am angry at you" variety would be viewed, not as a series of discrete and independently transformable events, but as bracketed joint propositional statements which would be negated as a unit. The negation of such joint propositions embed the separate features of both inverse and reciprocal operations and, as is the case with the defense of secondary projection, would transform the earlier statement into "You are angry at me."

The payoff from this formal job analysis of various psychological defenses lay in the fact that the hypothesized transformational tools of inversion, reciprocation, and the negation of joint propositions exactly duplicate the ordered sequence which Piaget has shown to occur in the development of various reversibilities of thought. According to this account (Piaget, 1970), the capacity to effectively unthink already completed thoughts—first through the application of simple inverse transformations and later through the use of reciprocal transformations—is a defining feature of the period of concrete operational thought, not yet available to children still functioning at the preoperational level. Formal operational reasoning, by contrast, was held by Piaget to consist of more propositional forms of logic, capable of achieving reversibility through the negation of whole bracketed statements about more concrete elements of thought. This apparent co-occurrence of common systems of transformations in the domain of both psychological defenses and cognitive operations made possible a series of specific predictions concerning the particular kinds of cognitive competencies which would be logically necessary to support an understanding of each of a series of defensive operations.

In order to test these interactional hypotheses, a group of 30 preoperational, concrete operational, and formal operational children were asked to interpret and explain stories formulated to portray each of eight different psychological defense mechanisms. The results of this study were seen to provide strong support for the general hypothesis that children's understanding of various psychological defenses is jointly dependent upon both their own levels of cognitive development and the structural complexities of the particular defenses they were asked to interpret. As anticipated, preoperational children, whose cognitive operations do not include the ability to process inverse or reciprocal transformations, were generally unable to decode any of the defenses. Instead, they appeared to take events at face value and settle for whatever misleading cover story was offered. Older, concrete operational children, by contrast, appeared aware that persons often go to rather elaborate lengths to obscure their true motives or feelings. Although less gullible than their preoperational counterparts, these concrete operational children nevertheless appeared to be limited in their ability to reconstruct events which have been obscured by defensive transformations. In general, such children were able to effectively decode defensive transformations which involve the outright negation (i.e., logical inverse) of unacceptable feelings, such as repression or denial. Defenses of intermediate logical complexity such as displacement and reaction formation, which hinge upon reciprocal transformations, also fell within the range of cognitive competence of some, but not all, of these concrete operational subjects. These same concrete operational subjects, however, remained unable to decode other more logically complex defenses such as projection and introjection, which hinge upon the transformations of joint propositional statements. Only formal operational children—whose available cognitive operations include the ability to deal with statements about statements, or second-order propositions—evidenced any success in decoding projective or introjective defenses, which require the simultaneous manipulation of two or more first-order propositions. In general, then, these results indicate a clear relationship between children's level of cognitive developmental maturity and their ability to fathom various mechanisms of psychological defense. What was communicated to and understood by these children proved, at every turn, to be a joint product of the structural complexities characteristic of their own cognitions and those of their present social stimulus environment.

Much of the potential relevance of this first study was seen to hinge on the possibility that these findings might provide a means for better understanding the course by which children sometimes do and sometimes do not re-create the psychopathology of their parents. Given the fact that the same defensive miscommunications had been shown to be either mystifying or comprehensible, depending upon the cognitive-developmental level of the child who witnessed them, it was postulated that the same explanatory framework might be used to account for the differential negative consequences of children's protracted exposure to various modes of parental defense, reported in the clinical literature. In order to explore this possibility, a second study was undertaken (Koch, Harder, Chandler, & Paget, 1979), in which the children studied were the offspring of psychiatrically ill parents. This research, which was carried out within the context of the University of Rochester Child and Family Project, involved the examination of 50 children between the ages of 4 and 10, drawn from families in which one parent had been hospitalized for a psychiatric disorder. The evidence available on these family groups included an index of the disturbed parent's primary mode of psychological defense, a test of the child's cognitive-operational level, and several measures of the child's level of social competence. Given these data and the transactional model described earlier, it was hypothesized that children whose parent employed a primary mode of defense too logically complex for them to understand would evidence a greater degree of social disturbance than children whose cognitive competencies would allow them to decipher the defensive transformations habitually used by their parent. The results of this second study again supported the theoretical assumptions which prompted it and indicated that children who, due to their relative cognitive immaturity, could not decode their parent's defensive strategies were rated by both their teachers and their peers as less socially and emotionally competent than children whose cognitive-operational competency placed them in a position to decipher their parent's defenses.

Cognitive Complexity and Moral Deliberation

The third of the research studies to be summarized concerned the general topic of moral deliberation (Chandler et al., 1980). Although quite different in its manifest content, this research effort followed the general plan of study urged in this chapter and illustrated in the work on psychological defenses just cited. As was suggested earlier, most previous studies of the moral judgment process have been carried out by investigators whose commitment to a lopsided, one-dimensional constructivism has led them to understand moral deliberation as a process, the outcome of which is determined exclusively by subject variables. Since, in this standard view, the component parts which make up the horns of various dilemmas are understood to be assimilated to each individual's current level of cognitive-operational competence, the free-standing environment is seen to lose its independent and objective character and revert to the status of another subject variable. According to this rationale, the dilemmas which set moral judgment processes in motion are routinely viewed as equivalent grist, equally suited for any cognitive mill. Views such as these—which focus attention almost exclusively upon the potentially distorting role of cognitive assimilation and fail to reinforce the independently organized social stimulus events to which persons must accommodate—fail, from the vantage point being presented here, to attach proper significance to the independently organized character of the moral dilemmas upon which moral judgments operate.

According to the alternative view adopted in the present study of moral deliberation, the exclusive emphasis which commonly has been placed upon subject variables, and the essential disregard for the particular character of the moral dilemmas which serve as stimulus materials, is seen as unwarranted. Instead, this research proceeded upon the converse assumption that the competing horns of moral dilemmas could be independently characterized as expressive of one or another of several structurally different levels of organization. This research had as its purpose the task of determining possible relationships between children's general levels of cognitive competence and the concrete outcome of their moral deliberation efforts, and it involved a direct test of the hypothesis that such morally relevant behavioral choices would be a predictable function of the interaction between cognitive complexity and the complexity of the independently structured moral dilemmas to be arbitrated. As was the case in the earlier study of children's understanding of psychological defense, this research began with a formal job analysis of the relevant stimulus environment—in this case the various sorts of prescriptive obligations which, when set in opposition to one another, form the competing horns of various sorts of moral dilemmas. Again, as in the previous study, the outcome of the empirical work undertaken rested heavily upon the reasonableness of this attempted characterization.

Drawing upon the work of authors such as Hare (1952) and Taylor (1961), it was argued that prescriptive obligations may be understood to vary considerably in the scope of their intended domain of application. At one end of this dimension are prescriptions such as "Open the door" or "Keep your mouth shut," which, whether issued to others or oneself, are intended as simple, one-shot *commands*, not meant to be generalized to all doors or to other occasions upon which "Open wide" or "Speak up" would be more appropriate. Commands of this sort are intended to apply to particular individuals, in specific situations, for specified periods of time, and are meant to have only the most minimal kind of generality. At the other extreme are obligations of a more unambiguously "moral" sort, involving prescriptions of unlimited generality, meant to apply to all comers, at all times, under all conceivable circumstances. Universal prescriptions of this golden-rule variety, referred to here as "meta-rules" or "principles," achieve their special status precisely because no hedge is placed against their unremitting generality. Intermediate between these extremes of particularistic commands and universal principles are concrete *rules* of real, but limited, generality, which are meant to apply to certain classes of situations but not others. While concrete rules of this sort are sometimes viewed as drawing their authority from still more general principles, this need not be the case, and their only necessary feature is that they prescribe to classes and relations between classes of events. As such, they are component features of interdependent systems of obligations, which bear upon one another in such a way that some rules may contradict or make logical impossibilities of others. Without attempting to prejudge the question of whether other intermediate distinctions might be drawn between such commands, rules, and principles, the present research proceeded upon the assumption that at least each of these brands of prescription refers to obligations of a different logical or semantical type (Tarski, 1956).

Commands, rules, and principles of the sort just outlined were understood as prospective candidates for outfitting, as component parts, the horns of various moral dilemmas. When set in opposition to one another, in all possible combinations, these three different brands of obligation generate an array of six structurally distinct dilemma types (i.e., one command vs. another, a command vs. a rule, a rule vs. a rule, a rule vs. a principle, a principle vs. a principle, a principle vs. a command). This typology, then, stood as the descriptive framework for characterizing the independent social stimulus environment of possible moral dilemma types with which subjects were asked to deal. A series of short, child-oriented story problems were written which pitted prescriptive obligations of each of these various sorts against one another and required that the subjects decide upon and justify which of these competing alternatives they would advocate.

While the descriptive framework just outlined provides a means of independently type casting various sorts of moral dilemmas, the number and kind of such dilemma types psychologically available to particular individuals are understood to vary as a function of their cognitive developmental level. According to this view, preoperational children, whose thoughts are understood to lack the systematic character required to appreciate either formal rules or universal principles, were expected to reduce all moral conflicts to contests between competing commands. Concrete operational children were assumed to possess the capacity to process both rules and commands, and they were consequently expected, by contrast, to accurately interpret contests between two rules or two commands, and to appreciate when a single command was pitted against a rule. When confronted with instances of conflicts between rules and principles, or between two principles, however, such concrete operational subjects were expected to fail to appreciate such higher-order principles and to reinterpret, and consequently misconstrue, them as simpler rules and regulations. Only children characterized by formal operational skills, by contrast, were assumed to be able to discriminate and accurately interpret all of these conflict types.

Given these separate accounts—detailing, on the one hand, an independent listing of possible moral dilemma types, and specifying, on the other, the kinds of transformations to be anticipated as these dilemmas are differently construed by children of various cognitive-developmental levels—one is forced into a kind of double-entry bookkeeping which attempts to keep separate track of the kinds of dilemmas actually being presented and the often seriously altered dilemmas to which one's subjects are responding. The result was an 18-cell matrix specifying how children at each of these levels of cognitive development might be expected to construe moral dilemmas of each of the six structured types presented.

On the strength of the rationale already outlined, it was possible to detail a testable model for anticipating the outcome of the moral deliberations of children at various levels of cognitive maturity as they attempt to arbitrate moral dilemmas of any one of the six different structural types identified. The model proposed a two-step process of deliberation. The first step involved the application of a transformational rule which specifies the manner in which moral dilemmas of various types are interpreted and differently construed by individuals representative of the three cognitive-developmental levels under study. This transformational rule states that individuals lack the cognitive means for adequately comprehending prescriptions justified by universality claims more general or abstract than themselves, and that persons will consequently construe and, therefore, reinterpret such obligations as representative of prescriptions of the same logical type as their own current level of operational competence. By this transformational rule, preoperational children will reinterpret and misconstrue all rules and principles as instances of concrete commands, and concrete operational children will reconstrue universal principles as instances of social rules. The second step in this proposed model of moral deliberation consisted of a single-decision rule which states that individuals of all cognitive-developmental levels will systematically prefer and advocate whichever of two alternative behavioral courses they judge to express the more universally prescriptive obligation (i.e., principles will be preferred to rules or commands; and rules, to commands for all who are in a position to make these distinctions). Conversely, the model specifies that whenever individuals of any given cognitive-developmental level construe both of two available morally relevant behavioral alternatives as being warranted at the same perceived level of prescriptive universality (i.e., as being obligations of the same logical type), their choices will cease to be a predictable function of their current level of cognitive development.

The implication of this proposed model is that, for all of the individuals under study, the various moral deliberation problems presented resolve into instances of one of two dilemma types. The first type consists of pairs of alternatives within which the subject in question is able to appreciate a level-distinction between the degree of universality which adheres to the two perspective alternatives presented. Dilemmas of the second type consist of those pairs of alternatives for which no such level-distinction is possible. The important point to appreciate is that membership in either of these categories is not an attribute of the subject alone or the moral dilemma alone, but rather a joint function of the interaction between relevant features of both the person in question and the situation which he/she is asked to arbitrate.

In order to test the validity of this proposed model, over 150 children were initially tested and a total of 60 children were selected, approximately one-third of whom were judged to primarily employ their preoperational, concrete operational, or formal operational modes of thought. These three groups of 20 subjects included approximately equal numbers of boys and girls, and were drawn from grades one to ten from both public and parochial schools in a middle-class urban area. Cognitive-development level was assessed via three Piagetian-derived measures of intellectual development (the Goldschmidt–Bentler

Conservation Assessment Kit Form C) and two measures of formal operational reasoning, adopted from the work of Diane Kuhn (Kuhn & Brannock, 1977; Kuhn & Ho, 1977). Following this screening process, subjects that could be clearly classified as to developmental level listened to six short tape-recorded stories meant to represent each of the six moral dilemma types previously discussed, each of which was accompanied by an illustrated line drawing. The subjects were asked, after each story, to decide how the central story figure should act, to justify the reasons for their choices, and to rate on a scale of 1 to 5 their level of confidence in these decisions. Responses were tape-recorded, and the order of story presentation was randomized.

The results of this study were analyzed by comparing the observed proportions of subjects choosing one or another of the "moral" alternatives provided with those outcomes hypothesized by the proposed transactional model. The data obtained, when reduced to statements concerning the proportion of subjects at each cognitive level who chose one rather than another of the pairs of six alternatives presented, consisted of a series of 18 different observed proportions. Each of these values was then compared with the proportion of subjects expected, on the basis of the proposed model, to elect each alternative. According to the rationale previously outlined, the expected proportion of subjects electing one or the other of paired alternatives posed by each moral dilemma should equal one of two values. In instances in which the individuals in question judged the available alternatives as being prescriptions of the same logical type, no structural grounds were assumed to be present for dictating a strong perference for one alternative over another, and the proportion of subjects electing either alternative should approach .5. When, by contrast, the competing alternatives were of different logical types and recognized as such by the subjects in question, then strong preferences were anticipated, and the expected value for the more universalizable of the two alternatives was anticipated to approach 1. As expected, the responses of these subjects neatly divided into one or the other of two categories. The first of these involved that subset of subject–situation transactions for which the structural complexity of the moral dilemmas presented equalled or exceeded the structural complexity of the inferential machinery leveled against them. As predicted, in these situations, where a kind of structural standoff was perceived to exist between the competing alternatives, no systematic preference was shown for one course of action over the other. The second response category included all of those transactions in which the subjects were expected to construe one of the available alternative courses as more universalizable or structurally adequate. Here, as predicted, subjects of all cognitive-developmental levels consistently chose as their preferred course that alternative which had the greater structural merit. Taken together, these results indicate that persons sometimes will and sometimes will not elect to pursue the loftier of two morally relevant alternatives. The edge which the proposed transactional model maintains over this otherwise commonsense conclusion is that it offers a way of establishing in advance precisely which of these outcomes will occur.

The overall conclusion of this study coincides with that of this chapter more generally. The outcomes of children's transactions with various aspects of their social environments seem best understood as the products of an interaction between their current level of cognitive organization and the independently, but comparably, structured character of social events.

REFERENCES

Barenboim, C. The development of recursive and nonrecursive thinking about persons. *Developmental Psychology*, 1978, *14* (4), 419–420.

Chandler, M. J. Social cognition: A selected review of current research. In W. Overton & J. Gallagher (Eds.), *Knowledge and development: Yearbook of developmental epistemology*. New York: Academic Press, 1977.

Chandler, M. J., & Boyes, M. C. Social-cognitive development. In B. Wollman (Ed.), *Handbook of developmental psychology*. Englewood Cliffs, N.J.: Prentice-Hall, 1982.

Chandler, M. J., Paget, K. F., & Koch, D. A. The child's demystification of psychological defense mechanisms: A structural and developmental analysis. *Developmental Psychology*, 1978, *14*(3), 197–205.

Chandler, M. J., Siegal, M., & Boyes, M. C. The development of moral behavior. Continuities and discontinuities. *International Journal of Behavioral Development*, 1980, *3*, 323–332.

DeCharms, R., & Shea, D. J. Beyond attribution theory: The human conception of motivation and causality. In L. Strickland, F. Abond, & K. Gergen (Eds.), *Social psychology in transition*. New York: Plenum Press, 1976.

Feffer, M. H. The cognitive implications of role-taking behavior. *Journal of Personality*, 1959, *27*, 152–168.

Feffer, M. H., & Gourevitch, V. Cognitive aspects of role-taking in children. *Journal of Personality*, 1960, *28*, 383–396.

Habermas, J. *Knowledge and human interests*. Boston: Beacon Press, 1971.

Hare, R. M. *The language of morals*. Oxford: Clarendon Press, 1952.

Hill, J. P., & Palmquist, W. J. Social cognitions and social relations in early adolescence. *International Journal of Behavioral Development*, 1978.

Koch, D., Harder, D., Chandler, M. J., & Paget, K. *Parental defense style and child competence: A match–mismatch hypothesis*. Paper presented at the biennial meeting of the Society for Research in Child Development, San Francisco, March 1979.

Kohlberg, L. *The development of modes of moral thinking and choice in the years ten to sixteen.* Unpublished doctoral dissertation, University of Chicago, 1958.

Kohlberg, L. Stage and sequence: The cognitive-development approach to socialization. In D. Goslin (Ed.), *Handbook of socialization theory and research.* New York: Rand-McNally, 1969.

Kohlberg, L., & Turiel, E. Moral development and moral education. In G. S. Lesser (Ed.), *Psychology and educational practice.* Glenview, Ill.: Scott Foresman, 1971.

Kuhn, D., & Brannock, J. Development of the isolation of variables scheme in an experimental and "natural experiment" context. *Developmental Psychology,* 1977, *13,* 9–14.

Kuhn, D., & Ho, V. The development of schemes for recognizing additive and alternative effects in a "natural experiment" context. *Developmental Psychology,* 1977, *13,* 515–516.

Lempers, J. D., Flavell, E. R., & Flavell, J. H. The development in very young children of tacit knowledge concerning visual perception. *Genetic Psychology Monographs,* 1977, *95,* 3–53.

Masankay, Z. S., McCluskey, K. A., McIntyre, C. W., Sims-Knight, J., Vaughn, B. E., & Flavell, J. H. The early development of inferences about the visual percepts of others. *Child Development,* 1974, *45,* 357–366.

Miller, P. H., Kessel, F. S., & Flavell, J. H. Thinking about people thinking about . . . : A study of social cognitive development. *Child Development,* 1970, *41,* 613–623.

Oppenheimer, L. *Recursive thinking and the development of social perspective-taking.* Paper presented at the workshop "Entwieklungspsychologie Sozialkognitiver Prozesse," Berlin, July 1977.

Payne, T. R. *S. L. Rubinstein and the philosophical foundations of Soviet psychology.* New York: Humanities Press, 1968.

Piaget, J. *The language and thought of the child.* New York: Harcourt, Brace, 1926.

Piaget, J. *The moral judgment of the child.* London: Routledge & Kegan Paul, 1932.

Piaget, J. Piaget's theory. In P. Mussen (Ed.), *Carmichael's manual of child psychology* (3rd ed., Vol. 1). New York: Wiley, 1970.

Selman, R. L. The relation of role-taking to the development of moral judgments in children. *Child Development,* 1971, *42,* 79–91.

Selman, R. L., & Byrne, D. F. A structural developmental analysis of levels of role-taking in middle childhood. *Child Development,* 1974, *45,* 803–806.

Shantz, C. The development of social cognition. In E. Hetherington (Ed.), *Review of child development research* (Vol. 5). Chicago: University of Chicago Press, 1975.

Shantz, M., & Gelman, R. The development of communication skills: Modifications in the speech of young children as a function of listener. *Monographs of the Society for Research in Child Development,* 1973, *38*(4, Serial No. 152), 1–37.

Tarski, A. *Logic, semantics, and metamathematics.* Oxford: Clarendon Press, 1956.

Taylor, W. T. *Normative discourse.* Englewood Cliffs, N.J.: Prentice-Hall, 1961.

Toulmin, S. Rules and their relevance for understanding human behavior. In T. Mischel (Ed.), *Understanding other persons.* Totowa, N.J.: Littlefield & Rowman, 1974.

Turiel, E. An experimental test of the sequentialty of developmental stages in the child's moral judgments. *Journal of Personality and Social Psychology,* 1966, *3,* 611–618.

Von Glasersfeld, E. *Assimilation and accommodation in the framework of Piaget's constructivist epistemology.* Paper presented at the Third Biennial Southeastern Conference of the Society for Research in Child Development, Chapel Hill, N.C., March 1974.

Wright, D. *The psychology of moral behavior.* Baltimore: Penguin Books, 1971.

Youniss, J. Another perspective on social cognition. In A. Pick (Ed.), *Minnesota Symposia on Child Psychology* (Vol. 9). Minneapolis: University of Minnesota Press, 1975.

8

Mapping the Social World of Adolescents: Issues, Techniques, and Problems

DALE A. BLYTH

Introduction

It has long been said that man is a social animal; that humans exist in a social world with its complex maze of actors and interaction situations. Generally, however, we do not think of the social world of an individual as changing in stages which are sequential, ordered, and universal, such as those proposed by Inhelder and Piaget (1958) for cognitive development, Kohlberg (1968) for moral development, or Selman and Byrne (1974) for social perspective taking. The individual's social world has always been seen as too complex to be easily categorized and too much in flux to be easily ordered into stages.

We are now, however, beginning to think of stages of the life cycle from infancy through old age and how each of these stages may have certain unique aspects as well as common threads. While these are stages which an individual passes through, they are also stages which are largely defined in social or relational terms. For example, we define a child as being in a dependent relationship to his/her parents and an adult as being in one of a series of particular relationships which we know as married, divorced, separated, widowed, or single, and which may also involve the additional relationship of parenting. Thus, as people move through different stages of the life cycle, they are taking on new sets of social relationships, which, at least in part, may serve to define particular stages in the life cycle.

DALE A. BLYTH. Department of Psychology, The Ohio State University, Columbus, Ohio.

Bronfenbrenner (1977) has introduced the notion of an ecological transition which he describes as "a change in role and setting as a function of the person's maturation or the events in the life cycle of others responsible for that person's care and development" (p. 526). The change which takes place as one makes the transition into a new role and/or a new setting may involve very definite changes in one's social world. The problem is one of trying to accurately capture these changes so they can be related to changes both in the environment and in the psychological development of the individual.

Even more formally developed stage theories (e.g., Piaget's theories of cognitive development) recognize the important relationship between the child's social world (i.e., interpersonal relations) and environment (i.e., physical and institutional surroundings). Unfortunately, these complex interrelationships have not been adequately conceptualized nor tested. This lack is due, in part, to the complexity of an individual's changing social world and the lack of a clear way to assess key aspects of that world.

Beginning with the assumption that a child's social relationships have differential meaning and salience as he/she develops, let us examine the social world of the child becoming an adolescent and discuss different ways to map or describe that world *as seen by the child*. We shall not elaborate on or conceptualize either the relationship between the environment and the individual's social world or the relationship between the individual's developing cognitive abilities and his/her social world. Rather, we shall focus on how to capture a meaningful picture of the adolescent's important social relationships and adequately describe characteristics of those relationships. Once such a procedure is developed, it may be used to explore how social relationships are affected by major transitions in the life cycle or alterations in structural features of the environment as well as how such relationships are associated with changes in an individual's cognitive development. (It should be emphasized that this concentration on the social world of the individual is done in order to permit a higher resolution of the details of that world and is not meant to minimize the reciprocal relationships between the individual's abilities to process information and his/her perception of that social world or the many structural features of his/her environment which shape that world.) In this chapter we first present a brief critique of other attempts at measuring an individual's social world, then delineate a set of issues which need to be addressed, and finally, explore some of the techniques which we are currently testing and some of the problems which still exist.

Delineation and Critique of Current Techniques

There are currently three broad classes of techniques which might be used to map different aspects of a person's social world. These broad classes are clearly interrelated and have developed historically from a common social-psychological theme. Nonetheless, each is analytically distinct and carries with it specific problems as well as special promise for different types of mapping. The three techniques can generally be referred to as classical sociometric techniques, social-network techniques, and techniques involving the identification of an individual's significant others. We briefly discuss each technique, how it is distinct from the others, and some of the particular problems associated with each.

Sociometric Techniques

Although the term "sociometry" has several meanings, we refer primarily to the classic work of Moreno (1934) and others in this tradition who use a sociometric test to examine the set of interpersonal relationships *in a defined population*. This type of study requires a clearly identifiable and finite group as well as a specific type of relationship or set of relationships between group members. Thus, in this technique it is necesssary to have a closed and reasonably small group of people and then have each of these people make a judgment about his/her relationship (on some specified criteria) with all other members of the group. This type of work has frequently been done with students in classrooms and other small groups.

One of the primary advantages of these techniques is that they permit the investigator to explore structural characteristics *of the group*, including second- and higher-order linkages between group members. For example, Hallinan (1979) studied the number and size of friendship cliques within different types of classrooms using a sociometric technique. However, because these techniques are devoted to completing the map for all people in the defined setting, less emphasis is placed on defining a single individual's *entire* map across settings. That is, although every individual's map *within that group* is complete, it is unlikely that any individual's total set of social relations occurs within the types of groups which can be readily studied. If we wish to study the social world of early adolescents, it is difficult to imagine how such a closed-group approach could incorporate both school and nonschool peers as well as parents and other significant adults. Yet, clearly these other individuals form an important part of the social world of most children and adolescents. This critique is particularly devastating if the substantive problem under investigation is one in which the importance of the defined group is minimal for the individual when compared to that of other groups and individuals. For such issues as educational or occupational aspirations, any given school-based group would leave out critical individuals influencing the development of a student's aspirations. Thus, the differential salience of the group and the relationship of that group to the specific topic under investigation are important factors to be weighed before utilizing this technique. To the extent that we are searching for a method of mapping and describing the social world of an adolescent in order to understand how that social world undergoes changes both developmentally and as a result of specific contextual transitions, the sociometric techniques generally used have only limited value.

Social-Network Technique

Another technique which has to some extent grown out of the sociometric approach noted in the preceding section is that of social-network analysis. Mitchell (1969) defines a social network as a "specific set of linkages among a defined set of persons, with the additional property that the characteristics of these linkages as a whole may be used to interpret the social behavior of the persons involved" (p. 2). It is not necessary for the members of the network to be individual people; the units could, in fact, be larger social units such as families, tribes, or corporations. Craven and Wellman (1974) make a distinction between a "whole-network" strategy and a "personal-network" strategy. Their reference to a whole-network strategy is identical to what was referred to earlier as a sociometric strategy. The personal-network strategy, on the other hand, is what we call a "social-network technique."

The personal-network strategy, or social-network technique, involves starting with a sample of individuals from a conceptually distinct population and then asking each individual to identify key types of relationships he/she has with any other individuals. The important point is that the entire population need not be involved, and that the relationships explored are selective from the point of view of ego and can include people from outside the sampled population. Furthermore, all those mentioned by ego are also interviewed. It is possible to take a given classroom and study it using both a sociometric technique and a social-network technique and come to somewhat different conclusions. The differences between the conclusions would result from the fact that most possible interrelationships between individuals within the classroom are explored in the sociometric technique, but only those interrelationships which exist among the sampled group or between the original sampled group and designated others would be delineated in a social-networks approach.

Another key distinction between the sociometric and social-network approaches is whether the individuals who are identifying their relationships with others are clearly specified beforehand (the sociometric technique) or can only be specified after the fact (as in the social-network technique). That is, in a social-network approach one must first go to the original sample and elicit the set of others that they consider themselves to be related to in the defined way and then go to each of these individuals in turn to elicit their set of relationships. This "snowballing" type of sampling is expensive and difficult to carry out. It also lacks a clear and distinct end point since it is theoretically possible for each new wave of respondents to identify another group of people. Most previous empirical work in this tradition has only followed up on those people first mentioned by the original sample.

One of the advantages of the social-network approach is that it does not *artificially* extend or cut off a person's social world by limiting it to a particular setting or group. This is a major improvement over typical sociometric approaches which must assume that all people in the setting are in the adolescent's social world and that no one else of importance exists.

There are two fundamental problems with a social-network approach for the type of social mapping that we are concerned with here. First, because of the expense involved, it is difficult to use a true social-network approach on a very large sample or to permit each member of that sample to identify a large number of others. To the extent that one must restrict the number of people an individual can mention, one will have considerable difficulty in drawing any conclusions about the size of an individual's social world or even significant subparts of that world. Furthermore, the cost of doing a social-network approach once is considerable, but to consider doing it longitudinally over a period of years is quite prohibitive on any large-scale basis.

The second major problem with the technique is that a considerable amount of energy is spent in exploring the relationships of the people mentioned by the original sample rather than in further understanding either the nature of their relationship to the original sample or other aspects of the original sample itself. To the extent that one goes beyond a single link to the individuals in the original sample, one has diverted a large amount of resources away from the individual's own immediate social world. This is not to argue that second and tertiary links are unimportant in influencing an individual and his/her development. Rather, we are simply arguing that if one is to understand an individual's social world it is of foremost importance to understand the immediate and direct contacts that the individual has. Whatever influence the second- or third-level contacts may have on the individual, they are not as important as the primary links. Moreover, such influences are probably filtered through the primary links.

Neither of these critiques are intended to discourage researchers from utilizing social-network-type analysis. Rather, they are simply an indication of the problems of a social-network approach when one is attempting to explore the immediate characteristics of a child or adolescent's social world. It is important to note that much of the work in the social-network tradition has been done with adults rather than children or adolescents.

Techniques for Eliciting Significant Others

The third technique which has been used to measure at least part of the social world of the individual is the Wisconsin Significant Other Battery (WiSOB), which was developed by Haller and Woelfel (1969, 1972). This technique was developed in order to better measure the influence of significant others on ego in a particular substantive domain. The WiSOB, for example, deals only with educational and occupational aspirations and roles. The technique involves selecting a sample from a population you wish to study and asking each person in the sample who his/her significant others are in the area or areas of concern. The technique distinguishes between two different types of significant others, those who act to define the role ego is to play and those who are models which illustrate the role by their example. The technique also distinguishes between the nature of the role itself (object) and the individual him/herself in that role. From the two distinctions four different types of influence emerge: definers for object, definers for self, models for object, and models for self. Thus, any given significant other may serve in one or more of these capacities for ego in a specific area. As the authors note, "the more of these modes of influence the other exercises, the greater is his proportional influence on the attitude, and the greater the significance as an other" (Haller & Woelfel, 1969, p. 398).

In order to help the individual think about the type of people who provide him/her with information in an object area, four different filter categories may be used in thinking about an object area such as education. These are: (1) the intrinsic nature of the object itself or what is essentially connected to it (e.g., attending classes is connected to education); (2) the extrinsic nature or the attributes of an object which are not essential to it (e.g., living in dorms); (3) intrinsic functions or the essential purpose of an object (e.g., learning); and (4) the extrinsic function, which refers to the ends an object may serve that are nonetheless not essential to it (e.g., gaining status) (Haller & Woelfel, 1969, pp. 398–399). By using these four different modes of influence and four different ways of thinking about the object area, researchers are able to help the person elicit as many significant others as possible. Obviously, the instrument developed to do all this was quite sizable.

Once a set of significant others has been elicited from an individual for a particular object area, questionnaires are sent to each of these significant others in order to further define the expectations these people hold for the individual. Haller and Woelfel describe these as "expectation elicitors." This approach is different from the social-networks approach noted earlier in that, although the questionnaires are sent to members of the primary individual's network, they are sent principally to obtain information about the others' relationships with or influence on ego and not to elicit the networks of these other individuals themselves.

The utility of this type of technique for drawing a map of an individual's world is twofold. First, the technique allows the individual to specify significant others from any area of his/her life and does not limit him/her only to people in certain groups. Second, the technique helps the individual to focus in on people who are particularly relevant in certain defined ways. This is important because it provides the individual with criteria for who should be defined as significant.

The major criticism of the technique is that it only elicits significant others for a limited domain of interest. While this is a strength if the domain of interest can be clearly specified and is limited in focus, it is a weakness if you are interested in a more general map of the individual's social world. In some ways, it is the equivalent of wanting to draw a map of Illinois and only including the Chicago metropolitan area. No matter how carefully drawn that map is, it is only part of the entire picture. One would presumably need to define multiple object areas and repeat the technique for each in order to get a more complete map of the individual's social world.

How can we develop a technique for eliciting a more general map of the important others in a person's life without losing information on the specific domains of influence or types of influence which such people exert? This issue is dealt with later in this chapter after we delineate several issues involved in trying to map the social world of an adolescent.

Issues in Social Mapping

Before attempting to map any territory, whether it be social or physical, it is necessary to make some decisions regarding several important issues. The issues have to do with key parameters which will define both the process used in mapping and the product of the mapping itself. There are four such issues which are addressed in this section. They are: What is the social world one is attempting to map? How does one define a social relationship? Who acts as the definer? How does one summarize or describe the individual's social map? Within each of these questions there are a number of subissues which are also delineated.

What Is the Social World One Is Attempting to Map?

Before one can begin mapping an unknown territory, it is important to define what one is looking for or the purpose of the mapping expedition. Since the social world of an individual consists of a very complex and interwoven set of relationships, it is particularly important that one give considerable thought to why they are trying to map this world.

In social mapping there are basically three strategies which might be used to define the social world one is going to map. The first approach is to attempt to map every relationship which meets a certain level of significance *or* is of a certain type. This is a global strategy since it attempts to include every possible important relationship in the individual's social world irrespective of how that relationship is utilized or focused on a particular object area. When such a strategy is used, it is particularly important to watch how one defines a social relationship since this is the only guideline which will be able to delimit exactly who is to be included in the map.

A second strategy is similar to that used by the Wisconsin Significant Other Battery, in which a specific domain or object area is specified at the outset. In this type of mapping, one is trying to explain a particular feature of the way the social world operates to exert influence on or direct the behavior of the individual whose map is being drawn. Thus, the more specifically the investigator is able to focus on the type of influence or expectations which he/she is interested in, the more useful this type of strategy becomes. For Haller and Woelfel (1969), their exclusive interest in educational and occupational aspirations allowed them to define a specific area of the social world they were interested in mapping. It should be noted that one of the costs of using a specific style of mapping is that you may miss significant others who can nonetheless influence that area. For example, while the Wisconsin approach attempts to elicit both role definers and role models, it may be leaving out a significant group of others who act as role interpreters: individuals who are not specifically defining what an individual ought to do, but who instead serve to interpret or discuss the information obtained from various individuals (e.g., a counselor may help an individual collate and evaluate information on college preferences). Furthermore, the use of a specific approach does not permit one to explore the degree of overlap in an individual's social world as one crosses different specific areas. We would argue that the extent to which there is overlap in specific social worlds is an important issue which needs to be empirically explored (see Verbrugge, 1979, for an illustration using adults). Once again, using the example of the Wisconsin Significant Other Battery, the issue of how much overlap there is between the set of people mentioned with regard to educational and vocational aspirations and those mentioned with regard to family aspirations should not go unexplored. Furthermore, it does not seem unreasonable to postulate that those people in an individual's social world who serve in multiple domains are likely to be more influential than are those who serve in only one or two isolated domains. Even this hypothesis, however, may well depend on the type of influence one is studying and the specific domains under investigation.

A third approach (which has some of the advantages of the global approach and yet deals with some of the problems of the specific approach) is to, in fact, elicit members of the social world for several specific domains. Thus, one could map the social world of an individual in different domains and then compare the overlap between areas. This strategy would be more repetitive in some ways than the global approach previously noted but would have the advantage of increasing the quality of maps which are created for each specific area. An alternative way of doing this is to use a global procedure to elicit others and then proceed to ask the specific types of domains in which each of the people elicited are important. This approach might provide a richer overall map of the social world but is not as likely to provide the high resolution desirable if only two or three specific areas are under investigation.

As is indicated later, the major attempts we have made so far at social mapping are ones which involve both the first and the third of these techniques. It is important to recognize that this issue, as well as each of the issues to follow, does not have a clear answer irrespective of the substantive interests of the investigator. Rather, how one defines the social world one is attempting to map is directly and intimately related to what one hopes to accomplish with the mapping procedure. The sooner such an issue is raised in an investigation, the greater the payoff in terms of the quality of information obtained.

How Does One Define a Social Relationship?

Once you have decided on an overall strategy to use in terms of defining the social world you are interested in, it becomes necessary to define the particular types of relationships that you are going to look for in that world. That is, how will one know whether or not a given relationship is one which should be placed on the map or left off? Furthermore, how will one illustrate or indicate the relationship on the social map? In this regard there are basically four issues which need to be addressed. First, what is the level of significance or degree of intimacy which you are interested in? Second, what type or types of significant relationships are you interested in? Third, is the relationship a single-strand or multiple-strand relationship? And, finally, is the relationship unilateral or reciprocal? We shall look at each of these issues separately.

In trying to define the *level of significance* or the degree of intimacy one is interested in mapping, it is important to realize that this level of significance can occur on any of several different planes. Each of these planes corresponds to the potentially different types of relationships that are explored later. But in addition to these different planes, there is the issue of how important the relationship is to the individual whose map is being drawn. For example, one could attempt to map an individual's world of close friends, or one could attempt to map that same individual's world of acquaintances. These represent different levels of significance or degrees of intimacy to the individual. Both, however, are equally valid, depending on the purpose of the map. One of the things to keep in mind in this regard is to try to elicit individuals who have some degree of intimacy and then attempt to actually access the degree of intimacy which exists in the relationship via other questions. That is, one should probably try to include as many people as possible in the social world of the individual and then *separately* explore exactly how close each relationship is. This is discussed later when we make the distinction between eliciting individuals and describing the characteristics of these individuals once they have been elicited.

Defining the *type of relationship* one is interested in is particularly important since the basis of the relationship is ultimately the basis of the entire social map. There are probably an unlimited number of different types of relationships which one could map. For example, the Wisconsin Significant Other Battery attempts to map two different types of relationships: those where the individual acts as a definer of a particular area and those where the individual acts as a model of that particular area. One might also want to map such things as the people that ego spends time with or does things with, people that ego goes to for advice, or simply people ego likes. Once again, which of these types one will want to use in forming the basis for the social map is a key decision which needs to be made in association with the purpose of the mapping process. It is, of course, possible to use several types of relationships within a single mapping procedure. If this is done, one needs to decide whether one is attempting to elicit a map of social relationships which meet *all* of the different types of relationships or one which elicits people who meet *any one* of the criteria for a relationship. The "and/or" quality of the map is quite important. In many ways it is similar to the next question on single versus multiple bases for a relationship.

Although a relationship between two individuals can be elicited in any number of different ways, it may also be important to establish whether or not there is only a single basis for the relationship or multiple bases for the relationship. That is, for example, if one is attempting to draw a social map of people ego spends time with or does things with, it may be necessary to also determine whether any of those individuals have other relationships with ego. Perhaps some of the people ego spends time with are also the people ego goes to for advice. Craven and Wellman (1974) refer to this as "single- versus multiple-strand" relationships. An obvious point, but one which nonetheless needs to be made, is that to the extent you have *elicited* people on the basis of only one type of relationship, it is not possible to draw conclusions about the social world of that individual with regard to other types of relationships. Thus, although you can talk about the number of people an individual spends time with who are also people he/she goes to for advice, it is not possible to describe all the people ego goes to for advice unless that is one of the ways in which others are elicited. A nested approach for questions simply does not have the same analytic capabilities as an independent approach. Hence, once again, the more clearly one can specify the form of the analysis one wishes to do, the more carefully one can plan how to draw the social map.

The final question which needs to be addressed in order to deal with the issue of how to define a social relationship is whether or not a relationship exists if perceived only by ego. That is, *is the relationship unilateral or reciprocal?* The importance of this question lies in whether or not one is going to seek verification or clarification of ego's map from the others he/she mentions. Such verification can take the form of either further definition of the basis of the relationship between ego and the other or actually asking the other about his/her own social world and seeing if ego appears in it.

Obviously, the more double checking one makes in such situations, the more empirically valid the map is in terms of demonstrated observ-ability, but this does not necessarily improve the quality of the map *if* one is looking for a map of the social world *as ego sees it*. This can perhaps best be illustrated by the well-known comic map of the United States as seen by a New Yorker. Such a map is quite distorted in shape and shows half the distance across the country as being within New York City, another fourth as extending to the Mississippi River, and the last fourth as including the entire Midwest and West. Obviously, this map has no verification in physical reality, but, nonetheless, it may bear an important resemblance to the way that an individual actually views the United States. Perhaps more importantly, a person's perception of his/her social world may have more bearing on the way in which he/she acts than would a map that has been checked by a neutral observer. This question is further commented upon in the next section with respect to who acts as the definer of a social relationship. The point to be made here is that the additional benefits of some social-network techniques may not be justifiable in terms of the original reason for doing the mapping.

Who Acts as the Definer?

To some extent this is a rhetorical question since we have already indicated that we are interested in the individual's social world. Hence, ego is the primary person we draw upon to define the set of social relationships we are interested in. There are, however, potentially three sources for defining relationships to be mapped in a social world. The first is ego him/herself, the second is some neutral observer who follows ego around, and the third is some combination of ego and the other people he/she mentions as being a part of his/her social world. The type of information you can get from each of these sources is quite different and will have quite different consequences for the type of map which results.

If, for example, we were to use only a neutral observer to attempt to map the social world of an adolescent, we would very quickly find that we have basically a count of the people whom ego interacts with, the amount of time spent with each person, and some description of the content of the interaction. The map would, however, be devoid of any qualitative interpretation of how ego defined that encounter or the relationship. This strategy was employed by Dunphy (1963) in his study of adolescent peer group structure. To the extent that the question under investigation requires ego's interpretation of his/her social relationships with others, it is important to incorporate ego's perspective into the mapping procedure. This is also true if one is attempting to establish multiple bases for a relationship between ego and someone. While an observer may see ego interacting with a certain set of individuals, he/she may not know the historical development of that relationship nor the multiple strands of that relationship through other settings. This is particularly true if the number of settings in which ego can be observed is limited. Hallinan and Tuma (1978), for example, looked at students *within* different classrooms but did not look at other settings which may have been relevant over time (such as walking to and from school) or even specific subsettings such as reading groups within the classroom.

If one decides to use a snowball technique in which ego lists the people in his/her social world and then each of these individuals is interviewed in order to follow up on the validity of ego's list, one has a different set of problems and advantages. The main problem is, of course, cost. The major advantages of this technique are that you can begin to study the structure of the groups within which ego exists and you can learn more about the reciprocal or nonreciprocal nature of the relationships. It is possible, for example, to see how accurately ego perceives his/her own social world on certain criteria. Once again, however, if one is interested in the accuracy of perception, one must deal with aspects of the world that are, in fact, verifiable. The point to be made here is that even without the opinion of other individuals within ego's social world, the map created by ego is useful. We are not disputing the potential advantages and additional capabilities of a map of someone's social world drawn from information gained from multiple sources, but rather wish to assert that there is great utility in a map drawn simply by ego. The issue to be dealt with is really one of how to stay within the restrictions that this type of perspective necessitates and how to empirically explore different factors which may affect the quality of the social map ego is able to draw. Obviously ego's cognitive ability would be one such significant factor. More is said on this in the last seciton of this chapter.

How Does One Summarize or Describe Individuals' Maps?

The final issue deals with what one does with the map once it has been created. We do not frequently think of taking a set of maps and comparing them to see how they are similar or different. Furthermore, it is not as if we are having 500 people each draw a map of a given territory. Rather, it is as if we were having 500 people drawing maps of 500 different territories. How one attempts to characterize or describe certain qualities of each of those maps so that they can be compared across individuals is a difficult issue. In dealing with this issue, there are four analytical possibilities which are discussed here. These are: (1) describing characteristics of the set of individuals mentioned, (2) describing characteristics of the set of relationships mentioned, (3) describing characteristics of the set of individuals within a given class of relationships, and (4) describing the characteristics of the set of relationships within a given type of individuals. The complexity of the analysis will grow or shrink depending upon the techniques used to elicit the members of the social world, the nature of the questions dealing with the relationships, and the variety of questions asked about characteristics of the other individuals.

DESCRIBING THE OTHERS' CHARACTERISTICS

In attempting to describe the characteristics of the set of significant others which have been elicited from ego, there are two basic strategies. The first of these is simply to count the number of individuals mentioned with different specific characteristics. This number then refers to the size of the social world with respect to that characteristic. For example, one could count the number of males and the number of females or the number of same-sex and the number of opposite-sex individuals in ego's social world. Each of these is an absolute number of points on ego's map.

In addition to counting the number of people with a given characteristic, one can calculate the percentage of individuals in ego's social world who have any given characteristic. These percentages are, of course, somewhat unstable due to the varying size of the networks and can fluctuate significantly for those people with small numbers of others. The major advantage of using percentages is that one can more readily compare the composition of the social world of different individuals.

Another way of looking at the set of others is to place them into different categories of a typology. Such a typology might deal with a variety of different characteristics simultaneously or with basically one characteristic at a time. For example, one could argue that an individual's social world is predominantly peer oriented or predominantly parent oriented in terms of the number of individuals of each type ego mentioned. A more complicated example would be to argue that an individual's social world consists primarily of nuclear family members and is further characterized by the absence of opposite-sex peers and the presence of a large number of same-sex peers. The number of possible typologies, of course, is endless, or at least only dependent upon the investigator's imagination and the number of variables measured.

An example of such a typology for seventh-grade males in a study we are currently analyzing is presented here. First, we have classified each significant other mentioned on the basis of his/her sex (the same as ego's or the opposite of ego's), age (young people, under 20; vs. adults, over 20), and family membership (nuclear, extended, or not related). Once each person mentioned by ego is classified on all three dimensions, it is possible to create a matrix which displays ego's set of others in terms of the typology. Table 8-1 contains examples of such matrices for two different individuals.

By averaging across egos for each cell of the matrix (either in terms of numbers or percentages), it is also possible to create a general picture of how significant others are distributed across the typology for, say, seventh-grade males (Table 8-2).

In looking at the results, a number of interesting features should be noted. First, almost two-thirds of the others listed by seventh-grade males were of the same sex as ego (64.3%). Second, on the average, seventh-grade males listed 14.26 others and these were almost evenly split between young people (7.55) and adults (6.72). Third, most of the young people listed (particularly those of the same sex) were not related to ego (5.07 out of 7.55), while most of the adults listed were related to ego (5.65 out of 6.72). Finally, nonrelated young people of the same sex, on the average, made up 28.5% of the list.

While there are a number of other interesting ways of looking at these data or comparing them to data for other groups such as seventh-grade females, this is beyond the scope of this chapter. The material presented here is primarily intended to illustrate the different ways of summarizing ego's social world. One comment concerning variance is needed. As can be seen in Table 8-2, the standard deviations for both the mean number and mean percentage are quite large. This suggests that the distributions are not normal and, hence, that the means may be affected by outliers. Care is needed when comparing this information across groups.

DESCRIBING EGO'S RELATIONSHIPS

In much the same way that one can describe the characteristics of the particular others in a person's social world, it is also possible to describe the relationships ego has with those others. Thus, while each member of the social world of an individual has characteristics which are inexplicably attached to him/her, there are also different aspects of the relationship between ego and that individual which can be measured. Thus, it would be possible to describe the social world of a person in terms of how many close friends he/she had, how many people he/she went to for advice, or how many people he/she wanted to be

TABLE 8-1. *Map of the Social Worlds of Two Seventh-Grade Males*

	Same sex		Opposite sex		Totals	
	Number listed	Percent of total listed	Number listed	Percent of total listed	Number listed	Percent of total listed
Person A						
Young people						
Nuclear family	2	18	1	9	3	27
Extended family	0	0	0	0	0	0
Nonrelated	4	36	0	0	4	36
Totals	6	54	1	9	7	64
Adults						
Nuclear family	0	0	1	9	1	9
Extended family	2	18	1	9	3	27
Nonrelated	0	0	0	0	0	0
Totals	2	18	2	18	4	36
Totals						
Nuclear family	2	18	2	18	4	36
Extended family	2	18	1	9	3	27
Nonrelated	4	36	0	0	4	36
Grand totals	8	73	3	27	11	100
Person B						
Young people						
Nuclear family	1	4	1	4	2	8
Extended family	0	0	0	0	0	0
Nonrelated	8	32	2	8	10	40
Totals	9	36	3	12	12	48
Adults						
Nuclear family	1	4	1	4	2	8
Extended family	0	0	0	0	0	0
Nonrelated	5	20	6	24	11	44
Totals	6	24	7	28	13	52
Totals						
Nuclear family	2	8	2	8	4	16
Extended family	0	0	0	0	0	0
Nonrelated	13	52	8	32	21	84
Grand totals	15	60	10	40	25	100

TABLE 8-2. *Mean Number and Mean Percentage of All People Listed by Seventh-Grade Males*[a]

	Same sex		Opposite sex		Totals	
	Mean number listed (SD)	Mean percent of total listed (SD)	Mean number listed (SD)	Mean percent of total listed (SD)	Mean number listed (SD)	Mean percent of total listed (SD)
Young people						
Nuclear family	.73	5.6	.71	5.5	1.44	11.1
	(.8)	(7.0)	(.8)	(6.9)	(1.1)	(9.1)
Extended family	.73	4.7	.32	1.9	1.04	6.7
	(1.2)	(8.0)	(.8)	(4.5)	(1.6)	(10.0)
Nonrelated	4.13	28.5	.94	6.2	5.07	34.7
	(2.8)	(15.3)	(1.4)	(8.4)	(3.4)	(17.8)
Totals	5.59	38.9	1.97	13.6	7.55	52.5
	(3.1)	(15.7)	(1.7)	(10.3)	(3.8)	(16.6)
Adults						
Nuclear family	1.08	9.2	1.08	9.2	2.16	18.4
	(.5)	(6.6)	(.5)	(6.4)	(.8)	(11.9)
Extended family	1.25	8.4	1.24	8.5	2.49	16.9
	(1.3)	(8.4)	(1.3)	(8.4)	(2.3)	(14.3)
Nonrelated	1.29	7.8	.77	4.5	2.06	12.3
	(1.6)	(8.7)	(1.2)	(6.6)	(2.4)	(12.4)
Totals	3.62	25.4	3.09	22.1	6.72	47.5
	(2.2)	(10.8)	(1.8)	(10.5)	(3.5)	(16.6)
Totals						
Nuclear family	1.81	14.8	1.79	14.6	3.60	29.4
	(1.0)	(10.2)	(1.0)	(9.4)	(1.4)	(15.4)
Extended family	1.97	13.1	1.56	10.4	3.53	23.6
	(2.0)	(12.2)	(1.6)	(10.0)	(3.2)	(18.6)
Nonrelated	5.42	36.3	1.72	10.7	7.14	47.0
	(3.7)	(17.1)	(2.0)	(10.7)	(5.0)	(20.4)
Grand totals	9.20	64.3	5.06	35.7	14.26	100.0

[a]Results presented are from 186 seventh-grade males.

like. Once again, this could be done in absolute numbers or percentages. The important thing to note here is that you are describing ego's relationships, not simply the type of people with whom ego interacts.

An example of describing ego's social world in terms of one type of relationship is found in Table 8-3. For seventh-grade males, on the average, 20.7% of all of the important others they listed were gone to for advice "a lot." Fully one-third of the important others were not sought

TABLE 8-3. *Mean Number and Mean Percentage of People from Whom Seventh-Grade Males Seek Advice, by Degree*[a]

	Mean number listed (SD)	Mean percent of total listed (SD)
Ego seeks advice . . .		
a lot	2.70	20.7
	(2.7)	(18.7)
some	6.35	46.3
	(4.3)	(22.1)
not at all	4.53	33.9
	(4.0)	(24.9)
Totals	13.58	100.0
	(6.1)	

[a]Although 186 seventh-grade males were surveyed, some "others" are included who did not answer the question on seeking advice. Therefore, the mean in this table is less than the mean in Table 8-2.

out for advice at all. While these results might differ depending on the technique used to elicit the others, they help inform us of key aspects of ego's social world.

If the investigation also involved contacting some of the other members of an individual's social world, a whole new set of variables can be created dealing with the interconnectedness of the members of the social world as well as the size of the social world through second- and third-order links. Much of the literature on social networks would then be relevant in terms of such concepts as density, interconnectedness, and quasigroups.

DESCRIBING COMBINATIONS OF OTHERS' CHARACTERISTICS
AND THEIR RELATIONSHIPS TO EGO

The third and fourth ways of characterizing the social world of the adolescent are based on whether one places priority on characteristics of the individual or on the characteristics of the relationship being investigated. That is, does one create a subgroup of members in the social world based on the characteristics they have (such as age) and then examine the different types of relationships which exist in that subset, or does one select only those individuals in ego's social world who have a certain relationship with ego and describe the characteristics of those people. In either case, the methods of analyzing the data are really quite similar. The analytical difference between the two can be clearly seen in the following example.

Suppose an investigator is interested in the usual question of parent and peer influence with regard to advice giving. If the investigator were interested in the composition of ego's advice-giving social world, he/she would select out those members of the social world who give advice and then count how many of these individuals are adults in the family and how many are peers. An example of this type of analysis is presented in Table 8-4. Here we see that nonrelated young people of the same sex and nuclear family adults (parents) of either sex are the type of people most often sought out for advice based on the mean number of people of these types listed. A total of 71.1% of the people that seventh-grade males sought out for advice were of these three types.

On the other hand, if one is interested in how often a person seeks advice from other young people, it is more useful to first delineate the social world of the individual which is made up only of young people and then look at how often ego goes to them for advice (see Table 8-5). The results for seventh-grade males indicate that, on the average, only 16% of the young people who ego said were important were actually sought out for advice "a lot." Another 48% were sought out "some" of the time. Obviously, these are different substantive questions, and it is the nature of the question which should dictate the form of the analysis.

SUMMARY

Although there are numerous ways to describe the social world once it has been mapped, we have tried to illustrate three analytically distinct approaches which we have found useful. These approaches involve using the characteristics of the others mentioned, the nature of the relationship between ego and the other, or some combination of both. In doing this type of analysis there are a number of statistical problems which need to be dealt with. For the sake of clarity, we have not dwelled on these problems, but the would-be analyst of such data should be forewarned.

With this understanding of what is meant by social mapping and how one might begin to describe the results of such a procedure, let us now turn to a discussion of alternate techniques which might be used to collect information for such maps.

TABLE 8-4. *Mean Number and Mean Percentage of People from Whom Seventh-Grade Males Seek Advice "a Lot"*[a]

	Same sex		Opposite sex		Totals	
	Mean number (SD)	Mean percentage (SD)	Mean number (SD)	Mean percentage (SD)	Mean number (SD)	Mean percentage (SD)
Young people						
Nuclear family	.09 (.3)	3.1 (12.9)	.08 (.3)	2.2 (7.6)	.16 (.41)	5.3 (15.1)
Extended family	.06 (.3)	1.6 (6.8)	.02 (.2)	0.9 (6.9)	.09 (.4)	2.4 (11.0)
Nonrelated	.58 (1.2)	16.8 (27.3)	.15 (.5)	4.1 (13.2)	.73 (1.4)	20.9 (30.4)
Totals	.73 (1.4)	21.4 (29.8)	.25 (.6)	7.2 (16.7)	.98 (1.6)	28.6 (34.5)
Adults						
Nuclear family	.50 (.5)	23.5 (26.2)	.58 (.5)	30.8 (31.6)	1.08 (.9)	54.3 (39.4)
Extended family	.17 (.5)	5.2 (15.5)	.14 (.4)	4.0 (12.1)	.31 (.7)	9.2 (19.8)
Nonrelated	.22 (.6)	5.4 (13.7)	.12 (.4)	2.5 (7.6)	.33 (.8)	7.9 (17.0)
Totals	.89 (2.0)	34.2 (29.0)	.84 (.9)	37.2 (31.4)	1.72 (2.7)	71.4 (34.5)
Totals						
Nuclear family	.59 (.6)	26.6 (28.0)	.65 (.6)	33.0 (31.6)	1.24 (1.0)	59.6 (38.0)
Extended family	.23 (.6)	6.8 (17.0)	.17 (.5)	4.8 (13.6)	.40 (.9)	11.6 (22.6)
Nonrelated	.79 (1.5)	22.2 (29.9)	.27 (.7)	6.5 (16.0)	1.06 (1.8)	28.7 (34.2)
Grand totals	1.61 (1.0)	55.7 (30.8)	1.09 (1.16)	44.3 (30.8)	2.70 (1.7)	100.0

[a]Of the 186 seventh-grade males studied, 25 reported that there was no one from whom they sought advice "a lot." These egos are excluded from the percentages.

Social-Mapping Techniques

In mapping an individual's social world, the investigator has control of basically two factors in designing the instruments. The first of these is how to elicit the list of people who are in the social world of ego. The second is the kind of information that is gathered for each important other. Although there are a variety of ways of eliciting the names of

TABLE 8-5. *Mean Number and Mean Percentage of Nonrelated, Same-Sex, Young People from Whom Seventh-Grade Males Seek Advice, by Degree*[a]

	Mean number (SD)	Mean percentage (SD)
Ego seeks advice . . .		
a lot	.58	16.1
	(1.21)	(27.8)
some	1.84	47.6
	(2.06)	(36.1)
not at all	1.36	36.3
	(1.78)	(36.6)
Totals	3.78	100.0
	(2.76)	

[a]Of the 186 seventh-grade males studied, 25 reported that there was no one from whom they sought advice "a lot." These egos are excluded from the percentages.

people (just as there were in the sociometric and social-network techniques), only two basic types are discussed here. There are also an almost endless number of different types of questions one could ask about each person that is mentioned by ego. We shall focus attention only on some analytically different types of questions which might be asked.

Eliciting Significant Others

There are two broad classes of methods for eliciting significant others. One approach stresses the need to get only the "relevant people" listed as members of the social world. This approach attempts to define very specifically the types of people that the investigator is interested in and then asks a limited number of questions about those individuals. In what is referred to here as the "global approach," a list of as many people as possible who are important to ego is generated, and then information obtained about each of those people is used to sort out those who are "most relevant." The second approach is broader in scope so as not to miss significant others. It relies on the more specific follow-up questions for each person mentioned (rather than the elicitation technique) to provide the basis for establishing the nature of the relationship.

With each of these strategies, there are two basic techniques for eliciting names. The first technique uses ego's relationship with the other as the point of departure, while the second uses some structural feature of the individual's social world as the organizing principle. These two approaches are referred to as the "relationship approach" and the "structural approach," respectively.

RELATIONSHIP APPROACH

By ego's relationship to the members of the social world we refer specifically to such things as people who are ego's friends or know ego well, or people to whom ego goes for advice. This technique attempts to make salient for ego the relationship between him/her and the other person that you are interested in his/her mentioning. In pure form, this technique uses only a relationship to define those that ego lists. An approach of this type was used by Garbarino, Burston, Rabel, Russell, and Crouter (1978) in a study where sixth graders were asked to list the people they knew best or who knew them best. Once the list was compiled, the subjects were then asked to indicate the ten most important people.

Another example of this approach is one used by Blyth and Garbarino (1977), in which they asked the following set of questions:

- Who are the people you consider your *friends*?
- Aside from the friends you just mentioned, are there any other people you feel *you know well*?
- Are there any other people that you *see a lot or spend a lot of time with*?
- Are there any people who *know you well that we haven't talked about*?
- Of all these people we've talked about, who would you say are the *ten people that really know you best*?

In examining this list of elicitors, it is important to note several features. First, the list of questions never refers to any demographic characteristic of the individuals you want ego to mention. It refers only to the nature of the relationship between ego and that person. That is, no questions ever draw upon such factors as sex or age, or context in which the individual is seen to delineate persons that ego is to mention. The advantage of this approach is that we have not attempted to define who ego's important others are likely to be. The disadvantage is that you have asked ego to scan his/her entire social world to choose individuals to fill a relationship category, when, in fact, the structure of the social world may be a more salient feature for ego.

The second important feature of the list is that it relies upon the interconnectedness of the questions in order to provide an ever-expanding set of others in ego's social world. This interconnectedness is not necessary and may, in fact, not be advisable in some situations. For example, just because you consider someone a friend does not mean that you feel that you know them well, or that you spend a lot of time with them, or even that they know you well. Each of these relationships could actually define a mutually exclusive set of individuals. When this technique is used it is frequently necessary to ask a final question such as "Who are the ten people that really know you best?" This type of summary statement has some advantages for analysis because it allows you to focus in on a relatively constant group of important others. It also has disadvantages in terms of artificially limiting the number of individuals ego considers important.

A third and final point to be considered in examining this "relationship approach" is that each of our four questions could be used independently to define members of the social world of ego and, hence, to draw up separate social maps. That is, one could draw a map of people that ego considers his/her friends or a map of people that ego feels he/she knows well. If a set of questions is used independently rather than interconnectedly as they are here, it is important to obtain enough identifying information about each person to know when the same individual has been listed in more than one social world. That is, for example, you may want to explore the overlap between people who are friends and people to whom ego goes for advice. Forcing the interconnectedness eliminates this possibility.

THE STRUCTURAL APPROACH

The "structural approach" is one which uses some structural feature of ego's social world as the basis for listing others. By "structural feature," we mean the ways in which ego's world is or can be organized. Such features as home, school, and neighborhood are both time and space locations which may aid the individual in thinking about his/her social world. In a structure-only approach, one might obtain a listing of many people in ego's social world who may not be important others in ego's life. That is, one could obtain a list of all family members for ego, and a list of all people ego sees at school, and a list of all people seen in and around his/her neighborhood, but still not have a good idea of how these people fit into ego's social world in terms of important relationships. If an investigator is interested in such a broad-level approach and has the time to deal with the relatively large numbers of people that ego is likely to list, then such a structural approach may be feasible. We believe that a combined structural and relationship approach overcomes the disadvantages of either single approach.

COMBINED RELATIONSHIP AND STRUCTURAL APPROACH

In an approach which uses both some structural characteristics of ego's social world and some relationship information about the members, one has helped ego to systematically think about possible others and evaluate their importance to him/her. In using this combined approach, it is necessary to define for ego a *set of relationships* or a single relationship which describes the type of person to be listed. Once this has been done, ego can then be asked to list individuals like this in each of a number of different structured contexts.

We have, in fact, used just such an approach in the study from which the previously presented data were drawn. In this study, directed by John Hill and the author, we chose to define a set of people that we thought were important or might be important in the adolescent's life. We provided the following definition of the type of people we were looking for:

> By important people, we mean
> People you spend time with or do things with
> People who like you a lot or whom you like a lot or both
> People who make important decisions about things in your life
> People you go to for advice, or
> People you would like to be like

As can be seen from this broad listing of possible relationships, we were attempting to encourage ego to think of people who could be important for any of a variety of reasons and to group all those under the common title of "important people." One could, at this point, follow this statement with instructions that ego make a list of all the important people in his/her life. We elected, however, to ask that general question *within* a set of specific contexts. The contexts we utilized attempted to capture two dimensions which we thought would be salient to ego. The first dimension involved the age of the person who was important. Here we referred basically to young people (those under 20 years of age) versus adults. The second structural feature we relied on was a general idea of what contexts were salient to junior high and high school youth. Four contexts were used: neighborhood, family, school, and outside of school activities. In addition, we added a final miscellaneous category which permitted individuals to list people who were not from any of these four contexts but who were nonetheless important people in their lives. By combining these five contextual levels with the two age levels, we come up with a ten-cell matrix (see Figure 8-1). For each cell of the matrix, we asked a specific question about who the important people were within that cell. For example, we asked students to give us the initials or first or last names of important adults in their lives from their neighborhood. Once they made such a list they would go on to make another list of names of important young people in their lives from their neighborhood. The same procedure was used until all ten combinations had been explored. Within each of these combinations there was room to list ten people. Thus, an individual could list a total of 100 people who were important in his/her life.

This approach was utilized because the specific context of the relationship was a particularly relevant issue and because we felt it would help an adolescent if he/she only had to scan smaller segments of his/her social world for possible significant others. By carving ego's social world up into ten cells, it was possible for him/her to scan each cell more quickly than it would have been to scan his/her entire social world. The net effect of this is to increase the number of people that ego can list as well as increase the number of particular types of people ego lists. Thus, for example, we found that this technique tended to elicit more adults than the technique used by Blyth and Garbarino (1977). We believe this is because we made the distinction between young people and adults more salient for ego and because we took adults out of competition with young people in terms of importance. This illustrates the power of the elicitors to dramatically alter the type of social map one creates. While this power is one which can be used effectively by the investigator to focus in on his/her research question, it is important to report these elicitors in great detail or it will be impossible to see whether different studies are, in fact, comparable.

SUMMARY

The specific elicitors used to help an adolescent define the important or significant others in his/her social world will have a great influence on the map one creates of that social world. We have discussed different techniques and philosophical approaches for eliciting individuals. We noted that one can use single relationships or sets of relationships which are either independent of one another or interconnected. To these one can add different types of structural features which divide the

Context where others are seen

	Neighborhood	Family	School	Outside-of-school activities	Anyplace else
Adults	• Next-door neighbor • Mother of a friend	• Mother/father • Older siblings • Grandparents • Aunts/uncles	• Teachers • Counselors	• Coach • Scout leaders	• Former teachers
Young persons	• Next-door neighbor • Younger children in area	• Siblings • Cousins	• Classmates	• Team members • Gang members	• Friend met while on vacation • Old friend from previous neighborhood

FIG. 8-1. *Structural matrix used in eliciting an adolescent's social world.*

social world into smaller and smaller units. Each of these approaches has advantages and disadvantages which must be weighed carefully by the investigator in light of the purpose of the particular study. In general, the only recommendation we can make at this time is that every effort be made to obtain as many people in the child's social world as possible, and then to use a separate set of questions to inquire about each of those people in order to obtain the finer details of particular relationships or characteristics. This recommendation is a result of the basic fact that if one cannot get ego to mention a person, one cannot ask further questions about that person. Once a person is mentioned, the analyst can choose to eliminate or keep the other in the analysis, based on the additional information. A discussion of the different types of further information which can be obtained on these individuals follows.

Filling in the Details of the Social Map

The second phase of social mapping is equally critical to that of eliciting the individuals. It involves collecting information which more fully describes a given other's characteristics and unique relationship with ego. Let us now explore some of the different types of information one might wish to obtain about a given set of individuals who belong in the social world of ego. As always, the exact nature of these questions will depend upon the specific problem being investigated.

Perhaps the first and most obvious set of questions to ask about each of the people listed by ego are some basic demographic questions— that is, questions dealing with characteristics of the other individuals themselves: sex, age, grade level in school, school attended, and possibly some idea of where the individual lives. These questions are useful if one is attempting to explore such things as cross-sex versus same-sex relationships or the age diversity of ego's social world. An additional advantage of the structure-plus-relationship approach previously noted is that the structure may allow you to separate lists in such a way that you can ask more specific characteristics about certain types of others. For example, by using the structural components noted earlier, we were able to ask grade-level and school questions only for young people who were mentioned and not for adults.

In addition to demographic questions about the characteristics of the members of the social world, one could also ask a series of questions about the relationship between ego and those members. As already suggested, it is particularly important to assess the relationship between ego and those members along the same lines as was used to create the list, in order to provide some indication of the reliability and validity of the people that were, in fact, mentioned as being in the social world. For example, in the second study, which used the elicitors noted earlier, we found that:

- Only 23% of the others mentioned were people ego "wanted to be like" a lot.
- Only 24% of the others mentioned were people ego "went to for advice" a lot. An additional 48% of the people were gone to sometimes.
- Over 47% of the others were people ego felt accepted him/her a lot, with another 44% perceived as somewhat accepting.
- Similarly, 41% were described as greatly understanding what ego was like, with 46% understanding somewhat.
- With only 27% of the people mentioned did ego say that he/she shared his/her feelings a lot. Another 42% were among those with whom ego shared some of his/her feelings.
- Over 80% of the people listed by ego were considered really close friends.
- Finally, only 2% of the people listed by all our subjects were not important in at least one of the ways already noted. Forty-seven percent were at least somewhat important in *all* of these areas.

Although there are any number of different characteristics of a relationship that one might wish to measure, a few additional characteristics include: the length or duration of the relationship in terms of years or months, the frequency with which the two people see each other, and the context or setting where the interactions most frequently take place.

It is also possible to ask ego to make judgments about whether members in his/her social world know each other. That is, you can ask ego about the interconnectedness of the members of the social world. Questions of this sort have unknown reliability at this point but do allow one to gain some insight into the interconnectedness of the social world of an adolescent. In this regard, it is possible to ask whether parents know or would approve of each of the friends that are listed in ego's social world. By asking this at different levels, it is possible to obtain information on whether the parents even know these people versus whether they like them. Likewise, if one is working with specific contexts such as the school, it is possible to ask whether students who have been mentioned as being in ego's social world are known to the other students in ego's social world. While this may be a poor substitute to actually going to the other members of the social world and asking them to describe their relationships with the people that ego mentioned, it is certainly less time consuming and may be more useful since it provides ego's own perception of how closely related his/her friends are.

In summary, the type of questions one asks about each of the particular individuals mentioned as being part of an adolescent's social world constitutes the key to the utility of the social map in terms of subsequent analysis. Therefore, one should attempt to build in validity and reliability checks in order to ensure that the lists of people created are, in fact, significant to ego. One should also attempt to formulate specific questions designed to measure not only the demographic characteristics of the others in the individual's social world but also the characteristics of the web of relationships that make up his/her social world.

Problems in Social Mapping

Once an investigator has adopted or created a social-mapping technique, it is possible to begin describing the social world of different sets of people in different contexts and to explore whether or not social worlds change as a function of development and/or the changing environment in which people find themselves. It is possible, therefore, to use these social maps as both independent and dependent variables in a larger frame of reference. In doing so, there are a number of problems which need to be considered. In this concluding section, three such problems are briefly discussed: first, the problem of different cognitive abilities and how these abilities might differentially affect the resultant maps; second, the problem of whether it is possible to talk about important people globally rather than talk about importance in specific areas; and finally, the degree of stability of the social world of an individual, both in terms of stability of individual members of the social world and in terms of the stability of the structure of the social world.

Perhaps one of the most difficult areas to be explored using this technique of social mapping is that of whether an individual's social map is primarily a function of his/her cognitive abilities or one's cognitive abilities are a function of the type of social world one lives in. Clearly, this is a developmental question of great importance. It would be necessary to study a group of individuals undergoing changes in their cognitive abilities over a period of time to see if changes in the size or diversity or nature of the relationships in the social world changed prior to, or as a result of, cognitive changes. Certain mapping techniques discussed in this chapter may be more or less subject to the influence of different cognitive abilities than others. This is particularly true for those techniques which use a structural approach in order to help the individual think about his/her social world. The structural approach may provide ways of thinking about the social world which require less complex cognitive abilities. Hopefully, this approach will be particularly useful for studying young adolescents. Those areas which are most likely to be affected by differential cognitive abilities are the more in-depth questions about the nature of relationships between ego and his/her others. To the extent that one asks for finer and finer degrees of distinction between relationships, one probably needs to consider the cognitive abilities of the individuals being studied. For all of these problems there is no quick and easy solution but only the suggestion that research in this area could prove quite fruitful, both for cognitive psychologists and for sociologists.

The issue of whether it is possible to create a map of a social world that is relatively global in scale and yet able to capture the important influence patterns operating on ego, is a serious question for both sociologists and social psychologists. Comparative work needs to be done on different ways of eliciting people from the social world of an individual and then exploring what can be said about the influence processes of those individuals with respect to different issues. The work of the Wisconsin group in the education and occupational aspirations area is a step in the right direction but one which needs now to be examined to see if similar results can be found using a global elicitation approach. Global- versus specific-domain approaches may be more complementary than contradictory. However, further empirical work in this area is clearly needed.

The final area, and perhaps the most problematic for the future of social mapping, has to do with the stability of the maps. As already noted, stability here refers not only to stability of the set of individuals in ego's social world, but also to stability in terms of the structure of that social world. The issue here is really twofold. First, how stable can we expect an individual's social world to remain in terms of the people who are important to him/her? Are the maps stable enough in this regard to investigate changes over relatively short periods of time? Second, with regard to the stability of the structural characteristics of the map, there are a whole series of interesting questions that need to be dealt with. Foremost among these is whether or not changes in the individual's context or environment can seriously affect the composition of his/her social world. In fact, it is this question which initially led us into the area of social mapping. Attempting to understand the types of changes which occur in an individual's development as he/she undergoes a transition in school environments and a transition into early adolescence necessitated knowing more about adolescents' social worlds and changes in those social worlds. This is an area which is still considerably lacking in empirical research.

Conclusion

In this chapter we have attempted to explore issues related to mapping the social world of an adolescent. We delineated and commented on some of the problems with each of three different techniques used previously and then discussed four issues in selecting a mapping strategy. We then described three basic classes of mapping techniques which might be used (relationship, structural, and combined). While these sections could not answer all the questions which are bound to come up in the development and application of these techniques, it is hoped that this discussion has provided new insights and new incentives which other investigators will pursue.

ACKNOWLEDGMENTS

This chapter is a product of an interdisciplinary research project directed by Dale A. Blyth and John P. Hill. Much of the material included came from discussions with John P. Hill, Karen Smith Thiel, and Keith McGarrahan. Also contributing to the overall conceptualization were Debbie Felt, James Garbarino, and Mary Ellen Lynch.

REFERENCES

Blyth, D. A., & Garbarino, J. *Transition to Adolescence study: Sixth grader's interview.* Unpublished instrument, 1977.
Bronfenbrenner, U. Toward an experimental ecology of human development. *American Psychology,* 1977, *32,* 513–531.
Craven, P., & Wellman, B. The network city. In M. P. Effrat (Ed.), *The community: Approaches and applications.* New York: Free Press, 1974.

Dunphy, D. C. The social structure of urban adolescent peer groups. *Sociometry*, 1963, *26*, 230–246.

Garbarino, J., Burston, N., Rabel, S., Russell, R., & Crouter, A. The social maps of children approaching adolescence: Studying the ecology of youth development. *Journal of Youth and Adolescence*, 1978, *7*, 417–428.

Haller, A. O., & Woelfel, J. Identifying significant others and measuring their expectations for a person. *Revue Internationale de Sociologie*, Series II, 1969, *5*, 395–429.

Haller, A. O., & Woelfel, J. Significant others and their expectations: Concepts and instruments to measure interpersonal influence on status aspirations. *Rural Sociology*, 1972, *37*, 591–622.

Hallinan, M. T. Structural effects on children's friendships and cliques. *Social Psychology Quarterly*, 1979, *42*, 43–54.

Hallinan, M. T., & Tuma, N. B. Classroom effects on change in children's friendships. *Sociology of Education*, 1978, *51*, 270–282.

Inhelder, B., & Piaget, J. *The growth of logical thinking from childhood to adolescence.* New York: Basic Books, 1958.

Kohlberg, L. *Stages in the development of moral thought and action.* New York: Holt, Rinehart & Winston, 1968.

Mitchell, J. C. The concept and use of social networks. In J. C. Mitchell (Ed.), *Social networks in urban situations.* Manchester: University of Manchester Press, 1969.

Moreno, J. L. *Who shall survive? Foundations of sociometry, group psychotherapy and sociodrama* (Rev. ed.). Beacon, N.Y.: Beacon House, 1953. (Originally published, 1934.)

Selman, R., & Byrne, D. A structural–developmental analysis of role-taking in middle childhood. *Child Development*, 1974, *45*, 803–806.

Verbrugge, L. M. Multiplexity in adult friendships. *Social Forces*, 1979, *57*, 1286–1309.

Index

273